The Man and His *Wings*

Mine was a clean battlefield, young men died up there, they were never buried up there—but their bravery still drifts through the clouds, like ghostly headstones.

—WILLIAM A. WELLMAN

The Man and His *Wings*

William A. Wellman
and
the Making of the First Best Picture

WILLIAM WELLMAN JR.

Foreword by Robert Redford

PRAEGER

Westport, Connecticut
London

Library of Congress Cataloging-in-Publication Data

Wellman, William A., 1937–
    The Man and His *Wings* : William A. Wellman and the making of the first best
picture / William Wellman, Jr. ; foreword by Robert Redford.
        p. cm.
    Includes bibliographical references and index.
    ISBN 0–275–98541–5 (alk. paper)
    1. Wellman, William Augustus, 1896–   2. Motion picture producers and
directors—United States—Biography.   3. Wings (Motion picture : 1927)   I. Title.
    PN1998.3.W454W45 2006
    791.4302′33092—dc22   2005032676

British Library Cataloguing in Publication Data is available.

Library of Congress Catalog Card Number: 2005032676
ISBN: 0–275–98541–5

First published in 2006

Praeger Publishers, 88 Post Road West, Westport, CT 06881
An imprint of Greenwood Publishing Group, Inc.
www.praeger.com

Printed in the United States of America

The paper used in this book complies with the
Permanent Paper Standard issued by the National
Information Standards Organization (Z39.48–1984).

10 9 8 7 6 5 4 3 2 1

Dedication

This book is dedicated to the love of my life, my beautiful wife of over forty-four years, my Flossie. She and my four children here and gone: Teresa, Cathy, Mark, and Chris; my grandchildren, Emma Grace and Jackson William, have truly made my life worthwhile.

Dedication must also travel to my steadfast brothers, Tim and Mike; my fiery sisters, Pat, Kitty, Cissy, and Maggie; and all the spouses and wonderful Wellmans far and wide.

To my incredible mother, Dottie, who raised all seven of us with such loving care and, amazingly, still found time—in her quiet and heartfelt way—to attach and embrace a web of devotion around the forcible figure of "Wild Bill."

Lastly, and most importantly, to the man who, even after his passing, has meant so much to me throughout my life—my friend, my companion, my inspiration, my hero, my dad.

Contents

Foreword *by Robert Redford*   ix

Preface   xi

Acknowledgments   xiii

Introduction   xv

1 The Waiting Game   1

2 In Love and War   25

3 The Homefront   49

4 The Slippery Ropes of Hollywood   67

5 The Director   85

6 The Picture   107

7 Judgments   141

Notes   163

Bibliography   165

Filmography   167

Index   179

Foreword

*M*averick is a worn term that has been batted around and has described many people over time. For me, William Wellman most authentically fits this description. Feisty, independent, self-taught, and self-made, he earned his stripes as a seeker and adventurer, sure of his passions and own mind, and not to be trifled with by authorities who were inherited or never saw the realities of hand-to-hand conflict or earned their way through the experience of real living.

Hollywood has always been tough on talent and independence; and his vision, his own brand of heroic storytelling, was sure to rankle those attempting to control the mind of the director. He stood his ground and fought his battles for artistic integrity, never wavering, always clear in his film sense.

He has given us great stories of great people, both light and dark and with a true understanding of what it felt like in the world of the underprivileged or those not born of a silver spoon. He could be rough, intimidating, and violently opinionated against hypocrisy or witless authority—but also warm and loving. I know. I grew up with his son Bill, and I met him once. He was friendly and kind, and he scared the hell out of me.

He has left a great gift in the annals of film achievement.

—Robert Redford

Preface

When my father began writing his memoirs, publication was of little interest, and only one of his works was published. He wanted to leave the generations of his family something about his life that they could hold in their hands.

I have been trying to further the process by gathering his life's experiences and, through his insightful voice, produce this book and future presentments. I have certainly enjoyed my many years (forty-nine and counting) in the film industry, and my passion for shining a light on my father's underappreciated work remains steadfast.

In 1958, the year of my father's last picture, it seemed to me that he was being quickly forgotten. In 1965, I began a lifelong quest to bring recognition to his vast and versatile body of work. Over the years, I have proposed a movie, a television special, a film retrospective, a documentary, magazine articles, and books based on the life and films of William A. Wellman.

Unfortunately, during his lifetime, only one of my magazine articles was published, however, in 1974, I successfully raised funds and produced the only film retrospective of his work ever done in the United States.

With the assistance of Tom Laughlin, better known as Billy Jack, we orchestrated a month-long tribute. Over a two-week period, 38 films were shown at the Royal Theatre in West Los Angeles. Included on the menu was a grand banquet at my father's favorite restaurant, Chasens. Dad was toasted by some fifty guests, including James Cagney, Richard Arlen, Buddy Rogers, Barbara Stanwyck, Robert Stack, Fred MacMurray, Mike Connors, Mae Clark, Ida Lupino, and others. Friends gathered at his home for another party, and he appeared on several of the most popular television talk shows. Dad enjoyed the whole damn thing immensely.

Since his passing in 1975, all of my magazine articles have been published, and my television special *Wild Bill*—written and sold in 1971, but never produced—turned into an award-winning documentary, *Wild Bill Hollywood Maverick*, in 1996. My screenplay *C'est la Guerre*, is completed, and I am in search of a production partner. This book is published, and more volumes are in the offing.

I have presented many of my father's films at international film festivals. I have appeared on-camera, in commentary, or made other contributions to a growing number of DVDs for Wellman films, including the recently restored *Island in the Sky* (1953) and *The High and the Mighty* (1954), both starring John Wayne. As of 2005, there are more than twenty-two films in video stores and over forty pictures playing on television. The global audience awareness is rising all the time!

Acknowledgments

Since the creation of this book dates back to 1965, when I first began my recognition crusade for my father and his work, many people have earned my gratitude. Not just the individuals directly involved during the writing period, but those in the industry who influenced and colored my life throughout the years—all share in the final edition.

It would be impossible for me, or anyone who writes about William A. Wellman, not to acknowledge the many decades of writing and research by two dedicated and talented people: John Andrew Gallagher and Frank T. Thompson. They are so distinguished and steeped in my father's tradition that I invited them to be the historians of *Wild Bill Hollywood Maverick* (1996), the award-winning feature documentary on the life and times of my father.

Of the same film, I am eternally grateful to the illustrious members of the film world who gave their time for interviews:

Mike Connors
Clint Eastwood
James Garner
Darryl Hickman
Arthur Hiller
Tab Hunter
Howard Keel
Howard W. Koch
Tom Laughlin
Burgess Meredith
Robert Mitchum
Harry Morgan
Gregory Peck
Sidney Poitier
Nancy Reagan
Robert Redford
Charles Buddy Rogers
Martin Scorsese
Tony Scott
Robert Stack
James Whitmore
Richard Widmark
Robert Wise
Jane Wyman
Joseph Youngerman

If it wasn't for my *Wild Bill* partners, producer Ken Carlson, and writer/ director Todd Robinson, I would not have this film that has meant so much to me. If any partnership is nearly perfect, our collaboration is it. My thanks to them is everlasting. I would also like to include our beautiful and talented film editor, Leslie Jones, and our narrator extraordinaire, Alec Baldwin. Lastly, thanks go to Michael Wayne of Batjac Productions, who, when everyone else said no, said yes. He believed in us and our film and my father.

To Marje and Bill Bullock for their support and assistance with the Wellman family history.

At Greenwood Publishing Group, I am grateful to Eric Levy for his confidence and guidance, before he moved to greener pastures, Lisa Pierce, and all those who worked on my book. A tip of the hat to my agent, Mike Hamilburg, for his support and finding Greenwood.

A collective thanks to the numerous journalists and authors who chronicled the writings listed in my bibliography.

All of the following share my special gratitude: (alphabetically) A. Scott Berg, Daniel H. Blatt, Kevin Brownlow, Reno Carell, Hoagy Carmichael Jr., Sue Clamage, Larry Cohen, Russell S. Doughten Jr., Scott Eyman, James Franciscus, Mary Harris, Maria Cooper Janus, Don Krim, Tom Laughlin, Ronnie Leif, Jerry Lewis, Leonard Maltin, Mimi Mayer, Andrew McLaglen, Betsy Newman, Douglas Odney, Sean Penn, Jan Rofekamp, Jerry Rudes, Richard Schickel, Frank Stewart, Donald Thompson, Gretchen Wayne, Vicky Wilson, and Mel Zerman.

My memory is good, but I have my limits, so please forgive any forgets.

Introduction

It has been said that my father, William A. Wellman, known to Hollywood as "Wild Bill," was a man who sprinted through life. Born in a leap year, he couldn't wait for the next year to arrive and the next adventure to unfold. His energy and his impatience wouldn't allow him to take just one step at a time. It was as if he wanted to spring forward, four years at a clip. His world was kaleidoscopic.

His fiery personality, roistering behavior, grim determination, and driving ambition were often on display, as was his unique ability to squint one eye while the other peered through a viewfinder and recognized a motion picture miracle.

I saw my father as a James Dean–like rebel *with* a cause. He was a square peg looking at round holes. He didn't fit in as a child. He didn't fit in as an adult. He preferred to exist outside the system, and yet he strove for stability in the rollercoaster life of Hollywood.

By the time he was thirty years old, he had already been a criminal on probation and expelled from school; been a professional athlete; served in the French Foreign Legion and flown in World War I as a fighter pilot in the famous Lafayette Flying Corps; married three of his five wives, including a Hollywood glamour star and a Ziegfeld Follies showgirl; and directed *Wings*, the first film to receive the Academy Award for Best Picture of the year.

With help from the Hollywood movie star Douglas Fairbanks, he began his film career as an actor in Fairbanks' *Knickerbocker Buckaroo* (1919). Hating how he looked on the screen, he switched gears and launched a long career behind the camera. His first job was that of messenger boy at the Goldwyn Studios. For over three years, he knocked around as a property man, assistant cutter, and assistant director. When his director went on an alcoholic binge, he finished the picture that led to his first directing job at Fox Studios, *The Man Who Won* (1923), starring Dustin Farnum—and was promptly fired.

Dad returned to the rank of assistant until he could wangle his way back to directing a lengthy list of B Westerns with Dustin Farnum and Charles "Buck" Jones.

After the artistic success of *You Never Know Women* (1926) with Florence Vidor, he won the job of piloting the legendary *Wings* (1927) at Paramount Studios. In the years to follow, he made many pictures and much money for nearly every major studio in Hollywood. He later said, "And I've been fired from every studio in Hollywood except Disney—they never hired me!"

My father wanted to make every kind of film, and he did. He made tough gangster films like *Public Enemy* (1931) with James Cagney and Jean Harlow, and *The Hatchet Man* (1932) with Edward G. Robinson; fast-moving action pictures like *Wild Boys of the Road* (1933), *Call of the Wild* (1935) with Clark Gable and Loretta Young, and *Beau Geste* (1939) with Gary Cooper and Ray Milland. There were comedies, too—movies like *Nothing Sacred* (1937) with Carole Lombard and Fredric March, and *Roxie Hart* (1942) toplining Ginger Rogers—along with hard-hitting melodramas such as *Heroes for Sale* (1933) and his Academy Award–winning *A Star Is Born* (the original 1937 film) with Fredric March and Janet Gaynor, *The Light That Failed* (1939) starring Ronald Colman, and *Star Witness* (1931) with Walter Huston.

Dad even made a semi-musical, *Lady of Burlesque* (1943), starring Barbara Stanwyck; and Westerns like *Yellow Sky* (1948) with Gregory Peck, Richard Widmark, and Anne Baxter; and the classic *The Ox-Bow Incident* (1943) starring Henry Fonda and Dana Andrews. There were war stories, such as *Battleground* (1949) and *The Story of G. I. Joe* (1945) with Robert Mitchum, a film that remains, perhaps, the greatest fictional tribute to the American soldier. No fewer than eleven films of aviation adventure streaked across the marquee, most notably *The High and the Mighty* (1954), starring John Wayne.

Even when my father's heroes were not airborne, he would focus on men who brought a similar grace and gallantry to other adventurous tasks.

My father's movie career began in the Silent Era. He was there when films began to talk. He was part of the golden age of comedy, the fabulous musicals, the gangster era, hero Westerns, the dynamic movie moguls, and the great stars of the silver screen at a time when Hollywood and its dream factories were at their most glamorous and finest hour. He was there when Hollywood's golden years began to fade. He saw those glittering empires crack and decay and wanted no part of their demise; and so, partly shunned by an industry he helped to create, and heartbroken by the treatment given his final passion project, *C'est la Guerre*, released under the title *The Lafayette Escadrille* (1958), he ended his career.

It was not until 1973 that the industry he had served so well relented and bestowed upon him the Directors Guild of America's Lifetime Achievement Award.

In his retirement, he wrote two books, *A Short Time for Insanity* (1974) and *Growing Old Disgracefully*, unpublished. He loved and enjoyed his devoted wife and growing family for as long as he could. At least five times he battled and defeated near-death encounters, but he could not conquer the cancer that took his life two months shy of his eightieth birthday.

When my father died, I lost three people: my dad, my companion, and my best friend.

As a director for over thirty-five years, Wild Bill fought many battles—some with his fists—for the right to make his pictures his way. He lived a life more adventurous, more confrontational, and more unpredictable than anything in his movies. After all, they didn't call him "Wild Bill" for nothing. He was feared and respected and even loved. After four unsuccessful marriages, his fifth lasted forty-two years and produced seven children, twenty-two grandchildren, and eleven great-grandchildren to date.

Just before my father died, he told me, "Bill, God—damn it! Don't feel sorry for me. I've lived the life of a hundred men." He sure did. He left wonderful memories to those who loved him, and a treasure trove of films that bring joy and comfort to all—especially those who reach out to touch that dream in the dark.

1

The Waiting Game

The journey to the making of *Wings*—the first movie to receive the Best Picture award from the Academy of Motion Picture Arts and Sciences, the last great silent film, the *Star Wars* of its generation—was long and arduous.

Besides the written story, the film's director is the most important component of the expedition, for he must steer the course and carry the load. He is the Noah, and the film is the ark. The ark holds the cast and crew and is like a studio. Everything and everybody is important and has a place on the voyage. It is important that the director be extremely knowledgeable on the subject matter, with firsthand understanding and life experiences to enhance the story and enrich the odyssey. Although the young William Wellman had no master plan to become that Noah, he was on course to destination *Wings*, and it would become well-navigated before his arrival.

William Augustus Wellman was born in a four-poster bed in a middle-class home in Brookline, Massachusetts, on February 29, 1896, a leap year. His grandmother, Cecilia Lee Guinness, was a member of the famous Guinness Stout family of Ireland. The family included royalty—Lord and Lady Iveagh. Cecilia was born in Ireland to a Roman Catholic family. She caused a great stir when she announced her intention to marry the Reverend Charles P. McCarthy, a Protestant minister. The family promptly disowned Cecilia and did not attend the wedding. The newlyweds left Ireland, settling in Cheltenham, England.

On August 12, 1869, Cecilia gave birth to a daughter, Celia. Three years later, the family set sail for America, settling in Boston, Massachusetts.

The red-haired, less than five-foot-tall Celia grew up in the Boston area, and before the Irish lass turned twenty-three, she fell in love with an Englishman, Arthur Gouverneur Wellman. Arthur's parents, William Augustus and Matilda Gouverneur (Ogden), had also come to find a better life in the new land.

William Wellman's parents, Celia and Arthur Wellman, circa 1892. *Courtesy of the author.*

Arthur was born April 8, 1858, in Boston. He had two brothers, Francis and Joseph, and a sister, Mary. All three brothers attended the Massachusetts Institute of Technology. Arthur was the only one not to graduate, opting to accept a position in an insurance brokerage in his hometown.

Arthur was never as successful as his siblings, nor his father. Francis L., born July 29, 1860, became an eminent attorney and wrote several popular books on law: *The Art of Cross-Examination, Day in Court, Gentlemen of the Jury,* and *Luck and Opportunity.*

Arthur's sister Mary Fairlie married Samuel Williston, a celebrated lawyer, on September 12, 1889. He was dean of Harvard Law School (1909), the first gold medal winner of the American Bar Association in 1929, and authored numerous articles and books on legal subjects, including *The Law of Sale* (1909, 1924) and *The Law of Contracts* (1920).

Arthur and Celia were married in 1892 and lived on his father's property at 4 Perry Street in Brookline, Massachusetts. Arthur's father, William Augustus, was a prominent banker in Boston. He built a Greek Revival-style house in 1843. Behind the main house was a carriage barn that was converted into a home for the newlyweds.

In 1903, the main house was moved to another location. The carriage house was given an address of 20 Linden Place. This is where Celia gave birth to two sons, Arthur Ogden (or Arch) and William Augustus, named after Arthur's father. Since Arthur's father had passed away before his grandson was born, no *Junior* or II was attached to the name of the newborn, William Augustus Wellman.

Unlike his more conservative brother, young Billy was a dashing, hell-for-leather maverick, who by age twenty-one had already been a juvenile delinquent kicked out of high school, a professional ice hockey star, and an ambulance corps enlistee preparing to join World War I before America was even a part of it.

During his ice hockey days, Douglas Fairbanks Sr. had taken a shine to the penalty-prone player and invited him out to Hollywood if he ever needed a job.

The day before going overseas, Billy had a final heart-wrenching meeting with his family and probation officer. Billy had a habit of borrowing cars. At night, he would find one on the street, get the engine started, and take off in it. After an evening of fun and frolic, he would return the automobile where he found it. On one particular night he was tardy with his return and, subsequently, got arrested.

In court, he told the judge that he never stole cars, but simply borrowed them. Sometimes he even replaced the gasoline he used. Even though young Billy saw a difference, the judge could not make a distinction between "stolen" and "borrowed" in this case. Since this was a first offense, Billy was given six months' probation and told to report every week to the probation officer of the city of Newton: his mother.

Celia Wellman with her sons, Arthur (Arch) and William, circa 1903. *Courtesy of the author.*

Wellman in 1914, pictured at bottom left with his dog Taffy and brother Arch at top left, was a four-year star on the Newton (Massachusetts) High School baseball team. In addition to baseball, Wellman was a standout in football and hockey and, during a brief professional hockey career, accumulated more than his share of penalties and attracted the attention of an important fan—Douglas Fairbanks. *Courtesy of the author.*

Celia was very successful at her job and was invited to speak to Congress on the subject of juvenile delinquency. She told them that of all the thousands of boys she'd worked with, the only one she couldn't control was her son.

On the morning of May 22, 1917, Billy awoke before daylight. Not wanting any more tearful goodbyes from mother and father or angry barbs from his brother, he packed one duffel bag, said goodbye to his old dog Taffy, tiptoed out of his home, and walked several blocks to the nearest main street. He hailed a taxi and proceeded to the New York Harbor and the French ocean liner *Rochambeau*.

Celia had given her son a letter, making him promise he would not read it until the *Rochambeau* was plowing its way to Europe. Billy kept his promise. On the first night, all alone, he opened the envelope and read the letter.

My beloved son—I cannot tell you what is in my heart for you—No one in all the world can ever love you as I have done, ever since God gave you to me. Remember this, dear, when you think of me, and how hard it has been for me to see you go. I know you are going to help and no one can do that better than you. Don't forget your prayers, and even through all the suffering and vice and other things that you will see, remember our heavenly Father watches over us all. I give you into His keeping and every breath will be a prayer that you will come home safely to us.

God Bless and keep you always. Your loving

Mother

Billy later wrote:

I cried. It was beautiful and I suddenly realized how cruel I had been to my mother, not wanting her to see me put to sea, thinking that she would stand on the pier covered with tears and make a big fool of me. How wrong can an idiot be.

My childhood was filled with many wonderful years, and I had never seen her do anything that would embarrass me or my brother. Our lives had not always been merry and bright. My dad had a drinking problem, was a partner in a brokerage firm and the good days were outnumbered by the bad ones.

All through this unreliable tempest, my mother was the strong one, my dad usually found his security getting loaded, good-naturedly. Despite all this I can't remember Mother ever losing her temper, she just seemed to suddenly have another son, a bad boy to be punished when all alone. My dad was an amazing man, weak in many ways, played the piano magnificently, loved my mother devotedly but wandered occasionally. I am sure she was conscious of his misgivings but her love of him was so strong that even after his rather early death, no one ever took his place. Her heart had but one love, and this lovely lady, my mother, I thought might embarrass me by crying. She would have cried, but it would have been all inside until perhaps in the seclusion of the taxicab taking her to a more empty home, she would have cried tears, each and every one a prayer for me. This is one more of the thoughtless mistakes I seem to make with such great ease.

I vowed to keep this prayerful letter with me at all times, safely tucked away in a thin flat wallet my mother had given me with my initials emblazoned on a small gold strip. It would be my good luck charm.

Onboard the French liner were other young Americans on their way to join the French Air Service. Like Wellman, some had joined other branches of service and would have to transfer into the Lafayette Flying Corps. After being turned down by the U.S. Air Service—mostly due to the lack of education—Wellman joined the Norton-Harjes Ambulance Corps, then transferred to the French Foreign Legion and to the Lafayette Escadrille. The escadrille, originally called the Escadrille Américaine, had been formed on April 20, 1916. It was composed of Americans only. Wellman and these young adventurers arrived in France on June 1, 1917.

The following was the first of eighty-two handwritten, pen-and-ink letters Wellman wrote to his mother, father, and brother Arch. Mother Celia had saved these glimmerings from the past throughout her long lifetime. When she died at ninety-seven years of age, the letters were passed down to caring family members and, in 2002, arrived at the home of this author.

I have selected some of them, and their excerpts, to appear in this and the next chapter. These letters chronicle the history of World War I through the eyes of a young American pilot in the battlefields of Europe. I have chosen to use his voice as a means to understand how his war experiences shaped and colored his path as a filmmaker in Hollywood and as director of *Wings*, one of the greatest air epics ever produced and winner of the first Best Picture Academy Award.

These letters and excerpts, written by this young voyager without a high school diploma, are included here in their original form, grammatical errors and all, with no editing of any kind.

HOTEL DE BAYONNE   June 4, 1917

Bordeaux

Dear Mother:

Had an eventful trip. Rough as blazes and I am beginning to believe me a <u>real</u> sailor, having passed without once getting sick. The last two days we spent looking for u-boats as the Rochambeau has been the boat to successfully evade these water-devils. They were laying for us and we zig-zaged in our course and did many other tricks. The last two nights we were not permitted to go below and were forced to remain dressed on deck or in the saloon. <u>Gambling</u> was the big amusement on board, at which I fortunately stayed clear. Many of the boys lost all their money shooting craps. Arch would have had a beautiful time.

There were several stage folk on board so we were not at all bored. Two bully little girls, both french, with their governess, acted the teacher to me and I learned quit a little french. The meals were typically french. Two courses of meat and fancy cakes and all varieties of cheese. Believe me I prefer the good old American meals every time.

I met a great crowd of fellows, most of them from the west. Older fellows but the real open hearted, happy-go-lucky type. Unfortunately but few of them are in the Harjis-Norton Ambulance Corps. Most of them are in the American Ambulance Corps. However there should be good chances to see them in the days to come. The question of writing is bound to be a bad one for from what I understand I will not all the time be in a position to write. My address will probably be 7 rue Francois Premier, Paris @ Harjis-Norton Ambulance Corps. If it changes I will let you know immediately.

France is certainly beautiful. It is just like a picture book, with its wonderful chateaus and marvellously cultivated fields, its cobblestones and odd buggies rattling over them. Everything is wonderful but I suppose the reason is because of its freshness and all the novelties that one sees. Paris tomorrow and then the real test. This red tape is hard and I am very anxious to become started. Not only because of the work but also the money one has to spend. New money, new language, new acquaintances, new experiences. That is a combination that sounds very, very, good to me.

The uniform we wear is a wonder. It costs $135 so should be worthy of a king. Bully Kakki and cut in the latest English style. Some little dishes.

I wish Mother that you would let Stan know about me. I won't have time to write another soul.

I hope Dad is coming along in business every day. He deserves it. Arch no doubt is doing well. He will be wealthier than I, but believe me <u>so</u> <u>far</u> I wouldn't swap for the world. Take good care of yourself, Mother and remember that there are just two letters that I have with me. Yours and Dads.

<u>Love</u>
Billy

Although no letter from Wellman's father has survived, it's safe to say that it contained references to his son's safekeeping: health, welfare, and behavior. Except for two local summer camps, Wellman had never been away from home before going off to war.

Wellman and the other Americans took their physicals, did their paperwork, and waited for their enlistment papers to come through.

Hotel Du Patais	June 8, 1917
28, Cours-La-Reine, PARIS	Friday P.M.
Champs—Elysees	

Adresse tel[e] graphique:

PALATEL, PARIS

Telephone passn 60-82

Dear Mother:

Rather than cable and so resort to only a few words, for my money is scarse, I am writing to tell you what I have done and the reasons for so doing. I have passed my physical and mental tests for the Franco-American Flying Corps. otherwise known as the Lafayette squad. My term is for the duration of the war and I am happy to say I have done the right thing. This ambulance job is considered really a joke. A good job for conscription shirkers or bums who want an excuse to come to Paris and raise h—l. Why Mother, we don't realize the seriousness of this war. France is practically wiped out. They are playing on their nerve. All their wonderful men and boys are gone. England has just started to do a little, and many claim that if we had not come to the rescue when we did, the Germans would have won the war inside of six months. Their ability and cruelty can't be deciphered. They are devils and believe me, unless all appearances are false those Germans will be able to hold out for a long time. America realizes a little bit, but not the public. The government will in all probability take over these Red Cross Units and then the ones will get put wherever Uncle Sam sees fit. That branch of the service is a good job for fellows like Francis Sketton not for real red blooded boys. This <u>service</u> used to be good, when Dave Douglas was here, but conditions have changed thus lowering the standard. Now, Mother, the casualty list is greatly exaggerated and a man with a clear head and a good training can get by O.K. I spend from three to six months training, starting at a big camp in Avord, France. Here we go through flying with a machine with clipped wings which makes it impossible to rise above the ground. Step by step you are carefully taught and then, after six months you are given a twenty-four days furlough in which to return to America. The pay to start with is small, something like two hundred francs a month, or ten dollars per week. Of course your board and lodging is free and this takes care of your extras. Believe me Mother I can't write what I could easily say about the conditions one gets to realize when in the real center of the trouble. There should be nothing in the world that our country wouldn't at this time, do for France. They have sent a big fleet and we have General Pershing and 9,000 in troops here, but what is that number compared to those really needed? I feel sure that you and Dad will think I have done the right thing, the only thing, after having chosen a brand of the <u>service</u> that appeals to me and at which I believe I can show the best service. There are so many (ambuscaders) as the french call them, men who by some pull have chosen a brand of the service in which there is practically no danger, that not for the world would I be classed with them. Arch should be getting busy. He will have to do so in a short time.

The hard part of this, is waiting for my papers to be vised by the French government. I will have to live here for two or three weeks doing nothing, just waiting for the word, and spending my precious little gold bag. Now Mother, write me just what you think and address the letter Lafayette Flying Corps, Avord, France. If you want to get ahold of me before the three weeks is up I will be here but I don't believe you will receive the letter until well into that period I surely hope Dad is having grand success, I know that you are Mother. Now don't worry for I have had a queer presentiment that all will turn out fine and that I will return safe and well to you, the most wonderful little woman in this world.

Lovingly,
Bill

Wellman wrote four more letters from Paris in June 1917. Excerpts are as follows:

Dear Mother: Thursday, June 14

Just a little note to tell you what I am doing. Am still waiting for my papers . . . A man who has joined aviation is considered above the others here in Paris. They understand that one is really serving his country by doing this, and that he is not an "ambuscadie" as they term the ambulance drivers.

The reception given Pershing and his staff, was remarkable. Paris
virtually went wild. God only knows every day is a wild day here, but on
his arrival they just about doubled in enthusiasm and believe me Paris
went crazy. Flowers were showered on the boys and all through the crowds
strong men were crying, for they realized that America will in all
probability win this terrible war. With Pershing would be seen Old
Marshall Joffre. He is a wonder and a fine example of a true military
man. I understand the object of Pershing's visit is to determine the
number of men required and then our boys will be immediately sent across.
It sure does seem as if America was awakening at last.

Monday, June 18

. . . Tell Dad I have safely come through the temptations he so much
feared for me. Also tell him I have seen more fellows who never knew
what hell meant in the United States, go there on arriving here in Paris
that I dare mention. It is a good place to stay away from unless you are
lucky as blazes or possess the gift Arch has shown.

This excerpt refers back to the letter from Wellman's father—which no longer
exists. Arthur's letter must have detailed the problems and temptations that his
young son would face. It may also have emphasized the fact that his more cau-
tious and mindful son, Arch, had the ability to stay clear of trouble and strife.

American Hospital of Paris   Friday, June 22

. . . I have been here for about a week laid up with a slight attack
of blood poisoning in that same old leg. Got it from a neglected cut in
the toe. By George I sure was disgusted for I was billed to go to camp
the next morning. I guess a week won't make so much difference, although
. . . the slightest delay makes you pretty mad.

Tuesday, June 26

. . . Yesterday I left the hospital feeling fit as a fiddle and
thankful for the wonderful treatment I received. Also for the bully food.
I am afraid it will be some little time before I again sleep between
sheets and before I once more eat real food. In spite of it all I feel
sure you understand everything and agree with me. I will come through
O.K. and will always be able to look back at this time with quiet pride.
   Yesterday while walking to the hotel from the hospital, along the
river Seine, with another fellow, we saw a girl commit suicide. Poor
thing jumped off a high wall and I apparently being the only one who
could swim went after her. There were crowds of frenchmen around, but
they showed their fear of water. I dove and dove for her for twenty
minutes in the dirtiest river in the world, but could not locate her.
Then the prefecture of the police in a boat came up and he and I grappled
for her with irons. We located the poor girl and succeeded in bringing
her in, but it was to late. Incidentally I spoiled some good clothes and
got very tuckered out just having come from the hospital. I am afraid the
Seine claims a good many such victims during the year.
   Somehow I couldn't get the girl out of my mind and I was awake all
night long thinking of her. The fact that she was in the river and that
I followed her so closely and yet could not reach her, just about drove

me crazy. God forbid I ever go through that again. She sank like a log
and never once came up . . .

   Keep in touch with me often Mother. Letters from home are like a gift
from heaven. By George things as they are, make me appreciate beyond
compare, all the luxuries and opportunities that I had in America. I will
do my best in writing you, but my chances will not be as good as yours.
Tell Dad to keep fighting. It sure would be wonderful to have the war end
as it should and to come home safe to see Dad high on top. He will get
there I firmly believe. Have you as yet been promoted into that office
you had offered to you?

   Tell Arch that unless he looks out he will have his license revoked.
That would just about spoil his good times this summer. I admit that I
envy him. Tell him to make the best of it.

Lovingly,
Bill

On June 27, Wellman found himself onboard a train bound for Avord, in
the south of France, for French aviation training.

The romantic notion of being a Foreign Legionnaire soon vanished against
the grim realities of Legion life at Avord. The American recruits found themselves living with hardened criminals and other assorted ruffians. Theft was
constant, their dwellings were infested with rats and lice, and graybacks hid
in their navels. Their uniforms were unclean and ill-fitting. Due to the lack of
toilet paper, finger-drawn feces paintings covered the walls, and the latrines
had to be whitewashed weekly. Boils and dysentery ran rampant from lack of
wholesome food . . . and the pay was 3.5 cents a day.

The fledgling flyers of the Lafayette Escadrille trained under hazardous
circumstances. Speaking only French, the instructors told them how to maneuver and pilot the various aircraft. Then, the recruits would take to the air
and try to perform. At no point in the training did an instructor actually get
into a plane with a student.

There were five basic steps in the so-called flight school, each using planes
called Bleriots. They looked like prehistoric birds. The recruits called the
first Bleriot a "penguin," because it could not fly with its shortened wings.
They were able to taxi only on the ground. The slightest crosswind or bump
in the road made the journey uncontrollable. However, the students learned
to handle the aircraft, with its three-cylinder Anzani engine, on the ground.

The next craft was called a "roller." It was a type of Bleriot with larger
wings that, at full speed, could get up to twenty-five feet off the ground. The
recruits then graduated from the roller to a full-scale Bleriot monoplane—a
model of the type first flown by Louis Bleriot across the English Channel in
1909. In this, the students cruised the airfield at an altitude of six hundred
feet, with speeds reaching fifty miles an hour. They learned to use the primary controls of rudder and ailerons, and made short turns and slow, careful
ups and downs. After a while, their self-confidence grew, and the crashes
rarely brought personal injury.

The final steps included two triangular cross-country flights of approxi-
mately one hundred and fifty miles each. They flew a route from Avord to

Instructor Adjutant de Curnier and Wellman stand in front of a Bleriot, the plane used to train all new recruits at the training center at Avord, France. *Courtesy of the author.*

Chateauroux to Romorantin. The terrain was picturesque from above, but it became a burial ground for many students who crashed due to bad weather, engine trouble, or simply getting lost.

Wellman described a typical morning to his family:

July 30, 1917

Dear Little Mother:

This Mother, is what happens every morning and night when the weather is good.

3:30 a.m.

Siren whistle.

4:00 a.m.

Awakened by Annamite [Indo-Chinese servant] bringing coffee. Took a small swig. Black as ink and no sugar. Possessing the power to keep a

fellow awake. Dressed for a chilly, foggy morn. Looks back longingly at
my hard bed, hard but oh so cozy at this ungodly hour.

4:15 a.m.

Run and catch camion [large military truck] in time to get a seat.
Annamite placing great loaves of bread and boxes of wormy cheese on the
floor under the seat of the truck. How dirty it looks at this hour and
with ones constitution in the condition that is bound to exist rising so
early. Will the bread and wormy cheese be appreciated in another hour?
Well I guess.

4:30 a.m.

Camion starts up. Past the long low barracks with its smelling, putrid
toilets just outside. Still very dark and gray. We have just drawn out of
the camp. What a relief now that we are on the beautiful dusty country
road. All around, the fellows are snoozing, some knaw at this infernal
war bread with a taste of strong French chocolate. Others, without a
snore, just think. Not a bit of muttering or complaining, and just as
little laughing and joking.

4:50 a.m.

Gradually getting light. The hangars loom in sight. Six of them,
immense things like circus tents. This is the 'Bleriot' school, the most
wonderful training for flying in the world. We drive up and jump or
rather stumble out.

5:00 a.m.

Up comes the machine with the Monitors [mechanics]. Things start to
look more business-like. The sounds of the mechanisms drawing open the
big flaps of the hangars, the machines, all 'Bleriots' are drawn out and
presently the roars of engines being tested. Classes are getting
together. I go to mine in front of the Hangars and on the main 'piste.'

5:15 a.m.

De Runye, our dapper little instructor runs up 'Good morning American
Bastards' is his greeting. Someone had told him that meant a cordial
greeting in our language. A general laugh and my name is called out.
"Willman trente-cinq," which means take machine 35. I do this. A mechanic
runs up and twirls my propellar as I give it the gas and the spark. A
little trouble, a few primes and she starts.

George what a thrill in the early morning, the cold wind going by your
face, the trembling of the whole machine, like a man nerving himself for
some great physical exertion. The blocks are withdrawn and I go up with
the wind. Rather rough this morning and I am forced to keep my 'marche-
balai' pretty well on the windward side. George the thrills one gets
touring high above all the earth. Beneath me the French peasants are
industriously pitching hay. I pass them by in a jiffy. 'My Trule-piste'
is just about at an end. I pass over the hangars and start my peek to
land. Wonderful, peeking from about such a distance. The ground just
seems to rise up, then the slow redress and the final settling. 'Tres
Bien' shouts the Monitor, "Aller" and off I go again.

Lovingly,
Bill.

After the sun and wind came up, all flights had to halt and the men came
back to their barracks. For the remainder of the day, they rested, gambled, or
were ordered to do close order drills—the free-spirited Americans did not like
to drill and worked hard to get out of doing it. On several occasions, the

recruits conspired to do the opposite of any commands given. After a while, the French considered them imbeciles and stopped the drills.

```
AMERICAN                                    ON ACTIVE SERVICE
Y.M.C.A.                                             with the
                                    AMERICAN EXPEDITIONARY FORCE
Dear Little Mother:                                 August 25
```

Have just returned from a forty eight hour stay in Paris. The luxury of it to once more stay at a real hotel. To walk on real rugs and to <u>lounge</u> in easy chairs. Also the sleeping between sheets. Above all, real good food. I was so dog-gone tired that I just gathered all the money I could possibly get and took the much needed change. Change from a life of monotony and hardships to one of excitement and ease . . . .Then again, the feeling of peace; everything here points toward war or in preparation of it. Everything, everywhere women in black. Truely, a women dressed otherwise is very conspicuous.

Every day, fellows are being sent away to different camps. I may go soon, for I have finished my Bleriot training and am waiting to go on my breve [pilot license test]. However, I must return here for prefectionere in Nieuport . . . How long this will take is a gamble. The longer the better for one cannot fly to much to get real good experience.

As you can see by the heading Mother, we have a Y.M.C.A. here. Established in a small room with a few eating and writing tables spread around. They serve hot chocolate and all kinds of sandwiches. Tobac, candy, soap etc. all at the lowest possible prices. Believe me it is a god send. Just a wee-bit of the good U.S.A. to cheer up the boys during their dull moments. Also they have a phonograph, not a Victor to be sure, but plenty good enough. Music, I miss the piano, and my singing. I have not sung for so long that I believe I have forgotten how. Singing is very seldom heard. So many of the boys are trying to sleep at odd intervals during the day, and this must not be sacrificed. . . . Then, the French music is absolutely opposite. No dreamy waltzs or raggy tunes. Not the variety that the American requires. Funny, for in almost all other things the Frenchmen demand variety.

```
Dear Dad:                                           August 30
```

Send that picture of yourself right along. Then I will have the whole family. Some family. Carry the whole crowd around with me. First Mother's and then Arch's, and Taffy's, now yours will be in line and the album will be complete.

Am waiting <u>anxiously</u> for those woolens. Believe me Dad they will come in handy . . . . at the present I go around "underwearless."

```
Dear Little Mother:                              September 15
```

Bully Arch, for yesterday I came home and found three bundles from you. Two of flannels (woolens) and the other my large sweater. George but I sure felt like a king. Now I am fixed to stand the coming cold weather. . . . Am getting accustomed to a bi-plane. They have it all over monoplanes, so much more sturdy and steadier in the air. It won't be long now before I am a regular pilote . . . Have met a fellow down here named Davy Judd. We have become <u>steadfast</u> friends. He is a Roxbury boy and went to Harvard. . . . We two are even here in the school and are going to try and go through everything to-gether. He is a wonder. Will send some pictures later.

Dear Dad: September 16

. . . Yes, believe me, this war is changing all the boys. Right here is an example, for the good I hope, but sometimes and today is one of them, I for one don't give a damn what happens. This letter had perhaps better not get beyond you. Just two days ago, a chap by the name of Billie Meeker, from Washington D.C.: One of the finest boys I have ever laid my eyes on, and with whom I had become a kind of "pal in misery" was killed at Pau. A wonderful pilot, so pronounced by the Captain of the school, yet he got his and in a very simple way. Motor stopped and he

Recruit Wellman sent this photo to his parents while he was training at Avord, France. *Courtesy of the author.*

went into a wing-slip not many feet from the ground. He bucked his
machine just a wee-bit to much. This is just the luck of the game.

Dear Arch: September 20

. . . Now to answer your questions. We were examined yesterday for the
U.S. to be given commissions as first Lieutenants when we receive our
brevit. I passed the exam (similar to that given in the States) but did
not <u>swear</u> in, for when you are once in, you are under orders and the
French training may consequently be eliminated. I intend to stick this
out as I have done, ever since starting training, go through my "brevite"
here and then to Pau . . . All this I will do on my french pay which is
just now about 38 francs a month or $6 in our money. When I get my
"brevite" I become a Corporal with an income of about twenty-five francs
monthly. This is damn little and if I am taken sick or anything I just
will have to stick it out unless Coffin and Gillmore come through as I
hope they do. As to my spending money (extravagently) I have sold just
about everything I possess and have spent that money on good eats, for
ever since I got mine on the "Bleriot" field my stomach has been bad,
very bad.

Dear Dad: September 20

This is the third letter, one to each member of the family in which I
have explained just what I have done concerning the U.S. . . . I may stay
with the French for six or eight months, getting good experience at the
front under old-timers. This will all help and the U.S. will be glad to
get seasoned men at all times. The money is the hard thing to give up.
Once in the U.S. providing you have your "brevite" (pilot's license) you
automatically become a first Lieutenant with its commission. This means
a monthly salary of about $200. A great help no doubt but I want to live,
and I am going to take the chance of doing so on my French pay, which
will be when brevited, but $11 per month. If however Coffin and Gillmore
come through, and I have asked Arch to do a little investigating for me,
that extra ten a week will be something on which to lean. God knows this
last three months have been hell for the food is bad and we have been
regulated to but <u>two</u> meals per day one at noon and one at ten o'clock at
night. The Frenchmen may be able to stand this and <u>I was</u> until I got a
slight strain cranking one of the propellars and then the after effects
acted where they always do, on my stomach. However, (c'est la guerre) and
kicking does no good.

Dear Little Mother: September 30

I have not written for over a week, due to my just having finished my
"brevit" and am now a full fledged pilote . . . Friday I started on my
first "petty voyage" from Avord to Chateroux a distance of about fifty
miles. I reached there O.K. against a tough wind and made the distance in
one hour flying at about two thousand meters high (7,500 thousand feet).
On the way back, my magneto went bad and I had to descend to a little
town about midway. Believe me those are the times you have heart thrills.
A dead motor and no good landing places. After I got down I luckily found
out what was the matter and was able to start again in an hour. Going up
with about a hundred open-mouthed peasants standing around in wonder.
They gave me several bouquets of flowers and you would have thought I was
some kind of a hero. The next day I did another petty voyage and then two
triangles going from Avord to Chateroux to a town called Romorantin (48

miles), Romorantin to Avord (55 miles) then reversed the order on my second triangle and my trials were all over. Thank the Lord for nine hours flying in one day is <u>enough</u>. My engine behaved like a watch after my first "petty voyage" and coming home on my last triangle I ran into a storm and was lost for over fifteen minutes. Then I pealed from 2500 meters to 500 m. and got below the clouds. After that all was well but flying was very rough at such a low level.

Thursday after to-morrow I start in on "Nieuport" perfectionner. It will take me about fourteen days, then "Pau." The front is very near now and I must admit I can't wait for it.

My Dear Little Mother: October 5

. . . You (people in general) in the states don't seem to appreciate conditions here. Especially at Avord, food very bad and very scarse. Pretty hard, for when one feels that he is giving everything he has for a good cause he also likes to have something in return. Why in all my life I never believed food was such an absolute needful thing. That is, good food. Indigestion is one affliction, that an aviator cannot have. Everything is against him anyway; the air is a hard thing to conquer, much harder even than the "Borch" [Germans] themselves. Many of these millionaire ambulance boys have newspaper articles written about conditions here in France. They say food is cheap. Perhaps for them (the embusces). I have yet to see a group of Americans I admire more than these that are here. They have hard conditions to battle against. You know what they are. . . . the more cynical ones in America may say "It will be a splendid experience for them. Make men out of them" they don't seem to realize that perhaps this is to be their last experience and a pretty sorry one at that . . . . but if I am not lucky enough to come through all this I should be and am, ready and willing to give my life to a cause that I realize will concern the happiness of the future generations. In spite of all keep Arch where he is. Make him keep up his good work and clean life. He is not impulsive, but has that serene, even going disposition that is to be envied. Encourage generosity, you should see it here among the Americans, they, and thank God I am one of them, would gladly give the shirt off their back, to one who needed it. If it hadn't been for one or two fellows here I don't know what I would have done, for about six weeks ago I got a pretty bad strain and with their aid I was able to see a real doctor and get fixed up all O.K. Now I am and have been for several weeks, well and strong again. Nevertheless, these two fellows have at least one life long friend. No matter what they do or what happens to them I will always be ready to return their kindness. After all, friendship is the most wonderful thing in the world and most of it comes from generosity, not be necessarily a "good fellow" in the sporty sense. Get Arch to cultivate this above everything. I often think of him. He was a good brother and perhaps on my return we will see more of each other. I will have quieted down a lot and with that help I hope we can have things more in common.

Keep a stiff upper lip Mother, make Dad do the same although he shouldn't have to be pushed. All my love dear little Mother.

                                                            Billy.

Dear Little Mother: Oct. 18

. . . To-day I had my first machine-gun conference. We took apart the "Vicker" Machine gun, the one we will in all probability use on our

machines. They are wonderful, shooting five-hundred and fifty shots per
minute and through the revolving propellar of a plane. That is sure some
stunt for the propellar of a "chasse" machine revolves about twelve
hundred times a minute. Just think how the gun has to be timed to do its
work successfully.

Adresse Telegraphique HOTEL EDOUARD VII

Edouartel—Paris Rue 8 Place Edouard VII

PARIS

Oct. 24

Dear Mother:

. . . Money is absolutely a lost chord with me, and after turning over
in a "Nieuport" at Avord my last day and fracturing the little bone under
my eye things pointed to an operation in Paris. As I am afraid of
anything near my eyes I went to the best surgeon I could find and he
fixed me up in grand style. . . . To-day I am a different sight. But for
a bandage over my eye I am O.K. . . . As yet I have not even received a
bill for the work done. The doctor is a fine old boy and he will let me
off as lightly as possible. For five months I have held off and gone
through everything without asking for help. Now I really need it, and
perhaps Dad won't feel so badly about it, when I can and will give my
word. . . . If I get the money from Coffin and Gillmore, Arch can deduct
what you send and thus everything will be as it should . . .

The front is very, very near. Pau is almost as bad. If I get through
there I should be able to take good care of myself later on. . . . My
letters to you will be getting scarser. Whatever does happen Mother, I
always think of you. Remember that and also that I am not artist enough
to voice my thoughts in letter. There is so much right now that I could
say if only I had the chance. . . . you must be satisfied with what I
have done. The first thing I go into in which there is any danger, you
are the one who urges me on and you are the one who I first think of when
it will be all over. Somehow I feel like offering my prayers to you
rather than to the allmighty. It seems as if there I would get more help,
more love, more everything that is pure and fine.

Dear Dad:

Oct. 25

. . . "Nieuport" is <u>the</u> machine. By George they can go. . . . The
great trouble is that the French want bombing pilotes, they are therefore
sending men from Nieuport to large machines. One has to go through the
school absolutely perfectly to get to Pau. A broken landing gear or any
other small offense and off you go. I have my heart set on Pau for after
leaving there you can really fly. It sure will be tough luck for me if I
do get in wrong and am shifted. The lease on life of course would be
improved if I went as a bombing pilote, but give me the "Chasse" machine
every-time and I will gladly take the added risk.

Hope Dad, that business is still on the go. You have no idea the
amount of confidence I have in you . . . if only you would keep up your
fight and confidence when the times are perhaps a wee-bit dull. Over here
we remember the words "It is easy to die, its the living thats hard."
That applies to everything not only here in aviation but also in the
common everyday walk of life.

Lovingly
Bill

When the recruits completed their primary training, they were sent to Pau in southern France and given courses in acrobatics and gunnery. The cadets were deemed pilots and attained their collar wings, corporals' chevrons, and a wreathed-wing insignia awarded to military aviators. The food was improved, they wore tailored uniforms and, after their grim life at Avord, received seven days' permission (furlough). The recruits often chose Paris.

Ecole d' Aviation Militaire   Oct. 30
B. P. Pau.

Dear Mother (le petite)

. . . Here I am at Pau. I have done my first group of acrobatics and am in "vol de group" flying [group formations]. Everything is done in, wonderful little "Nieuports" Fifteen meter and thirteen meter. Nothing larger. . . . Over a hundred miles an hour and the landing speed is terrific. So fast that one has to have perfect eyes in order to judge the landing correctly. This is the most beautiful spot. The place is but fifty miles from Spain. We are separated only by the Pyrannes which at this time of the year are snow-covered. The view from the ground is wonderful but from the air it is awe-inspiring. The marvellous sunsets and sunrises. Seems as if life really was worth while living. Palms are everywhere. This is the famous English resort in the winter. Since the war it has died down considerably but lots of life still. In Pau itself there are two suburb Hotels and the shops are snazzy. Someday I hope to return here when the war is a thing of the past.

Dear Dad: November 2

Just received notice from Morgan, Harjis Co concerning the money cabled me (280 francs). Bully of you Dad to answer so promptly and you can believe me it is needed and will be paid, (a portion of it which as yet I do not know) to my doctor on arriving in Paris, perhaps in a weeks time. . . . My work here has so far progressed rapidly. Am well into vol-de-group flying and with a few more perfect days "Pau" will be behind me. This morning Juddy and I were sent up to-gether vol-de-group. The trick is to stay within fifty meters of each other all the time. We flew this way for a couple of hours and at times were so close that I could read the small printing that is on his "essence tank." This is the manner by which the front is patroled so one cannot have to much practice. We are traveling at over a hundred miles an hour so you can imagine how readily and quickly two can become separated.

Have got to go out for roll call now Dad for we have barely time to eat lunch before the afternoon flying starts.

Dear Arch: November 4, 1917

Just received word from Dad about your visit to Coffin. Perhaps in the end it is the best thing. It will mean my ending with him if I desire when getting home from the war. With a little adjustment I can finish there and be in a position to get with someone else. You have done and am still doing so well that perhaps you can have a place for me. No use of talking about this, it is so far away. George you are a wonder to help me out. Dad mentioned my getting 400 francs per month. No such luck, at the start off we all received 200 frs per month, that soon bid out and left me with nothing further than the French pay. You are a great help Arch and it means more to me too know that you are so ready to help me. In the course of time I may change to the U.S. then money should be easier to get and I can quickly repay your gifts. Remember Arch, Morgan, Harjis & Co, 31 Boulevard Haussmann Paris, is to be my address from now on. I will not change it even when arriving at the front. They can take care of me in grand style. The cable, thank the Lord came through, right along with it, (the next day) a check for 100 frs. from the Comptor's National

Wellman and Reginald "Duke" Sinclaire met and trained together at Avord. This was the beginning of a lifelong friendship. *Courtesy of the author.*

D' Escompte de Paris. Feel like a millionaire now for it is the first time in months that I have had real money in my pockets. Most of whats left after I fix things up in Paris will go to-wards a new pair of field shoes. Winter is here and "Poilus" [infantry] boots are supposed not to be worn by aviators.

Eye is practically well now. A slight scar, but the job was done with such fine instruments that only a slight mark is left. To-day I had your long hours vol-de-group, flying at fifty meters, and then at three thousand meters. Some change. Low flying is the fun. Duke Sinclaire was the leader this morning on the low stuff and Juddy and I were each fifty meters to the right and behind. He spotted a train coming from a nearby town and we circled around it as if it was anchored. We can only go about 110 miles per hour. George it is fun. Tough if the motor gives at such a low altitude. None did however and we furnished a few thrills for the occupants of the cars.

Should be here but a few more days. Thank God when this place and the acrobatics are over. Also an altitude we have to do of over five thousand meters. This gets a lot of the boys, the fine air etc. Will write again soon. Good luck and a real sincere thanks.

Faithfully,
Bill

Trust the car is O.K. Have you received a little gift I sent you by one of the boys returning to New York?

Dear Mother: Sunday November 11

Just a word to say I have passed through "Pau" and with good success. In fact have been recommended for a "Monoplane" which means I should go to the front in one of the fastest machines there are. . . . Arch and his letters their cheer and the confidence I get from them all just like some wonderful times. He has shown what a wonderful brother he can be when the real test comes. . . . Don't let him get in the game until it is really the last thing. When he does go, get him to choose anything but <u>aviation</u>. Arch with his knowledge of figures could find something far better than flying. One in the game is enough.

Dear Little Mother: November 14

. . . Arch is a wonder. I have written him my thanks. I couldn't get on without his help for at the front we have to buy our own share of good food. Everything costs. I am trying to save for another uniform. The French insist on you looking well in case of being taken prisoner by the Borch. . . . Am very tired Mother dear so will close. Of you my last thoughts.

<u>Billy.</u>

Those pilots who survived the advanced training at Pau were sent to Plessis-Belleville in northern France, about thirty miles from Paris. Plessis provided airfields with every type of plane used in the war: Voisins, Breguets, Sopwiths, twin-engined Caudrons, Letords, Morane Parasols, Nieuports, and Spads. The flyers flew many different kinds of aircraft while awaiting assignment to a fighting escadrille. When a pilot was killed in one of the sixty-four escadrilles, a new pilot took his place. The average time the fully trained aviator spent at Plessis-Belleville was about three weeks.

CHATHAM

Bar and Grillroom

17, Rue Daunqu

PARIS

Dear Dad: November 14

. . . Was in Paris on a twenty-four hour permission from Plessis-Bellville. Have been recommended for a mono-place machine, a "Spad" so am doing a little flying in that machine to become used to it. Wonderful machines with "Hispano-Suiza" fixed motors, two hundred and twenty horse-power. Should be at the front very soon and as you know under the French. . . . I have received your money, (the cable) and Arch's twenty-five, the other, on the National Comptor is lost . . .

Mother is certainly a wonder. Keep up the pep so that she won't have any extra worries. Go out a little more and everything will be O.K. . . . I am afraid my Xmas will be spent in an entirely different manner than yours. Perhaps I can get to Paris, but even so I don't look forward to it very much.

Section 92 G.D.E.

Division <u>Spad</u>   ON ACTIVE SERVICE

                                                                with the

AMERICAN   AMERICAN EXPEDITIONARY FORCE

Y.M.C.A.   November 17, 1917

Dear Mother and Dad and Arch:

Has to be for the three for I have not had much time. Things toward this last stage are getting busy. I fly when the weather permits and also practise shooting. You can readily see how my hours of daylight are utilized. Things here are in a general uproar. The cantine is closed and we have to buy our meals. The barracks are full so I am hiring a room. One franc a day but at present I am dead broke and waiting for that 25 of Arch's. At the front we have to pay so much for good food and everything costs. Goodness only knows where my next uniform and shoes are coming from. Perhaps Santa will be good to me.

My plans now are very definite. Am staying with the French until my period for a permission is around. Will then come home for thirty days which should be sometime in April or May. Then I will try and change at home. Better chance for higher commission. A release can be gotten through the French Consul. Of course this is all premeditated. I may get it the first time over. Be sure and send all things to Morgan, Harjis Co. The $20 sent through Comptors has been lost and is probably at Avord. It may turn up. I have written for it.

In reference to Dad's letter. You all may rest assured that I will not use any of my funds for any extravange. I am sorry, so sorry I can't buy presents for you all. Mother you will understand, for to be true I have been worrying wether I will be able to take any permissions when at the front. Am afraid I will have to just stick there until something happens. Get Dad to talk things over with Uncle Sam concerning my possible transfer in six months. A man who goes through what I will have to and does it successfully should command quite a position and should be able to help a lot. Get any dope you can and let me know about it.

Will close now and remember I think of you all everyday. The old times we used to have to-gether. The times you used to listen to my playing and

Wellman flew two types of aircraft in combat: a French Spad similar to the one shown here and a French Nieuport. *Courtesy of the author.*

singing (if I dare call it such). May they come again and soon. Nearly six months since I left.

Lovingly,
Bill.

To the boys: November 22

Good luck to both of you Arch and Dad. Get after the old man joy. He is the chap that can bring you through anything. Believe in Douglas Fairbanks and this world will be brighter. Believe me when I say that through all the wild planes I have been in the last six months old Doug and his book "Laugh and Live" have been a wonderful inspiration. Just two days ago I had motor trouble out in this country. I was in a "Spad" Machine that is used at the front. Two hundred horse power "Espano-Suiza" fixed motor. Imagine the speed. I decended in a field and hit the barb wire trenches, for this country once belonged to friend "Boche" Little Willie was not scratched but was cold for fifty minutes and the first thing I thought of when I was found, was of "Laugh and Live" and I am just as O.K. as usual. I have gotten to pretty near worship that Chap just on account of his view on life. Eat lots of turkey for me and remember somewhere over here I am eating just as much only perhaps of the wrangler variety.

Lovingly,
Bill.

Dear Little Mother: November 27

I have finished all my preparatory work. Am now on this "dispensable list" and will probably go to the front this friday. All my time has been devoted to gun practice and to flying in a "Spad" Terribly busy and just as tired at nights. About a week ago I had an accident in the country. My motor went bad and I made a forced landing in the improvised trenches that abound here, for we are in territory on a hill by the "borch" and very near the front. I ran into the barb wire entanglements and lit on my head some fifty yards away. They picked me up about fifty minutes after it had all happened, (a youngster having time to run to town and get help) and brought me home in an auto. I was laid up for two days and am once again O.K. Trust me to get by when a hard head is the thing to be hurt. The machine was smashed beyond compare, costing the French government about six thousand dollars. However this cost is no rarity, a very daily occurrence in fact. Nothing else has happened, am grudging along and hoping with all the rest, for the end of the war. My writing has fallen off, but sincerely Mother dear I have very little time. I will always manage to get news to you: and Arch and Dad must share it with you. All my letters of thanks must have arrived. Arch knows how I feel about this aviation in reference to his getting into it. He also must know that his money is a Godsend to me, for it is practically all I get with which to cloth myself and often times to feed myself. Will write a full letter to Dad very soon, on arriving at front, telling of my future plans and how he can be a great help to our looking a few things up in the states.

Take good care of yourself Mother dear. Do not overwork. A happy thanksgiving to you all.

                                    Lots and lots of Love Billy.

2

In Love and War

On December 3, 1917, Wellman was assigned to the Black Cat squadron, Escadrille N.87, stationed at Luneville, in the Alsace-Lorraine sector of eastern France. This escadrille was a famed group of French flyers, and Wellman was the first American to join the squadron. A slow, crowded troop train carried Corporal Wellman to Luneville, located only ten miles behind the first line trenches on the eastern front. The town was emptied of nearly all civilians except those caring for the army. Most of the houses and stores were vacant, and few vehicles were seen on the streets. Except for the sounds of distant bombardment, Luneville was a quiet little town.

```
Wil. Wellman                                          December 3
Pilote Aviateur Americain
Escadrille N.87 Sector 44
Dear Little Mother:
    My official address. However keep Morgan Harjis as yours. They will
forward things to me. I arrived here after a long trip from Paris. We are
at "Luneville" two hours beyond "Nancy." The aviators are all Frenchmen.
I being the only American. We have wonderful living conditions, in this
little village. Houses, abandoned temporarily are used as lodging
places. We eat ensemble at a little hotel. This is what costs. They all
are sergeants and get more pay than I. The food costs us 70 francs every
fourteen days. That just uses up Arch's money. I must get along with my
pay which as you know is but forty francs per month. If you ever do get
flush at odd intervals, for the love-o-mike, remember your little son in
France. If I have good luck, it won't be long before I am a sergeant,
than I will be much better off.
    Funny to sit here and write with the guns banging away. Some sensation
I must say.
```

An escadrille comprised fifteen pilots. Since N.87 had recently lost a pilot, Wellman was the replacement. Most of the French airmen had never seen an

Wellman was the first American member of the famed Black Cat squadron, N.87, stationed in Luneville, France. *Courtesy of the author.*

American, much less lived with one. Unlike the louse-infected barracks at Avord, or the second class hotel at Pau, or Wellman's tiny rented room at Plessis, the aviators lived in a comfortable chateau across a dirt road from the airfield.

The three-story chateau was rectangular, built of wood and stone with a ten-foot high wall surrounding it. The rusty iron gate fronted a wide pebble street, and the sidewalks were lined with old trees. Inside the gate was a narrow pebble path that worked its way up to a large, double, wooden door. Patches of snow covered the yard, which contained a fountain in the center of some leafless trees.

The interior of the chateau was similar to a hotel, having bedrooms for the pilots, community bathrooms at the end of each hallway, and a large kitchen on the ground floor next to a spacious combination living and dining room. The room had a high ceiling and gray walls, and no pictures hung down. In the center of the room stood a large oak table capable of seating all fifteen aviators at one time. Near the table was an upright piano; several smaller tables and chairs filled out the room. A huge fireplace looked out onto the fourteen French pilots, with their many "aces," and one lone American.

For a pilot to receive the designation of ace, he must shoot down at least one enemy plane and have a "kill" confirmed. The act must be witnessed by at least two other flyers from the same squadron; or be seen from the ground by military observers; or be witnessed from the air by observation balloonists; or the pilot must land his plane, tear off the black cross insignia from the downed aircraft, and return it to his escadrille. One can well imagine that few flyers received all the credits they deserved.

```
W. A. Wellman                                        December 4
Pilote Airateur Americain
Escadrille N.87 Secteur 44
Dear Little Mother:
    . . . Things are going smoothly enough. The front is very different
than anything I have ever even dreamed of. A life of thrills and luck and
I feel sure I have both in my favor. I am not permited to say much . . .
When I have had about fifty hours over the lines I will be made a
sergeant than things will be much easier. Am depending on Xmas for a new
```

A German observation balloon under surveillance from a French Spad. These balloons served an important communication function in World War I. Soldiers positioned in the basket would signal troop movements, enemy aircraft sightings, and combat results to their counterparts on the ground. Wellman and his fellow pilots were constantly on the lookout for them, shooting them down whenever possible. *Courtesy of the author.*

uniform and shoes. . . . One more thing, will you send me a lot of music. Old and new stuff for we have a piano here and with music I can amuse.

Dear Arch: December 6

   Well we are in the real thing now. To start with, my writing will have to be careful for not much gets by. . . . Dad writes me you are going into aviation. That is up to you. I have not and never would advise it. The time you spend in training is perhaps the most dangerous so if you do start flying take care and go easy. Let the other fellows get the name of dare-devil. Just plod along and when you get to the front, then you can show them. Often times getting Germans is not the sign of a wonderful flyer. A man may be in the war for years, do his work every day and still not have any fabulous number of "Boche" to his credit. As an example "Thaw" the Americain with the Lafayette Escadrille since the start. He is one of the best in the game yet, in pretty near three years has only one boche to his credit. . . . These are just a few of my ideas Arch but the big one is for you to keep out of it. You have to much ahead of you. In my case it was different. I am not brilliant in business as it is very evident you are. If anything should happen to Dad I could not take care of Mother in the proper way. All these things you could do. . . . In my notes that my Captain heard of my work at all the schools. I was pronounced a "bon pilote" but crazy. I had luck, but am sorry for that last word on my notes.

                                                    Faithfully
                                                    Bill.

Dear Dad: December 7

   At last a letter to you. . . . When I went into this; for perhaps the first time in all my life, I sat down and reasoned the whole thing out, giving special thought to the fact that I would not be a drain on the folks at home. Then Coffin, the man who went back on his word, failed me and you know the rest. My ideas on him are best where they now rest. I can only say that if his position was the last one in the world open for me I would not accept it. Two can play the same game and if I ever get through this all, he will loose me, wether for his good or bad remains to be seen. One thing I can swear for. If he had stuck to me I would never have even thought of failing him in future years.

   Across the road from the pilot's chateau was the airfield and escadrille pilotage or headquarters. The building was attached to one of four hangars. Each hangar could hold ten airplanes. For morning briefings, all fifteen flyers sat in chairs listening to their commandant, Captain Azire. He was a talkative, distinguished-looking Frenchman who wore a pointed black mustache. His command of the English language was quite good. He discussed everything from weather to flight plans to the current state of the war. He explained to Wellman that patrols took place twice a day at two-hour intervals, in the early morning and late afternoon, when the wind was light. When the weather was cruel, they waited for it to improve—sometimes hours, sometimes days, even weeks in wintertime.

   One morning, Azire asked for a volunteer to fly a risky-sounding mission.

Since it was common practice to send five or six planes to bomb and strafe an enemy airfield or position, Azire believed that one pilot, flying close to the ground and under the eyes of the balloon observers, could surprise the enemy with a swift attack and return to base before the enemy could counter. Azire asked for a show of hands. Since the idea seemed like suicide to the Frenchmen, no hands went up at first. After a few moments, only one hand was raised: that of Corporal Wellman. This act of volunteering brought murmurs from the other pilots. Azire was surprised at the replacement's response. Wellman explained that he wanted to get into the action as soon as possible.

The first rays of dawn heralded a lone French Nieuport as it taxied out to the runway. A mechanic followed on foot a short distance behind. Captain Azire and another officer stood near the hangar watching the one-plane dawn patrol takeoff.

Wellman's Nieuport traveled at over one hundred miles per hour as it raced against the early morning sunrise, hedgehopping across fields, over low hills, and down valleys on the way to the enemy airfield.

There was normal, early morning activity at the Boche airfield. A dozen planes, Fokkers and Albatrosses, were parked on the runway. Several mechanics worked on the planes, and a group of pilots stood some distance from one of the hangars. Wellman's Nieuport appeared over the treetops at the end of the airfield. It was a complete surprise. Wellman's plane dropped down just above the ground and sprayed the flyers with his tracer bullets. The flyers ran toward the nearest hangar. Two of the five pilots were hit and fell to the ground.

Wellman was instructed to make two passes only. Additional passes would not only end the surprise, but increase his chances of running out of petrol. He was able to release all six of his ten-kilo bombs. His strafing left several dead mechanics and pilots lying on the runway. A number of Boche planes

Wellman and the famed flyers from N.87 in front of their pursuit planes at Luneville, France. *Courtesy of the author.*

were destroyed and in flames. Ground troops ran in different directions and took positions in bunkers and trenches. Some returned fire with pistols and rifles. Two Huns [Germans] manned an anti-aircraft gun in one bunker, and three pilots dashed across the field to their waiting Fokkers.

Puffs of black smoke exploded near Wellman's Nieuport. Before turning for home, he surveyed the damage below and considered making one more pass. At least, he thought, why not stop the enemy planes from taking off? He made a third pass at them.

Back at N.87, Wellman's mechanic waited patiently for the hopeful return of his pilot. Realizing how long Wellman's plane could stay airborne with one full tank of petrol, Azire and the other officer walked out of the pilotage and stood on the tarmac looking skyward. They checked their watches.

It must have seemed like forever before Wellman's Nieuport came into view gliding over the treetops at the end of the runway—completely out of gas. All the mechanics shouted praises. The breezes pushed the plane from side to side as it fluttered and sailed to a bumpy but safe landing.

The excited mechanics helped Wellman from the cockpit, kissed him on both cheeks, and pumped his hand many times, voicing high-pitched enthusiasms. Wellman removed his goggles and helmet as he walked over to the waiting officers. He saluted and gave his report. Azire complimented him and offered three days' leave. Paris, of course, had become the designated R&R destination. The pilot mentioned nothing about the third pass, but from this day forward, Captain Azire referred to Corporal Wellman as Wild Bill.

Over the next few weeks, there were many days when the weather turned cruel—bringing strong winds and sleeting rain. Again, Wild Bill would have to deal with the "slow time" of an aviator. Sometimes the English translation of the French slang came out as *quiet time* or *down time*.

Wellman felt that these terms were unsatisfactory for the French flyers of N.87. They were rarely quiet, and "slow" was not in their personality. They moved quickly and talked rapidly with great enthusiasm.

Down time made the most sense to him, except that there seemed to be other connotations as well. For instance, rather than doing laundry at the chateau, Wellman noticed that the pilots often took their soiled clothes, even small amounts, to a laundry in town.

There was nothing unusual about this, except for the fact that they sometimes set out for this laundry with no dirty clothes at all—and returned with no clean ones either. They always came back smiling and laughing, with excited conversations.

Wellman, of course, understood little French, and kept hearing the word *chaussure* shouted about. He wondered what that word meant, and what was so entertaining at a laundry. Miot, one of the most daring French aces, spoke some English and told the American that *chaussure* meant wooden shoes. Then he explained the down-time laundry story.

Two French women, Marie and her grandmother, ran a laundry out of their farmhouse near the airfield. They washed and ironed all the pilot's clothes.

Wellman remembered,

They lived alone in what was once a not too large but neat little busy farmhouse. That was before the war, when there was a father, mother and brothers around, all working, eating, having a good time, a happy family. The war had devoured them, there were just these two left, all alone, unhappy, frightened, and angry with memories. Marie had taken the wooden shoe route.

The French pilots brought her their soiled clothes which she washed and ironed spick-and-span; for a small amount of extra money gave of herself to each of them. This was not done in the lush confines of a boudoir but on a confused so-called cot which had no legs, just sat not too firmly on the cobblestone floor—occasionally during a rainy spell when all the wet clothes were hung up to dry in this, the kitchen, the living room, the every room, one performed beneath the drippings of the swarm of drying underdrawers, socks, shirts, sheets, blankets, you name them, and before the curiosity of an old asthmatic dog, an older peeking goat, and one noisy clucking hen.

The Frenchmen being interested in sex found but little of it in a panic-stricken blackedout little war-ravaged village—to them Marie was the pacifier, their tranquilizer, and their means of a very unusual game. They were all judged by their sexual performance—of the eight competing pilots there were four no wooden shoe men, which meant that during their sexual endeavors with Marie, who held her feet ceiling-wise, her wooden shoes remained unconcerned on her feet. Three were one wooden shoe men testifying that enough excitement had been generated within Marie to cause one of her wooden shoes to leave the warm safety of her dainty little foot, and take off, landing on the very busy ass of the pilot trying his best to be not only a great lover but an ace of the wooden shoe combat. One was an ace, he claimed, and it was homologated each and every time the joyful shooting off of both of Marie's wooden shoes, proving his technical prowess. It started slowly and oh so gently, but it ended in rhythmic savagery and Marie was like a sail weakly flapping in a gentle breeze.

Wellman could hardly wait to trek on over to the farmhouse to meet Marie during his down time. Of course, the young American aviator brought some dirty clothes. Wellman introduced himself to Marie and her grandmother. He gave them his soiled garments but did not go any further with the French laundress. In the days to come, an unusual relationship developed between Marie and Wellman. He wrote:

My relationship with Marie was entirely different. I had been in numerous whorehouses but never once taking part in the pay for play, there was nothing wrong with me, it just didn't appeal to me. I wanted something about a girl that interested me—something about her that made it a little difficult to reach the hunting grounds—paying for it was like playing with myself, which bored the hell out of me. I liked Marie very much, she stuttered slightly, making her voice a little unusual but intriguing . . . but I couldn't erase the wooden shoe festival from my afterthoughts. . . . One rainy night . . . I was lonesome alone, and began to think about Marie, a young hard-on thinking, maybe I could pantomime her into coming to a little apartment—get her clothes off, give her a bath, and go to bed the way it should be done, away from the drippings, the cobblestones, the confused cot and the wooden shoes. So I decided to visit the bakery; they might have a few éclairs, French éclairs, little ones, about three inches of delicious yum yums. I was lucky, there were six left, I bought them for Marie, it might help.

When I arrived in the rain, she was just finishing hanging up the drippings, grandma had gone to bed, there were no French pilots, it was my night.

She seemed glad to see me, maybe because she was a little tired of the wooden shoe acrobatics. I had never made a pass at her, god forbid I might be the brother image, that would be the end, so I held out my hoped for sex inflamers. She was curious and reached for them, I pulled them back, she reached again, getting close, again I pulled them back, she literally attacked me, it was wonderful, I had her in my arms but she was so quick she got away, and with her, the éclairs. She started running among the rows of leaking clothes with me after her. We were laughing, tearing off pants, drawer, undershirts, sheets, socks, everything the eight pilot lovers wore, finally I caught her, we both were as wet as if we had just come in from the rain. I held her in my arms, she stopped struggling. I kissed her full on the lips—it was like kissing a dried crust, passion flew out the window into the rain.

Six crushed eclairs, one crushed desire, and a pathetic woebegone confusion. . . . Renee would be different.

During Wellman's stay in Le Plessis-Belleville, he had met an enchanting brunette named Renee. Her mother had died when she was very young; her father had been killed in an air raid at the beginning of the war. Renee had a sister who was married to a French soldier and living in Paris. Although Renee worked in a bakery in Plessis, she kept a small apartment in Paris to be near her sister and to pursue a career in painting.

Wellman's winter uniform included a fur coat. *Courtesy of the author.*

When Wellman happened upon the Plessis bakery and gazed at the stunning French girl, it was love at first sight. That instantaneous cupid-shot was shared by Renee. As soon as she could manage it, she followed Wellman to Luneville, gaining employment in a small bakery near the airfield. During the harsh winter weather, when no flying was scheduled, their romance continued to bloom.

Wellman did not write or talk about this relationship until he was seventy-seven years old.

She was older than I, but beautiful beyond compare, not only in appearance, in every other way imaginable—she was one of the great number of women who, despite each and every known handicap, persisted in being close to the one and only man that meant everything to them. No matter where they had to go, wherever the war was that their man was a part of, that was where they went, living on the outskirts, cold and hungry, but existing for the few heavenly dwarfisms of time they were able to get together. She was that way with me at Luneville, working in a bakery shop.

For the time being, Wellman decided to keep his first real love affair a secret from his family.

It was common practice among the pilots to name their planes and have a good luck moniker painted on the fuselages. Wellman chose "Celia I," after his mother. On Wellman's next experience with the enemy, he was on an early morning patrol in Celia I. It was bitter cold, and there were no Boche planes in sight. After about an hour, boredom and the chill caused him to leave the patrol and dive to a lower altitude where it would be warmer. He spotted a camouflaged two-seater machine called an Aviatik. It had been on a photographic mission and was on its way home. Wellman had been well instructed not to dive on a two-place machine from above, as the gunner, with a swivel machine gun, could fire in any direction except downward.

Instead of coming up from underneath and under the control of wild excitement, Wellman swept down from above in the attack. By every rule of the game, he should have been shot from the skies. But luck was on his side, as the gunner was an extremely poor marksman. As a matter of fact, Wellman wasn't any better. He fired many times without registering a single hit; then his gun jammed, which was a good thing, for it made him realize his foolishness.

The remains of Wellman's plane, Celia I, after crash landing in Luneville in 1917. Wellman emerged from this accident unscathed; however, several months later he was seriously injured in a crash landing over the Forest de Parroy. *Courtesy of the author.*

After speeding past the Aviatik, he turned and scooted for home. Wellman was so overwhelmingly happy to see his own airfield that he forgot another cardinal rule and failed to pull his control stick back and so bring the machine parallel to the ground at the moment of landing. He plunged into the ground nose first. Six thousand dollars' worth of Celia I was smashed to splinters. Only Wellman's ego was wounded.

The pilot's self-esteem would receive another jolt. Ever since joining N.87, he had been on a collision course with a French flyer, Sgt. Jeannot. From day one, Jeannot kept needling the new pilot. Maybe it was because he was an American, or because he had volunteered for the one-man dawn patrol when no Frenchmen would raise their hands, or because Wellman was the replacement for Jeannot's friend, who had been killed in combat. Maybe it was all of the above or something else. In any case, their clash was a certainty. Wellman did his best to ignore the Frenchman's mocking, staying as far from him as possible.

Wellman had spent much of his early years not mixing well with his peers; he wanted very badly to fit in with the other aviators in N.87. He didn't speak the language, and he didn't know their customs, but he was trying to be one of them.

During a mail call in the chateau living room, the Frenchman provoked the American for the last time. When Wellman received the last letter handed out, Jeannot remarked, "Une lettre de Maman?" Wellman answered, "What'd you say?" In broken English, the Frenchman translated, "Letter from Mommy?" Wellman placed the letter in the upper left pocket of his jacket before replying, "Get off me." Jeannot replied, "Connard d'Americain." Wellman knew a few French swear words; *connard* meant "asshole." Without another word, Wild Bill walked over to the Frenchman and belted him in the chops. The fight was on.

Wellman was shorter than Jeannot and fought from a crouched position. The Frenchman was an upright fighter displaying stiff-legged kicks with sharp punches; he was experienced in savate, a popular French martial art.

Sgt. Jeannot moved with grace, speed, and accuracy. He was able to kick from many angles, even with his back to his opponent. This fight resembled a choreographed dance, a kind of ballet, as Jeannot's feet performed a tattoo on Wellman's face and body. Before long, the American was bleeding profusely from the nose, mouth, and cuts over both eyes. The living room furniture was taking a beating as well.

In the first five minutes, Wellman had scarcely touched his adversary, with most of his punches too wild to catch up with the deceptive Frenchman. Even though the American was taking a serious beating, there was no quit in him. But he realized that his tactics were incorrect; he stopped momentarily, faking injury, to think it over.

From the circle of Frenchmen gathered around, Miot stepped forward to stop the slaughter. The other aviators pushed him back. Now, Wellman tried a different strategy as he moved toward Jeannot. He bobbed and weaved, trying to become a more difficult target. The Frenchman missed a few kicks and threw some sharp punches that missed the mark.

As the aggressive American moved closer to the dancing Frenchman, the front doors swung open and Captain Azire, with another officer, entered the room. They stood near the doorway and watched the battle royale.

Settling arguments with fists was quite common at Luneville, but when one of the combatants was being destroyed, the fight got stopped.

While Azire and the other officer were watching, Wellman caught up to Jeannot, hitting him on the hips and thighs instead of trying to land blows to the stomach and head. This tactic slowed the Frenchman's foot speed and brought his guard down. The American landed his best punch of the fight, a left hook to the thigh and right cross to the jaw. This combination dropped the Frenchman to the floor; he got up quickly and danced away from the swarming American.

Seeing the American bathed in blood and obviously losing the battle at this point, the commandant stepped in to halt the brawl. The other officer grabbed Wellman from behind, while Miot moved in front of Jeannot. Now Azire took a position between the fighters.

"Ça suffit. Qui a commencé? Who started this?"

Neither Wellman nor Jeannot said anything. Several pilots answered from the group.

"L'Americain a frappé le premier."

Azire glanced at Wellman. "Is this true? Did you strike first?"

Wellman, breathing heavily, answered. "Yeah . . . sir."

Azire thought for a moment before replying.

"I'm disappointed in you, Corporal. Disagreements between pilotes are common. Oftentimes they serve a useful purpose. But they can cause deep resentments that are not good for the morale of the escadrille. You are the first American in this escadrille. Others will follow. You are setting a bad precedent."

Azire scanned the flyers' faces and the room as well, which was littered with broken chairs, lamps, tables, and the like.

"Furniture can be replaced. Good pilots are more difficult. Do you have anything to say for yourself?"

Wellman looked straight at his commandant and said, "No, sir."

Azire answered without hesitation.

"I have put men in the stockade. I put you on probation. Attend to your wounds. Dismissed."

Wellman was handed bandages and disinfectants. He waved off any help from the other pilots. Renee would become his nurse.

From this day forward, the young American began to receive respect from the French aviators—not only because he fought the valiant fight and took responsibility for it, but also due to his comradeship and prowess in the air. Wellman would return that respect, but would always feel like an outsider looking in.

Wellman's best wartime friend, fellow American Thomas Hitchcock, was a ten-goal polo player. *Courtesy of the author.*

Dear Arch: Dec. 12

   . . . Another American arrived here yesterday. Thomas Hitchcock of New York. His father is a very wealthy man and Tommy is a wonder. Just nineteen years old, a whale of a pilote and we two, in the same escadrille can fly to-gether and should be able to work up a good team. A lot of this work is volunteer and two chaps who absolutely understand each other in the air, can pull off a lot of good work. However that all remains to be seen.

Thomas Hitchcock Jr. of Westbury, Long Island, became an important player in the Lafayette Flying Corps. From a renowned family, he excelled as a sailor and horseman, particularly in the sport of polo.

Hitchcock had joined the French Aviation on June 25, 1917. From the beginning, he astonished his instructors with natural ability, a double dose of courage, and an unflinching demeanor. He performed outstandingly with all types of aircraft. He was brevetted on September 17 and sent to Escadrille N.87, where he arrived on December 10.

Hitchcock and Wellman teamed up immediately and were called the "A-Team." They were fast friends and fearless flyers. During the next three months, they would record five confirmed "kills" and receive multiple medals and citations, including one of France's highest honors, the Croix de Guerre with Palms. Each palm was like getting another Croix de Guerre.

It was Christmas morning, and snow sparkled on the ground and roofs in Luneville—a picture-book scene. Captain Azire mentioned a quick "Merry Christmas," and it was back to work—war knew no holidays.

Wellman was scheduled for patrol duty protecting a three-place machine, a Letord, on a photographic mission. He wore his winter wardrobe: three suits of underwear, three pairs of woolen socks, and a heavy winter uniform. This was supplemented with a fur-lined flying combination and helmet, fur-lined boots, a sweater, and a muffler wrapped about his neck, ears, and forehead. It took two mechanics to hoist him into the cockpit and strap him in place. Santa Claus had never looked like this. In the six pockets of the combination suit were placed small boxes, covered on the outside with velvet, and containing a slab of charcoal that could be ignited at the last moment by a fuse at one end. It glowed and shed heat for a short time.

Six escorting Nieuports came online and followed the cumbersome Letord as it taxied across the snowy field and slowly floated into the crisp air. The mission was to photograph troop movements over the town of Saarburg, about an hour away. As soon as the squadron crossed over into enemy territory, the sky came alive with the black puffs of anti-aircraft explosions—a "Merry Christmas" from the enemy.

After completing the picture-taking, the group turned for home. There were no enemy planes in the sky as it turned dark and deadly with rain, hail, and increasing wind. Before they had gone halfway back, snow began to fall. Icy particles covered the glass windshields and the pilots' faces. One by one the planes lost sight of each other. Wellman's motor began to misfire and he struggled to keep Celia II in the air and on course. He was able to follow a bare outline of the Vosges mountain range and later the Forest de Parroy, which ran some three miles from French territory and crossed the front lines into Germany. Still working to keep his engine alive, he spotted a bright light in the black storm coming from ignited gasoline on the airfield for the returning airmen.

The high-velocity windstorm buffeted Wellman's small aircraft as it neared the snow-covered ground. The slender wheels sunk into the snow, sending the machine over and over in three complete somersaults. When the plane stopped rolling, it was smashed to bits, with the back end of the fuselage bent around until it almost touched the front, its wings both separated from the fuselage. Wellman was amazed to still be alive and able to walk away from the final gasp of Celia II.

```
Dear Little Mother:                                    December 26
   Day after Christmas and believe me Xmas was a pretty lively affair.
True there were no happy greetings in the morning, but I was fortunate as
to gifts. Money that was much needed. Two packages from Aunt Sarah, one
of candy and the other smokes, Pall Malls and Philip Morris. Then my "old
Americain Friend" as she terms herself, Miss Wood sent me candy,
cigarettes, holly and a beautiful combination wallet and cigarette case,
with my initials W. A. W. inscribed in silver . . .
   Things going along famously. Xmas noon I spent twenty five miles in
Germany on a photographing expedition. Thrills every minute but we got
back safely in spite of a snow storm. Then, your beautiful letter was
waiting for me. That was the best Christmas present of them all.
```

```
Dear Little Mother:                                    December 27
   When I finish this note to you I will write one to Arch having
received news of his joining the U.S. aviation. Will give him all the
dope I know and let him profit by it if it is any good to him. . . .
Weather terrible. Snow very deep and consequently our landings have to be
made with a great deal of care. Christmas was spent over Germany as I
have already written you. Believe me Mother it was cold, very cold, in
fact I never before knew what cold really was. Am just waiting for this
winter to get over, then the summer and perhaps a permission home. . . .
Then we can talk all things over. . . . My health is wonderful. Feel like
a "fighting cock" all the day.
```

In Arch Whitehouse's *Legion of the Lafayette*, he gives this account:

On one occasion Hitchcock and Wellman came upon a German two-seater and began a relentless chase, each one taking turns darting in from tight angles to taunt the gunner. Still, the biplane stayed in the air and started to glide for its field near Nancy. Wellman and Hitchcock tried every trick in the bag to torch them, but the rugged two-seater crew hung on, so the two Nieuport pilots turned their attention to the field itself. They shot up aircraft standing on the line, then dove on hangar after hangar trying to hit something inflammable that would start a good fire. The defense machine guns tried to drive them off, but Tommy and Bill forked the gun teams out of their pits, and when they had driven everyone to cover, pulled out and raced back for their own lines. By the time they returned to their field neither one had a round of ammunition left. They heard later that one of them had killed the German observer in the two-seater.

On a photographic protection assignment, Wellman and Hitchcock, expecting some real excitement, encountered no enemy opposition of any kind. Boredom set in as the mission was completed. As they started for home,

Hitchcock moved closer to Wellman and, pointing toward the Vosges Mountains, pantomimed their next mission. Wellman signaled his understanding.

Wellman said, "I knew immediately what was up. Last night we lay in bed talking about how quiet it had been for over a week. One patrol of Germans flying and by the time we got there, they were gone. Strange, but Tom had an answer that might possibly stir things up. He had noticed on one of our flights a small town close to the mountains that had a wide straight roadway that ended on a church with a good-sized belfry with a very good-sized church bell. He wanted to ring that bell by flying up the street and just before he had to fly up and over the belfry, to let go with as many shots as he could, cut his motor and hear if he had rung the bell.

"I was to circle to one side and above and cut my motor at the same time, continuing my circling, and perhaps I would hear the church bell ring. I bet him I would hear them and the only bells ringing for him would be those that were constantly ringing in his head.

"When he finished we were going to change positions and give me a chance to be a bell ringer. It sounded like fun so off we went to awaken a sleepy little town.

"We arrived at our destination, Tom flying down the outside of the town preparing for a fast turn and a swift flight up the main street, full motor, while I lazily circled above and very close to the belfry. Here he came, just a few feet above the street, people ducking into doorways, full motor with one hand on the gun ready to pull the trigger and the other doing the flying with the thumb on the coupe contact button, to stop and start the motor and listen. He did a great job hitting the bell with a cluster of shots and just clearing the top of the church tower as he started his motor again. Meanwhile I lost altitude as I circled with my motor shut off and I heard the sharp pings as the bullets caromed off the bell. I gave it full motor and went the same way Tom had done. I did it exactly the same speed, cut the motor as he did, and Tom duplicated my previous maneuver. He heard, as I did, I heard as Tom did, nothing but the rotation of my motor even before giving it full power to get me over the tower.

"You can hear a church bell ring without pulling on a rope, and incidentally scare the hell out of a group of quiet homey townspeople. They must have held a town meeting to try to decide what two enemy planes were doing, not shooting at anybody or anything except the church bell, maybe they were heathens and that was a warning, or an odd way to defame God, or perhaps it was just a couple of young crazy fliers playing games. Which it was."

Because of the strict rules forbidding flyers to divulge war information to the home front, Wellman wrote only one such letter.

```
Escadrille N.87                                      Jan. 19, 1918
Section 44

Dear Dad,

    Just a letter to follow the cable. Was so tickled after everything was
over that I just sent the good news the quickest way possible. Trust you
have received the photos and various things I have sent. Today I am
```

enclosing a few more photos for Mother. Pictures of machines, pilotes, snow and other points of interest. Study them carefully and you can learn a lot.

Now for the real thing. Today I was sent out to do protection work for a big machine taking pictures over the lines. With me was another pilot named "Miot" a Frenchman and a wonderful chap. We of course have as you know, small, fast, fighting machines, and when a large two-place machine is sent to take photographs it has protection from us little, but faster chaps. This usually is a terrible bore, nothing to do but get a lot of trouble from the anti-craft batteries. Usually the big machine is well protected so that no enemy interferes from the air. The photos were all taken and the big chap descended to the home grounds when I saw the black puffs of a French battery giving it to a German, who was just above our little village. "Miot" saw him the same time and we both started to climb after him. "Miot" going to the right and me to the left. I got to just four thousand meters and the "Bosche" dead ahead coming toward me when I saw "Miot" make his first and last attack. He dove at the Bi-plane "Bosche" and one of his wings snapped off. Probably one of the vital points had been hit by the "Bosche". Imagine Dad he was just perhaps fifty yards from me and I saw the poor boy drop into a tree and not come out of it until he hit the ground. His machine was smashed to bits. (he landed in the French lines) and he of course had to be identified by various papers on his body.

Well, by this time Tommy Hitchcock, the other American with me here, had arrived on the scene and together we tackled the "Bosche". First, Tommy diving from above and coming up underneath him and then shooting when as near as possible, then I would repeat the performance. He, the "Bosche", was descending all the time and finally at two thousand meters his engine must have given out for his propellor stopped. The rest of the way he had to vol-o-plane and believe me Dad we gave it to him in great style. Also they were a couple of gamsters for they were shooting at us all the time. The pilot when his machine was in a good position and the gunner, (the man behind) all the time, to make a long story short, the Bosche smashed just between the trenches and as Tommy and I had followed him down to the ground, we started a lot of fun in the trenches. We were just twenty yards above the trenches and they gave us hell from their rifles.

Although we were not touched the machines were pretty badly. One wing has to be changed and the other is well patched up with cloth coverings over which an iron cross is painted. This Dad, is the whole story and is the first experience of my new machine, the "Celia III."

May I have as much luck always and be able to add a few more palms on my "Croix de Guerre" for I will now have that medal with one palm, a citation from the Army of France.

Love,
Bill.

Wellman continued to spend as much time as possible with the beautiful Renee. One can only imagine her constant torment at waiting for her pilot's return from so many missions.

War changes people, and this young, impetuous, American flyer was changing with it. He was discovering the force of love while living with the continual threat of death. He was holding onto hope and the power of prayer for a better tomorrow. He was understanding that the future might only be now—just this moment in time.

Still keeping the love affair a secret from Mother and family, only Tommy Hitchcock served at Wellman's wedding in a small church on the outskirts of Paris. Renee's pregnant sister was her only confidant. The groom and best man were dressed in their first-class uniforms complete with Croix de Guerres. The bride wore her sister's wedding dress. Hitchcock provided a plain gold wedding band.

Mrs. William A. Wellman enjoyed only one night of bliss before her husband and Tommy Hitchcock returned to the war.

During the war, propaganda was a flourishing issue. One form of it was the dropping of leaflets and pamphlets across enemy lines. This paper trail sounded everything from Allied victories to President Woodrow Wilson's speeches to Congress and the American people.

Over time, bundles of propaganda began building up. Hundreds of pounds of Wilson's speeches were taking up space across the war zones. The French pilots were less interested in disseminating paper than in sending bombs across German lines. However, maybe a couple of crazy American pilots might jump at the opportunity to harass their enemy with their president's words.

On the morning of February 11, Wellman and Hitchcock were summoned by Captain Azire. With a twinkle in his eye, he offered the A-Team a special mission together. "Together" was nothing new, but the "special" part was electrifying.

The two American flyers were invited to drop President Woodrow Wilson's messages to Congress—translated into German and French—over the lines in enemy territory. Their excitement was soul-stirring. However, their enthusiasm for the actual delivery process was somewhat less.

Bundles of pamphlets had to be rolled up into small parcels and tied lightly with thin twine. Two bundles each, one in German and one in French, would be dropped at the same time. To the flyers it all sounded like great sport and very patriotic, but they soon discovered that simply tossing bundles overboard at a hundred and thirty miles an hour caused an entanglement with the wings and fuselage. Frequently, the strings would break or slip off in midair, and the pamphlets would go fluttering down like so much confetti. The process needed research and experimentation, but there was no time for research, and the experimenting would have to be quick.

When Wellman and Hitchcock took to the air, the weather was less than ideal. The sky was gray with heavy, low-hanging clouds; the wind was turbulent. They separated so that their sectors could be covered in half the time. Time was of the essence, since the "Archies" (anti-aircraft shells) would be launched in their direction, to say nothing of machine gun and small-arms fire. It had to be a hit-and-run affair.

The flyers discovered that by executing vertical virages (turns in the air), tossing the bundles over when flying perpendicular, and at the same moment kicking the machine around sharply so that its tail would not hit them, the plane could pass before the bundles had dropped a foot.

It seemed amazing that both pilots could successfully fly at low altitudes for several miles at a time, through a hailstorm of bullets and shrapnel while doing acrobatic stunts, and escape scot-free. Wellman was amused to look back and see men below and behind dropping their rifles and scrambling for the messages fluttering down.

Hitchcock completed his drop-task first. He waved a salute to Wellman and sped for home, thinking Wellman would follow right along. However, Wild Bill's exuberance gave him another idea. He had one more package to deliver and one more showoff to accomplish.

Instead of performing the usual virage, he sped directly upward for several hundred feet, turned, and dove vertically at the enemy troops and trenches. Just before crashing into the earth, he did a renversement—turning the machine up, flipping it over on its back, then pulling up so that he came out in exactly the same line in which he had started—before shooting up again in a loop. At the top of the loop, his motor quit. The magneto had broken, leaving him in an upside down position, just a few hundred yards above the ground without any power. As bullets buzzed around him, some hitting the plane, he turned the machine on its side and coasted away from the enemy.

There was enough wind to help carry his machine back over No-Man's Land and the first-line French trenches. The poilus (French soldiers) beneath him shouted encouragement as he passed over their heads and landed in a shell-hole big enough to accommodate Celia IV. As Wellman slowly unhooked his harness and leisurely gathered up his compass, maps, and a few personal things, the French soldiers began shouting. Wellman could understand only carefully spoken elementary French, but when he heard the discordant sound of an artillery shell passing overhead and landing some twenty-five yards beyond, exploding with an earsplitting roar and shower of dirt and rocks, he understood their French perfectly. He accelerated his exit from the plane and ran full tilt to the nearest of the trenches. The shelling, in his honor, continued for some time; when it ceased, Celia IV was unidentifiable.

Wellman thought, talked, and wrote about having more than his share of good luck. Good luck and bad made strange bedfellows. One never knew which would get up with him in the morning. It seemed that Wild Bill Wellman had good luck as his constant companion. But when Renee sent word to him that her sister's husband had been killed in battle and the baby was ready to deliver, good luck stayed in bed for a long while.

"The weather was lousy," Wellman wrote.

It was raining day after day and I got my captain to let me go to Paris for a short few days of funmaking. We went to Paris together, to her small little apartment where she did her painting when not following me. She left to hurry to the hospital to be with her sister, hopefully before the birth of the baby—she said she would be home sometime during the night and showed me the little café nearby where I could get a light dinner. It was late and dark when I got there. The Germans had been bombing Paris with the first long distance cannon of the war. It started as I was eating and I lost my appetite. A poilu came flying into the café—the hospital had been hit—a direct hit—there was nothing left of it.

I explained as best I could that my wife had gone there to visit her sister and he took me there. He was right, there was nothing left—a direct hit, with the police digging into the still burning rubble for dead mothers and babies. My poilu friend told them who I was, so I joined the rubble searchers looking for my wife. Some of the people that were found were just blackened bits and pieces. My poilu pal stuck with me—he found a burned leg and arm, God knows who they belonged to. All I was certain of was that I had no wife, I didn't get sick, I didn't stop searching but an anger encompassed me so frightful and so welcome that I went completely berserk, digging into smoldering rubble and finding nothing but burned flesh and guts and coming up with a charred finger with no fingernail joint, a little of the knuckle and a ring, a plain gold ring that I had placed on my wife's beautiful finger when we got married exactly one month ago. I stopped digging, that was all that was left of my beautiful wife. An ashen finger, it looked like a bone you would throw to your dog. I got sick to my stomach and threw up. My poilu pal took the finger from me and asked me what to do with it, did I want the ring? No—nothing to keep reminding me of the slender beautiful fingers, that used to wander through my hair, a face like an angel—she was an angel. You knew her sister, find out if there is anybody else and take care of everything. I've got to go back to Luneville, I want to talk to Tommy. He dropped it gently into a pile of burning wood—a funeral pyre for my love.

Only Tommy Hitchcock would know the whole story, and his lips stayed sealed for his buddy. Wellman placed this entire chronicle on his life's back burner for the next fifty-five years.

Good luck continued to be a distant memory on March 6, 1918. Conflicting tales speak of another tragic event in the life of William Wellman. He and Hitchcock were two members of a five-plane patrol when they attacked a six-plane group of German Albatross fighters. An action-packed dogfight ensued. Wellman and Hitchcock became separated in the combat. When the smoke cleared and the pilots from Escadrille N.87 landed, Hitchcock's plane was not among them. Wellman's Nieuport was badly damaged, so he couldn't go back after his pal. He waited the rest of the day and night on the tarmac and paced the airfield. Tommy Hitchcock never came back.

Combined reports from the history books *Lafayette Flying Corps* and *Legion of the Lafayette* give the following account. A German bullet entered Hitchcock's back and another cut his aileron control wire, which deprived him of maneuverability. The enemy pilots forced his plane to the ground.

Wellman poses in a German two-seater he and Hitchcock shot down. *Courtesy of the author.*

Tommy's wounds placed him in a German hospital, and later he was imprisoned at a military compound at Lechfeld. From the minute he was put behind barred gates, he planned an escape. After several failed attempts and over five months of imprisonment, on August 28, 1918, he was successful in one of the most thrilling escapes of the war.

While traveling at night during a prisoner transfer, he leaped from a speeding train full of German soldiers. He moved mostly under the cover of darkness. By daylight, he covered ground through thick wooded areas until reaching the Swiss border and crossing into safety.

With Tommy gone, Wellman felt lost. They had been an inseparable team, as close as brothers. Wellman recalled,

---

We trained together at Avord. Went through acrobatics together at Pau. Ended up together at the front at Luneville in the Alsace-Lorraine. Flew patrols together, shot up enemy airdromes together, shot down a German Rumpler and a Fokker together. Lived together. Dropped President Wilson's messages to Congress, translated in German, in the front-line trenches together. Went to Paris together. Hell, we did everything together, and on two occasions he saved my life. Tom was a ten-goal polo player. Tom was a ten-goaler in everything.

Hitchcock and Wellman, the A-Team, had flown so much together, sharing complete trust in each other's support. If Wellman made an attack, he knew Hitchcock would be right there and vice versa. However, on the occasion of March 6, Wellman was not right there.

How could Wellman have known that Hitchcock had suddenly left the aerial combat, diving hundreds of feet into a flock of Albatross fighters below? Wellman didn't know and wouldn't find out any of the story until after the war had ended.

Consumed by personal loss and guilt, Wellman asked and received permission to fly as a one-man patrol, except, of course, when called upon for squadron duty.

On March 21, just fifteen days after Hitchcock's disappearance, while on solo patrol, Wellman was shot from the skies by anti-aircraft guns over the Forest de Parroy. His Nieuport crashed into treetops. He was thrown from the cockpit and, as he fell to the ground, he clung to the boughs of a tree before sliding down beside the wrecked Celia V.

French soldiers rescued him and took him to the hospital. He was partially paralyzed, suffering from moments of blackout. There was internal bleeding. His back was broken in two places. The control stick of his plane had been forced through the roof of his mouth, and a piece of shrapnel was embedded in his nose, an eighth of an inch from his eye. But good luck lay beside him, for he had escaped death.

During World War II, a comic strip commemorated "Wild Bill" Wellman's heroism as an aviator during the First World War. *Courtesy of the author.*

Surgery removed the shrapnel, and a silver plate was inserted into his skull. He would wear a full back brace for many weeks, and one doctor believed he would not walk again.

On March 29, 1918, Sergent William Augustus Wellman received his honorable discharge from the French army and Lafayette Flying Corps.

Decorations: Croix de Guerre, with two Palms
             Medaille Militaire
Citations: A L'Ordre de L'Armee
             Le Pilote Americain, Marshall de Logis
Final Rank: Sergent

After a brief recovery period, a more subdued Wild Bill Wellman sailed to New York aboard the French liner *Espagne*.

Two hundred and ten Americans saw combat duty with the French. Sixty-five were shot down or killed in accidents. Thirty-five were wounded or taken prisoner. There were 100 casualties. Seventy-two pilots were credited with official victories. This meant that observers were able to confirm the kills or the pilots themselves retrieved the black crosses from the fuselages of the downed planes. The Americans accounted for 199 confirmed victories, with hundreds unconfirmed.[1]

There had been great camaraderie between Wellman and the other Americans he befriended in the Lafayette Escadrille and Lafayette Flying Corps. His closest pals were Thomas Hitchcock, Frank "Jules" Baylies, David Putnam, Reginald "Duke" Sinclaire, David Judd, William "Billy" Meeker, and Staff Brown. Baylies, Putnam, Meeker, Brown, and Hitchcock were killed in the wars. Of all Wellman's friends, only David Judd and Reggie Sinclaire survived the battlefields.

3

The Homefront

Upon returning, William Wellman and other veterans were treated as heroes. There had been a great deal of media attention praising the gallantry of those young Americans who risked their lives for France before America entered the war. This worship would last only as long as the war. From the boat to Wellman's neighborhood, hundreds of well-wishers received him back home. What a sight he must have been, arriving by taxi to his family's home in Newton, Massachusetts, a suburb of Boston.

Wearing his best blue uniform, medals, two wings—French and Lafayette—and back brace, he carried a duffle bag and walked with a limp up the steps onto the porch and into the waiting arms of his mother and the handshake of his father. Lieutenant Arch Wellman was not home to greet his brother, as he was down in West Point, Georgia, testing planes for the U.S. Air Service.

As amazing as it sounds, Wellman's old dog, Taffy, partly deaf and blind and quite arthritic, was waiting also. Man's best friend took his last breath the evening of his master's return. Wellman buried Taffy in the back yard, where both had spent much of their youth.

At the dinner table that first night, Celia and Arthur showed their son pages of names, addresses, and phone numbers of people wanting to see him. The list included calls from local newspapers, magazines, the mayor, and even Teddy Roosevelt. It seemed to Wellman that the whole world wanted a meeting.

Among the personal items Wellman displayed for his parents was a cablegram sent to France by Douglas Fairbanks, congratulating the Croix de Guerre recipient and again offering an unspecified Hollywood job.

Later that evening, Wellman, still in uniform, accompanied his father to the local watering hole. Arthur had suggested to Celia that the men have some quality time together. The two Wellmans pushed open the front door of the neighborhood establishment, right into a surprise party. The bar was

William Wellman returned from the war a decorated pilot with no real career direction. Here he is pictured in civilian clothes and holding some of the medals he earned flying for France. *Courtesy of the author.*

crowded with local gentry singing, "Over there, over there, the Yanks are coming, the Yanks are coming, the Yanks are coming everywhere," and the like.

Wellman soon found himself in the center of a rip-roaring, drunken ca-rousal. There were shouting, applauding, hand-shaking, back-slapping, and drink after drink pushed in his direction. Everyone wanted to hear about the war and Wellman's exploits in it.

The embarrassed pilot, trying to get with it, answered a few questions while Arthur tried to restore order to the boisterous crowd. Later that evening, with the party still in full swing, Arthur, two sheets to the wind, be-gan clanking beer mugs with his son and the closest merrymakers. The toasts covered many thoughts and future notions—from Billy's safe return, to the end of the war, to Billy's future job possibilities, to thanking God for John Barleycorn.

The evening climaxed when Arthur sloppily discussed his son's state of health and the ugly back brace. Billy, with slightly slurred speech, explained that he felt fine, had worn the brace for a number of weeks, and was supposed to keep it on for many more. After another gulp, Arthur announced to the room that his son should take the "goddamn" thing off, throw it across the bar, and never wear it again. Billy downed the rest of his beer and began to undress. In his inebriated state, he had some difficulty taking off his coat and shirt, revealing the laced-up leather and steel-ribbed brace. He began to untie the laces. The crowd started to shout and applaud their approval, some thinking it was strip time. With Arthur's less-than-expertise assistance, Billy pulled out of the back brace and threw it. The brace flew across the top of the bar, taking glasses, bottles, and dishes with it before crashing to the floor at the end of the bar.

When Wellman awoke the next morning, he was greeted by two things—a head-pounding hangover and a sharp pain in his back. After wobbling to his feet, he laced up that "goddamn" back brace, where it would cling for several more weeks. Then came a zigzag trip to the kitchen for some strong java.

The decorated airman's popularity brought a steady diet of meetings, interviews, lunches, and dinners with reporters, photographers, and local dignitaries. Even the mayor got into the act with a first-rate parade in his honor. The war ace waved to the mob scene from the back seat of a convertible.

Wellman was a guest speaker at several war-bond rallies. The fuss made over this returning aviator was enormous. His enjoyment of coming home was fast fading. As the days rolled by, the business of being a war hero turned his smile downward. He didn't feel like a hero; rather, he felt like a busted-up, ex-fighter pilot who had lost his wife and buddies and had no future in sight.

When called upon to speak at the war-bond rallies, he even told the audiences, "We airmen are not the heroes that we are acclaimed. I say it now. Flying is safe, under ordinary conditions, and under extraordinary ones it is nine-tenths luck—and the other tenth is foolishness. It is the men in the trenches who are the real heroes of this war, for theirs is the hardest work; theirs the most horrible conditions. All honor to them."[1]

The forlorn flyer began turning away from the media attention until Teddy Roosevelt called again. Wellman went to see him.

By 1918, the former president of the United States (1901–1909) had reached sixty years of age; retired from public life and lived at his home in Oyster Bay, Long Island; and been somewhat forgotten. According to historians John and Alice Durant, "Theodore Roosevelt had been the youngest man to become president, the wealthiest (up to this time), the most popular since Andrew Jackson, and by far the most athletic, dynamic, colorful and adventurous. No shrinking violet was our twenty-sixth president."[2]

In March 1909, Roosevelt left the presidency, sailing to Africa to hunt big game. Soon after his return, and finding his Republican party in disarray, he formed a new party, the Bull Moose Party. During an election speech, he was shot by a deranged assailant. He recovered but lost a close election to the Democratic candidate, Woodrow Wilson. When the war with Germany began, Roosevelt offered to organize a troop division, but was rejected by the president.

Wellman's only personal contact with a Roosevelt had been Quentin, Teddy's youngest child by his second marriage. Quentin was a sophomore at Harvard and engaged to Flora Payne Whitney when the war broke out. He enlisted in the U.S. Air Service and was sent to France. It was difficult being separated from his Flora, and she was denied permission to go to France and be married. Like Wellman, Quentin trained at Avord, but was later assigned to the 95th Bomber Squadron.

Wellman met Quentin once, in Paris, with his pal Tommy Hitchcock. On July 14, 1918, twenty-year-old First Lieutenant Quentin Roosevelt was shot down by two German fighters, crashing behind enemy lines. His body was recovered and buried in France. His grave was later moved to rest beside that of his brother, Ted, in the U.S. Military Cemetery in Colville, France. In 1919, the French government posthumously awarded Quentin the Croix de Guerre.

To illustrate the cruelties of prison camp, a returning pilot told about morbid photos of dead flyers being shown to prisoners in the camps. One postcard displayed the photo of Quentin's mangled body beside his crashed plane.

In 1918, it was rumored that Teddy Roosevelt never recovered from the death of Quentin, his youngest son.

Roosevelt sent a driver to pick up Wellman and take him to Oyster Bay.

I was driven there to meet a great man. It's funny, but I don't remember meeting anybody else. I must have, but he was such a titan that it is only he that I can remember. I can't even remember eating lunch, if we ate at all, just sitting on the porch of a spacious home in Long Island and listening to a man that I felt sorry for.

At first we talked mostly of me and how I learned to fly "the Blériot Method," which is a polite way of saying "by the seat of your pants."

Then he asked me about Tom Hitchcock and how he was brought down. I told him it was in a dogfight; that I was there and was so busy taking care of myself that I didn't even see Tom. Things can pass awfully fast in the air, especially if someone's on your tail, and he's a persistent bastard. Oh, I'm so—Never you mind, I understand perfectly. He chuckled a little and then asked me if I thought Tom was still alive. I told him I had no way of knowing, just hope. Sometimes they would let us know; sometimes they wouldn't. I felt that this was a "wouldn't," because of Tom's importance and reputation as a great polo player. He had a good trade-in value. He thought that made good sense. The only time you can be sure is when the flier crashes inside our lines. I knew whom he was thinking of. We just sat there quiet for a minute or two, then he asked me how well I knew his son. I told him I didn't know him at all, just met him once for a few minutes, with Tommy, and that was it. He looked away off as if trying to remember something. He had a strong, powerful face, but there was a sadness in it.

The two men talked on for some time. Roosevelt mentioned stories of his children and both discussed their current state of health. Roosevelt shared a less-than-widely known fact: People knew he was deaf in his left ear, but few knew he was blind in his left eye. He confided in Wellman:

I never said anything about it. I learned to see with one eye as well as a lot of people could with two. It's like a game, doing something better than the other fellow who has more to do it with than you. Wilson had too much more. I can't understand that man. In 1914—Germany, a ruthless, militaristic country, and he wouldn't even start getting ready, just in case; and then finally after we are in it, I ask permission to raise a division of troops to fight in France, and he said no. So I sit here alone. It's peaceful and quiet, but the whole world is so noisy.

Theodore Roosevelt died January 6, 1919, of a broken heart.

Soon after, another very important phone call grabbed Wellman's full attention. On the other end of the line was a Captain H. Clyde Balsley, calling from Washington DC. Wellman noted,

---

I met him at Le Plessis Belleville, waiting for his papers that would transfer him into the U.S. Air Service as a Captain in the Pursuit Division in Washington.

I had heard all about him, member of the American Ambulance Service, enlisting in the Aviation Section of the Foreign Legion. After receiving his brevet militaire in French Aviation, he spent six weeks at La Bourget as a member of the air guard of Paris. On May 29, 1916 he was sent to N.124 and one month later was shot down in one of the squadron's earliest battles, as a matter of fact, it was his first and last combat.

Balsley was seriously wounded, shot in the hip by an explosive bullet that left a gruesome wound. Unable to use his right leg to work the rudder bar, he soon crashed his Nieuport into a wheat field. His plane flipped over and threw him out. He managed to drag himself away from danger until found by

French soldiers. After a lengthy period in a French hospital at Vadelaincourt, near Verdun, he was transferred to the American hospital at Neuilly. Balsley probably would have died in that hospital had it not been for the extraordinary care given him by his American nurse, Miss Wolf. During a year's stay, he received six operations to remove the many tiny bullet fragments from his body.

On one of Wellman's sojourns to the same hospital, he and Balsley were reunited and developed a friendship. Wellman also received splendid care from another American nurse, Miss Wood, and a lasting friendship developed through letters and occasional visits. After nearly a year and a half from the time of his combat, and although permanently crippled, Balsley was sent back to America.

Captain Clyde Balsley had heard about Wellman's homecoming and was now calling to offer a job.

"Can you still fly?" he asked.

"You're goddamned right I can. What's up?"

"I am working in the Pursuit Division, United States Air Service, and we need a couple of veterans to teach combat, one at Mineola and one at North Island in San Diego, California. Which one do you want?"

"I'll take California."

"Good, you get First Lieutenant."

Wellman said goodbye to his family and the devouring media and was on his way to Washington to add another pair of wings to the French and Lafayette. The officership brought with it respect and a good starting salary, far better than his three and a half cents a day in the Foreign Legion.

He later wrote,

I made my landing in Clyde's office in civies. He looked much better than when I bid him good-bye, and joined the gentlemen who were going to save the world from an idiot called the Kaiser. I was much older, not necessarily in years, and you can strike out one of the words of the report from Pau, "A born flyer but a little crazy," erase the "a" and change the little to completely. That I was, and most of the pursuit pilots I knew were, in fact the French encouraged it.

Balsley was well-respected and pleased with his job. Wellman was again happy as he went through a short indoctrination period.

The only stumbling block was the physical examination he would have to take; one that he could not possibly pass. Clyde told him not to worry, for they had their own system there. Wellman took off the back brace and arrived at a doctor's office in one of the Air Service buildings. Wellman recalled,

He was a Lieutenant Colonel, which made me a little wary.

He told me to strip, which I did, and then the comicality started. They pounded me, they rubber-fingered me, deep throated me, looked at everything I had, including a very bored penis, at last came the moment of truth, a long white line down which I must tight rope walk without a stutter. Unfortunately I had not listened to Clyde and did not keep the brace on until the last minute, so I had a tired and painful back to help me walk the white line like a drunk.

The charming lieutenant colonel chimed in with a dilly, "You haven't had anything to drink, have you?"

Wellman in his U.S. Air Service uniform with French wings over his right pocket and U.S. wings over his left. He is also adorned by the Croix de Guerre with two palms. *Courtesy of the author.*

"Not this early in the morning."

"Get dressed and come into my office." A comforting invitation.

This I did, and my nonflying pal got right to the point and said I could never be a flyer, and his advice to me was to join the Signal Corps. That, to a flyer, is a third-rated insult, you can't sink any lower, so I left his office saying nothing, you can see I was growing up. I could have said go fuck yourself, but that would have been so untidy.

Wellman returned to Balsley's office, took his pants down again and, with great relief, hooked on his brace. When Clyde returned to the room, he was carrying a new uniform draped over his left arm. He handed it to the surprised Wellman. Clyde's right hand sprung forward for a handshake. Wellman said, "What's this for? I flunked the test." Clyde smiled when he answered, "Remember, we have our own system around here. You passed with flying colors." Wellman shook his hand.

Wellman dressed in the uniform, thanked Clyde for everything, said good-bye, and marched out of the Pursuit Division of the United States Air Service, a virgin first lieutenant on his way to California.

The days at Rockwell Field in San Diego, California, were filled with flying, but a different kind than Wellman was accustomed to. Instead of searching the skies for the enemy, the dogfights, and the thrill of battle, Wild Bill was doing classroom aeronautics and aerial tactics, teaching students to become pilots. Instead of Vickers machine guns, cameras watched the action and took pictures of the results.

For a while, this schooling business suited Wellman fairly well, but he missed the excitement of aerial combat. Boredom reared its ugly head; that lost feeling returned to Wellman's world, and he wondered where all this would lead. After all, the war would not last forever. Where was the future for a battle-tested fighter pilot in civilian life? An invitation arrived for First Lieutenant Wellman to be the honored guest at a Hollywood party at the Del Coronado Hotel in San Diego. The dinner affair was given by French filmmaker Louis Gasnier.

"He was producing the Pearl White serials with Tony Moreno and a beautiful little ingenue, Helene Chadwick," Wellman wrote.

This was my introduction to a new wonder world, the land of cinema. There were a lot of strange new people there, actors and actresses, and they liked me and the uniform, and the medals; and I was very humble, and my limp was eye-catching. [Wellman had made the decision to give up the back brace for good.] Then I met her. The ingenue. She was lovely, and her voice was low and much older than she. I forgot to limp, and my humbleness began to leak. I was like an airplane trying to get into a fogged-in airport.

A beautiful girl and a crazy flier and youth and desire. An unbeatable combination. But all good things must come to an end: I met her mother.

She looked me over like a judge inspecting a prize dog, even walked behind me to see the position of my tail. I saw a dollar sign twinkling in the pupil of each of her ferretlike eyes. Her husband had deserted her—deserted her, hell; he fled from her. There wasn't one single thing about her that even suggested that she was the mother of this beautiful, dainty, talented daughter that I had fallen head over heels in love with. She talked—oh how she talked, a never-ending babble of dull words. Her horn was stuck.

From the get-go, Helene's mother began working against their relationship. Wellman thought back,

---

I can just hear her. Oh, he's a nice boy, but he's a flier, and they are all unreliable . . . You are going to be a great star, but he can only be an aviator, and what good will they be after the war is over . . .

Helene signed a new contract with the Goldwyn Studios, and I was within flying distance of her. We spent the weekends together, either in Hollywood or at the Del Coronado Hotel in San Diego.

On one occasion, Wellman invited Helene to an air show at Rockwell Field. It was an important few days as a twelve-member inspection team of high-ranking officers—including two generals—and a large group of Washington politicians were arriving to inspect the base and view the Air Services' newest pilots and planes.

A large red, white, and blue banner, spelling out "Rockwell Field–U.S. Air Service," hung over the grandstand that was filled with civilians, military people, and Helene Chadwick, dressed to the nines. She was surrounded by a cadre of statesmen.

Between the grandstand and the field stood the two generals, the inspection team, and the ranking officers of the base. A young, enthusiastic captain spoke for the air base and introduced the final event of the weekend—the air show.

A squadron of planes, manned by the best young pilots, took off and flew over the airfield. They performed a number of simple stunts in various formations. As the aviators landed their planes in perfect order, Helene and the hoi polloi showed their appreciation with energetic applause and shouts of *hurrah!*

Next, the captain announced the finale: one pilot, one plane, performing a series of spectacular stunts. Over the loudspeaker came the captain's booming voice: "Ladies and gentlemen, this is our newest and best chase machine, the Spad-17, flown by our top instructor, Lt. William Wellman, a decorated fighter pilot. . . . I told him to show you something you hadn't seen before. Take it away, Wild Bill."

Wellman, in his silver Spad-17, taxied past the grandstand and heard the clamor from the spirited spectators. He looked over and saw the frantic waving from his Helene. He smiled and returned a salute.

Wellman's Spad roared into the blue skies with all eyes on it. He executed the acrobatics—vrilles, loops, tournants, a Russian mountain, and some complex stunts of his own.[3]

Four times he passed the grandstand low enough to cause the throng to duck and grab for their hats. On his next pass, less than fifty feet off the ground, he barrel-rolled toward the officers. As the plane approached, the officers scattered and ran for cover. One of the generals tripped, fell, rolled over, got up, and raced toward the stands.

Wild Bill figured he had given them enough show, but wanted one more showboat. His final stunt would be a close-to-the-ground renversement, a vertical virage, and then a wing-slip.

The book *The Lafayette Flying Corps* defines these terms as follows:

> Renversements—a method of turning by pointing the machine up, flipping it over on its back, and then pulling up so that you come out in exactly the same line in which you came; vertical virages—another way of turning by snapping the machine around a 180° corner; and wing-slips—a way of losing altitude very quickly, by reducing the motor and turning the machine on its side.[4]

Unfortunately, Wellman's grandstanding was less than successful; however, he did show them something they hadn't seen before.

His renversement went perfectly well, and the virage was proper, but when he went into his wing-slip—reducing his air speed and turning the plane on its side—he was too close to the ground and crashed into the turf, somersaulting several revolutions before stopping in a heap. The wings and fuselage collapsed around him. Shock waves rippled through the crowd.

Wild Bill woke up in the base hospital. Next to his bed, seated in a straight chair, was Helene. She told him how lucky he was to have no serious injuries—a few minor fractures and the loss of his front teeth.

Wellman's air show calamity gave his future mother-in-law more lowdown for her attacks on her daughter's "good-for-nothing, crazy-flyer" boyfriend.

The movie star and the aviator continued their torrid romance. A short time later, they met halfway between Hollywood and San Diego, at the old Mission Inn in Riverside, and tied the knot. Wellman dressed in a sport coat

Hollywood starlet Helene Chadwick became the second Mrs. Wellman in 1918, shortly before the armistice. The young actress supported the couple and encouraged her retired warrior husband to choose any career that would make him happy. *Courtesy of the author.*

and tie, Chadwick in a white suit with fox fur cuffs. They stood before a Spanish minister in the mission church and exchanged vows. The only job left—to tell her mother.

Mr. and Mrs. William Wellman motored up to Helene's apartment to drop the bomb. It exploded. There were shouting and crying and all sorts of verbal utterings from Mother. Eventually, she fainted; Wellman didn't catch her.

My mother-in-law never just looked at me, she audited me, over and over, up and down, inside and out, and with never a change of expression. . . . It made Helene very unhappy. I began to get worried.

Then came the two armistices. The first, a false alarm. The second, the real thing. I got a short wire from my wife with but two words, "Thank God."

We—by we I mean the fliers—celebrated the false alarm. We all got loaded, had a fight with the navy, made a shambles of the Coronado bar, and twelve of us goose-stepped off the long pier that used to extend out from the beach of the hotel. It was at night, there was a strong wind, and the waves very very high. We had on our uniforms, complete with the officer's high boots. It was great fun. We did pretty well. We managed to reach the beach, half drowned . . . and then, we found out the armistice was just a rumor. That sobered us up, but it was a little late. C'est la guerre.

The real armistice [November 11, 1918] was celebrated with a little quiet drinking. No fights, no laughter, no talk, no goose-stepping, just silent sorrow. I went to bed early. I didn't sleep.

I asked for, and got, a complete divorce from the air corps. During the time I waited for my discharge papers to come through, I became a member of the ever-growing group we called the Ruptured Penguins. There was no more flying. You reported in and then retired to the Coronado Hotel bar. You were forgotten.

You drank a lot and did a lot of thinking, trying to decide what to do now. This was a new kind of war. A war that you had not trained for. A lonesome war.

I got a letter from my wife. She was on location at Catalina and would be away for another two or three weeks. She said that she was so thankful that I was through with flying, that I could now come home and wait for her and concentrate on choosing a career. Whatever I wanted to become would make her happy.

It sounded so simple. What if I wanted to become a bum? What if I didn't want to, but just became one?

My discharge came through. I bought a couple of suits and became a civilian again. It was an empty feeling, and I was lost. A Joe Doakes with a couple of little narrow, colored ribbons in my buttonhole. You had to get real close to notice them, and even then they didn't mean anything; probably just came with the suit. I threw away my limp and joined another war.

Before going home to his wife, her mother, and Hollywood, Wellman received some momentous news—his buddy Tommy Hitchcock was alive and well!

Wellman contacted the Hitchcock family and discovered that the report was true. However, Tommy had remained in Europe. Wellman left his Hollywood address with the family.

Wellman had never mentioned anything to his family about his first wife. Knowing his second marriage would certainly show up in newspapers and fan magazines, he would have to call home and break the news.

Celia was completely surprised and equally disappointed in her son. Wellman explained that everything had happened so quickly and that his family was so far away at the time. He promised to bring Helene home after she finished her film.

Realizing all that Billy had been through, and trying to keep a proper perspective on the whole affair, Celia remarked that both she and Arthur had always liked the Pearl White serials. They looked forward to the visit.

With Helene out of town on location, Wellman was in no hurry to spend time in the apartment with his mother-in-law. Where would he go? What would he do without his wife?

"Then I remembered," Wellman wrote. "I got out of bed and dove into the dufflebag, and I found it, a worn cablegram from Douglas Fairbanks after the news services had proclaimed to the world that I was winning the war single-handed. It read: 'Great work boy we are proud of you when you get home there is a job waiting for you—Douglas Fairbanks.'"

Wellman found out about one of Fairbanks' grand parties. He awoke early the next morning, dressed in full uniform, shined boots, decorations, and all— a one-day re-enlistment. He had the only Spad airplane at Rockwell Field. He prepared it for takeoff and then split the early morning skies on his way to Douglas Fairbanks.

Fairbanks was hosting a Hollywood polo party. On one side of the polo field was a sea of umbrella tables with chairs, and a long buffet table with portable bars at either end. The rest of the field was devoted to the spirited game, with eight players on horseback involved in the contest. The list of well-dressed guests struck a virtual who's who of the glitter capital: Charlie Chaplin, D. W. Griffith, Harold Lloyd, Buster Keaton, Will Rogers, Rudolph Valentino, Norma Talmadge, William S. Hart, Mack Sennett, and Mary Pickford.

Considered by many to be the world's first superstar, Pickford, in 1915, was the first female to found her own corporation. She was known to movie audiences as "America's Sweetheart." She, along with Fairbanks, Chaplin, and Griffith, had formed the United Artists Corporation in 1919.

Everyone knew Fairbanks and Pickford cared for each other, but since both were already married, their nuptial would not take place until 1920.

Some of the elite guests were glued to the polo match while others roamed through the crowd, socializing. Many sat in the shade of their umbrellas enjoying the sumptuous bill of fare—liquid and solid. Several violinists played background music while waiters and waitresses, in formal attire, moved through the action. Dressed in white, Fairbanks and Pickford paraded through the swarm and gestured their hellos.

The sound of a loud airplane engine caused the celebrities to look skyward. A silver Spad, at maximum speed—132 mph—with First Lieutenant William Wellman at the controls, descended on the attentive gathering. Attitudes swung from concern to fright as the plane dove at the now-scattering mob. It buzzed over their heads, causing some of the polo ponies to skitter and

During the war, Douglas Fairbanks had cabled Wellman with the message "When you get home there is a job waiting for you." After the war the unemployed young pilot landed his plane at one of Fairbanks' famed polo parties, hopped out of the plane, and, with characteristic audacity, asked the Hollywood star for a job. Fairbanks cast him in a co-starring role as a young cowboy in *The Knickerbocker Buckaroo* (1919). *Courtesy of the author.*

rear up, and some of the guests to run for the protection of their umbrellas. The Spad performed a few special stunts before returning for another zoom by.

Wellman pulled back on the throttle, slowing his plane to a landing speed. The Spad glided down to a smooth, perfect landing at the far end of the field and away from the startled horses.

The plane taxied to a stop some sixty yards from the astonished audience. The pilot unhooked his harness and stepped from the cockpit. Dressed in his best blue uniform with three sets of wings, ribbons, and medals, he limped toward the amazed celebrities. All eyes followed him to Douglas Fairbanks and Mary Pickford.

Wellman: Remember me, Mr. Fairbanks? You said if I ever came to Hollywood, to look you up.

Fairbanks: Mary, I'd like you to meet Wild Bill Wellman. He's a helluva hockey player and a war hero. Fairbanks shook Wellman's hand, then passed it to Mary.

Pickford: We've read about you. You have an unusual way of dropping by.

Wellman: I hope I didn't cause any trouble.

Fairbanks: Can you ride a horse?

Wellman: No, but I could. I've ridden everything else.

Fairbanks: I've got a part for you in my new picture. Come with me, I'll introduce you to my director, Albert Parker.

Wellman: Thanks, Mr. Fairbanks.

Fairbanks: Call me, Doug. Excuse us, Mary. I'll be right back.

Wellman left Rockwell Field, San Diego, for good. He traded in his flying uniform for the uniform of a cowboy, boots and all. He was now an actor, playing the juvenile lead with Douglas Fairbanks in *The Knickerbocker Buckaroo* (1919) for $250 a week.

Wellman's next move was another big one—into Helene's apartment with his mother-in-law.

I didn't ring the bell, I just walked in; after all it was really my home—now. She was in the kitchen getting dinner ready. I hoped, for me. She hadn't heard the front door close, so I Hi'ed my presence, but the Hi had a western twang to it. In she came. She had a dress on, and all her hair was showing. She looked very presentable. On her face, a struggling smile, which quickly changed to a look of puzzlement. I told her I had flown out of the air corps and onto the back of a horse, that I had landed a very important role with Douglas Fairbanks, who, thank God, was her idol. I was in. . . . I had risen from a bum to a western Sir Galahad. Dinner that night was in my honor.

Wellman snuck out of the apartment and returned with some bottles of wine. His mother-in-law hit bottom while drinking the second bottle. Her horn got stuck again and Wellman learned the whole history of her life from childbirth. He said but three words: "yes," "no," and "really."

After she wobbled up the stairs to bed, he was left alone and exhausted. When he went upstairs to bed, he passed her room; the door was ajar. He couldn't help peeking in and saw her sitting in front of her dressing table, fussing with her hair. In the next moment, she jerked off a wig, revealing a bald pate. Wellman was shocked and horrified. He wondered how he could ever forget the sight of that large, ruffled, drunken woman, bald as a billiard ball.

Wellman spent the next several days meeting Fairbanks' production team, reading the script, taking riding lessons and photographic tests, and doing rehearsals and wardrobe fittings. He tried to emulate the way a cowboy talked, walked, and rode. Fairbanks told him to wear the western outfit as much as possible, so that it would become a part of him. Wellman recalled,

---

We were not going to work during the weekend.

I made arrangements, with the help of Doug's business manager, to get passage on a water taxi to Catalina Island Friday night. It wouldn't get in till rather late, but I knew Helene wouldn't mind what hour it was, and it would be a wonderful surprise. She was staying at the Saint Catharine Hotel.

It was close to midnight when I arrived at the desk in the Saint Catherine Hotel. I told the night clerk who I was and asked the number of my wife's room. He gave it to me . . . She was on the second floor. The elevator was too slow. I went up the stairs three at a time. I was so excited that my hands were perspiring. I forgot where I was. I didn't knock, I just opened the door, and it opened. I wanted to make the surprise complete, so I stole down the little inside corridor to the bedroom that was dimly lit. Not too dimly. The light came from the lamp on the nightstand. One bed was untouched; in the other were two figures entwined in sleep. Christ, I had the wrong room. One of the dim figures turned in its sleep. It was she. I never got so goddamned mad so quickly. I ran to the bed, he awoke and started up. He didn't get far. I hit him and he fell back with a groan. This awakened her, she sat up staring at me, not believing what she saw. She pulled the sheet around her to hide her nakedness. For the first time, she looked just like her mother. I did something I had never done before or since: I hit her. She let out a shriek like a little dog who's had its tail stepped on, and she crumbled up and fell back, naked. I left them the way they were when I came in, sound asleep.

I spent the night in the water taxi with the skipper. He could tell something rugged had happened to me, but he didn't ask any questions, just broke out a bottle, and we drank ourselves to sleep.

It was midmorning when I arrived at what was my home. When I came in, the old shrew was as usual in the kitchen. When she came out to greet me, she was attired as usual, robe, slippers, and the nightcap with the fake curls sticking out like little angry black tongues. She greeted me, as usual, nastily. Where have you been? You might let me know when you're not going to be here. I told her that I didn't think she would miss me. She said she didn't, but at least she could take care of me for her lovely daughter's sake. I told her that I was sure she would appreciate that now. Then she asked me the sixty-four-dollar question. Where will I tell her you've been? Oh, just tell her I have been to see an old whore I knew. This unstuck the horn, and I went upstairs to pack and get the hell out of there for good. She went back into the kitchen and took it out on the pots and pans. I went into my room, packed quickly; and on the way out as I passed by her boudoir, I got a novel idea. I sneaked in to her dressing table, found her wig in one of the drawers, a pair of scissors in another, and I retired to the bathroom, gave it a butch haircut over the toilet, pulled the chain, and went out of that den of horrors as happy as a lark.

Once again I was homeless . . . so, I found me an inexpensive room in a house on June Street in Hollywood. It was within walking distance of Doug's studio . . . .

In makeup at 7:30. On the set at 8:30. Finished shooting at 6:00 or later. . . . One thing it was doing for me, at least during the day: I wasn't thinking of that other business. . . . Nighttime was not so easy. I eased things a little by helping the cowboys bed down the horses and then drinking beer and eating with them. This usually took a couple of hours, and I didn't get home until around ten o'clock. I was tired physically, but not mentally or imaginatively. I was having a rugged battle on June Street. One night it rained, and I thought I would go crazy. Rainy nights are such wonderful nights if you are in love and together, and so lonesome if you are alone.

———————————————————

4

The Slippery Ropes of Hollywood

The Catalina caper signaled the end of Wellman's second marriage but the beginning of his film career. The production of *Knickerbocker Buckaroo* went smoothly, but Wellman never felt comfortable in the actor's boots.

A second role, in Raoul Walsh's *Evangeline* (1919), got him a raise to $400 a week with a four-week guarantee. He was cast as a young lieutenant in the British army. His costume consisted of a red and white uniform, leggings, and a white powdered wig.

In his first scene, Wellman was to wade out into the ocean to a small boat, pick up the beautiful female star, Miriam Cooper, and without getting her wet, bring her back to shore. While carrying her in his arms, Wellman took it upon himself to kiss her, just before stepping into an underwater hole and disappearing from sight. Because she could not swim, she came up frightened and fighting. In order to subdue her, Wellman was forced to cold-cock her, then swim the rest of the way to shore and deposit her sleeping body at the foot of the director, Raoul Walsh—who turned out to be her husband. Wellman was fired on the spot but paid off in full. His only scene shot was edited out of the final edition.

When *Buckaroo* was released, Wellman went to see it all alone. He left halfway through, rushed to the men's room, and threw up. The next day, he went to Fairbanks and told him he wasn't cut out to be an actor. Fairbanks understood and asked him what he wanted to be. Wellman told him he wanted to be a director. Fairbanks, of course, couldn't make him a director overnight, but got him started in the production department of Goldwyn Studio—as a messenger boy.

Wellman went from $400 a week as an actor to $22 a week as a messenger boy. His duties included delivering mail to the studio stars—including his ex-wife, Helene Chadwick.

The production manager was less than enthused with Wellman. He had

Wellman, shown here on set, had to battle his way through the ranks of Hollywood to become a director. *Courtesy of the author.*

been forced to take him on and made that fact known. The manager ridiculed actors and flyers and seemed to enjoy Wellman's salary demotion. He smiled when he said that Chadwick was in a position to fire Wellman.

Wellman reminisced,

I was given my sack of mail and my route. It included my wife's dressing room. . . . I passed by the directors' board on my way to my first stop, or maybe my last. . . . I looked up at all those big names that were doing what I hoped to do someday. . . . What a list . . . Reginald Barker, Clarence Badger, Harry Beaumont, Hobart Henley, E. Mason Hopper, T. Hayes Hunter, Frank Lloyd, William Parke, Victor Schertzinger, Wallace Worsley. . . . I wondered if I would ever get on a list like that. . . . What had they all within themselves that made them successful directors? There was no school for directors, no particular education that was necessary, no college degrees, just the complete know-how of the making of a picture, great desire, unending work, and the great privilege of having lived unusual and exciting lives.

I seemed to fit into that pattern: no college degree, great desire, willingness to work, and, for a kid, I had lived a couple of lives already. . . .

I knocked on the door. It opened, and there she stood, in bedroom slippers, dressing gown, and, so help me, a towel around her head with a few brown curls sticking out. She looked like her mother, only her horn was not stuck. She was speechless with surprise and confusion.

I broke the spell as I handed her a big bundle of fan mail. "Red Arrow messenger bringing tidings from your growing public—congratulations." She tried to pull herself together and stuttered four world-splitting words: "Well—how—I don't—"

"You don't have to say anything until the end of my small talk, and I hope you don't. I got sick of acting, or acting got sick of me, or I am just a sick actor, so I got Doug to get me a job in a production department and unfortunately it was here. I am starting, as you can see, at the bottom, way down. I am a messenger boy. My very personable boss is worried about what your attitude might be on seeing your outgoing husband grazing in your green pastures. This is his method of finding out, as it is mine. Of course your lawyer has described in detail my feelings on the demise of our bastard romance, and they will remain that way as long as we don't interfere with one another. Is that acceptable to you?"

She stuttered three more words. "Yes—of—course. . . ." I picked up my bag of goodies and started on my route whistling, "I Left My Love in Avalon" [Wellman's version of "I Found My Love in Avalon"].

She closed the door slowly and softly, and on her deceitful little face was just a trace of remorse, not much, just a little wisp.

Wellman moved to a small apartment near the studio. During the following weeks, he busied himself with his messenger talents. He was on time and worked diligently. He hung around the important places, studying sets, the casting office, and cutting rooms; and watching directors at work and reading scripts—old ones as well as new.

With whatever money he could spare, he went to the movies. He studied them. The best ones he saw over and over. He lay in bed at night trying to figure how he could direct them better. His dreams were filled with scenes from the pictures. He drew inspiration from films, which helped him endure the menial tasks of a messenger boy.

On Wellman's delivery route were the likes of Geraldine Farrar, Rockcliffe Fellowes, Pauline Frederick, Jack Gilbert, James Kirkwood, Cullen Landis, Mae Marsh, Tom Moore, Mabel Normand, Jane Novak, Jack Pickford, and Will Rogers.

Rogers had been born November 4, 1879, in Oologah, Indian territory (Oklahoma). Considered America's folk hero of his era, he was part Native American Cherokee and part Irish. His homespun humor made him hugely popular, especially during the Great Depression. Using his homely-virtues brand of wit, he attacked the country's tide of sophistication and sex, bringing laughter to everyone who heard, saw, or read him. His celebrity soared in vaudeville, on stage, on radio, and in pictures. His film career lasted more than fifteen years; he made many pictures until his untimely death in 1935.

No matter how famous he became, he always remained the common man. His best remembered statement was, "I never met a man I didn't like."[1]

Rogers took a special liking to the young messenger boy, helping him take the next step as an assistant property man with a slight raise in salary. Wellman worked on five Rogers' pictures, all from 1920: *Jubilo, Jes' Call Me Jim, Cupid the Cowpuncher, The Honest Hutch,* and *Guile of Women.* Wellman was promoted to head prop man on this last film.

After almost two years, another opportunity came his way, and he made the most of it.

Wellman with Will Rogers in 1926. Wellman worked on five Rogers films in 1920, working his way up from messenger boy to head property master. *Courtesy of the author.*

Wellman recalled,

... and I was still an assistant property man with a head full of dreams. Then it came like a bolt out of the blue. Word from the front office for all the ex-servicemen to report at the front gate at noon, twelve o'clock sharp.

We were all there, grips, electricians, painters, construction men, assistant directors, property men, cutters, musicians, animal trainers, cowboys, messenger boys, but no actors. All wondering what the hell it was all about, and suddenly Mr. Vice-president appeared. This was important.

He said that he would take but a few minutes of our lunch hour and then announced the arrival the next day of a very important general and that he wanted all of us in uniform, to form a line down which the general was to traverse to the promised land, the stars. Nobody cheered this proclamation, and the deadly silence angered Mr. Vice-president. He continued: "Of course you all realize the importance of this; so, to put it in military terms, this is an order." Again silence, whereupon he decided to find out what the score was.

"All those who will be in line in uniform at twelve thirty sharp tomorrow noon raise your right hands." Slowly and reluctantly hands were raised, all but mine.

I was standing directly in front of him, and he singled me out for a blast.

"Wellman, we particularly want you, in the blue uniform of the French Flying Corps with the medals; gives the welcoming ceremony an international flavor. Why is your hand not raised?"

All eyes were on me, and once again I was on the spot. This little unpretentious derby-hatted vice-president of a motion picture company had suddenly become a monster of memories. He looked like a despicable little drill sergeant who made my life miserable at Avord. There was that about him that reminded me of four-letter Fleming of the Butterick Lumber Company, of the insufferable foreman that I scaled soles at in a shoe factory; and, by God, if he had nothing on his head, including hair, he would have looked like my ex-mother-in-law. In short, I didn't like him.

"Well, Wellman!"

This was a big decision to make and a fast one. If I told him to stick it, he would have kicked me off the lot, and the directors' board would crumble all around me.

Everything that I had learned from six [five] rugged pictures would go by the boards. I couldn't go to Doug again and ask him to get me another job. To hell with it, I will try one bit of acting, throw one lame excuse at him, and maybe it will work; but at least I will keep my job, and the directors' board will remain intact.

"I am sorry, sir"—that "sir" damn near killed me—"but my blue uniform has everything but a seat in the pants; it is so worn and torn that I can't wear it anymore."

I didn't get to first base.

"You in production now?"

"Just preparing."

"Splendid. You go get your uniform, take it to the wardrobe, and they will rejuvenate the seat of your pants." He thought that was very funny and laughed like hell, dismissed us, and I went home to dig into the dufflebag once more.

Twelve thirty, and everything was in readiness: the long sixty-five-man line, at the end of which the stars and, of course, Mr. Goldwyn. It was the most bastard-looking line I have ever seen—soldiers, sailors, fliers, marines, coast guard, from doughboys to gobs up to a few second lieutenants. All the uniforms looked as if they had just awakened, that is all but mine. Mine had a fresh press and I stood erect, very erect. Mr. Vicepresident reviewed the line and gave me a smile of satisfaction and a compliment.

"What a soldier."

Soldier my foot, I was a broken-down ex-flier with a half-soled ass. I stood erect because I didn't dare bend over.

The sirens, the iron gates swung open, and in came the cars. Out of the first one stepped the general, and by God it was Pershing. I snapped myself into attention, as they did all the way down the line. This general was *the* general.

––––––––––––––––––––

During the war, Wellman had met, however briefly, the famous American general John J. "Black Jack" Pershing—in a Paris brothel. Wellman spotted the general coming into the parlor house and taking refuge in an upstairs boudoir away from prying eyes. As a prank, Wellman snuck into Pershing's room and, under the cover of darkness and the commotion of lovemaking, crawled across the floor and stole the general's uniform pants.

When Pershing completed his premeditated engagement, he discovered his britches were missing. He howled and stomped about, calling for their return.

After a long few minutes, Wellman marched up to the trouserless general, saluted, and showed him the pants. An astonished commander glared at the uniformed flyer, who introduced himself and told the general that he had been the only American pilot in the air supporting Pershing's "Rainbow Division" when the Yankee troops made their historic first over-the-top attack on the Germans.

General Pershing smiled, shook Wild Bill's hand, and they shared a long, loud belly laugh.

General John "Black Jack" Pershing, center in overcoat, tours Goldwyn Studios in the company of its vice president (left, in derby hat). Wellman (far right), in his airman's uniform, was one day away from being promoted to assistant director. *Courtesy of the author.*

Wellman later wrote,

He looked over at this motley lineup of ex-everythings, with not a particularly happy expression on his face. He was much more interested in what was gathered in a sweet-smelling handful at the end of the line. But it had to be done, so he started shaking the sixty-five hard-worked calloused hands to get to the lovely, soft, well-manicured ones that awaited him.

I, the international flavor, was first in line. He shook my hand, then the next and the next, then he turned back to me and said, "Where have I seen you before?"

"General, I had better not say where, right here."

He snapped his fingers and said, "That's it," came back to me, started pumping my hand. "How have you been, it's good to see you—been a long time."

I said, "Too long," and we quieted down a little bit. Then he asked me how I was really doing, and I told him "Not too good." He thought for a moment and then very sincerely asked how he could help. I told him "By making me important in this hotbed of fakery."

He said, "You're damn right, what do you suggest?" I suggested that he take me under the fig tree right behind us and talk to me for a few minutes.

He did, and it worked like a charm. The next day, I was called into the vice-president's palatial office and taken into the president's superpalatial office and introduced to Mr. Goldwyn, who shook my hand and said in perfect English that I was the type of young man he wanted working for him, then turned to Mr. Vice-president and shouted an order. Make him an assistant director to start with; and then he turned to me and asked me to sit down, that he wanted to hear all about me.

Sit down—I goddamn near fell down. He started asking me questions, but for a moment I didn't hear a word he was saying. I was thinking of the general: you meet the nicest guys in the strangest places.

For the next two and a half years, Wellman worked as an assistant director under eight different directors on twenty pictures, fourteen of them Westerns. Eight of those films were directed by Bernard J. Durning, an action director of mostly Westerns. "A big, handsome, hard-drinking, tough, lovable guy with a terrific temper" was Wellman's definition of his director.

Durning took his young assistant under his wing and they became great friends—after a fisticuffs. When Durning first hired Wellman, he told him there were two rules he insisted upon: One: loyalty; two: dames in his pictures. "No fooling around with any of them, at any time," he said. "On the set, on location, or in your stalking time. . . . There are lots of happy hunting grounds all around, but stay out of this fakey love nest."

Wellman received a passing mark on number one, but an early failure on number two. He had helped a struggling young actress get a small part in their picture. Later, she came to his office at the studio to thank him. One thing led to another, and while in the midst of solidifying that thank you, Durning caught them, and the fight was on. It was a brutal battle with Durning losing the most blood, but Wellman losing consciousness.

Durning shook his young assistant into consciousness, telling him, "You can't be like this. I'm going to need you soon." Then he told him to put some raw meat on his swelling eye and be on the set bright and early the next morning. Wellman apologized and promised that this would never happen again—it didn't.

Durning's film, *Iron to Gold* (1922), was a Western starring B-picture hero Dustin Farnum. Farnum had been born in Hampton Beach, New Hampshire, on May 27, 1874. He began his acting career on stage before finding a prominent place in film history.

After starring in the successful Broadway play *The Squaw Man* (1901), the striving young filmmaker Cecil B. DeMille chose Farnum to reprise his role

Wellman with his directing mentor Bernard Durning. *Courtesy of the author.*

in the film version. *Squaw Man* (1914) was Hollywood's first feature-length film. The story deals with an Englishman who marries a Native American woman in the Wild West.

Soon after securing his high place in the annals of filmdom, "Dusty" made an historic blunder. He rejected DeMille's offer to take a partnership in the latter's studio in lieu of his upfront salary for this eighteen-day, $15,450.25 picture. DeMille's studio became known as Paramount Pictures.

In Farnum's defense, money was tight, the underfinanced picture looked risky at best, and DeMille's present studio was a barn shared with farm animals. However, Dusty went on to forge a fine career starring in a string of popular pictures until his passing in 1929.

Iron to Gold was shot on location in Eureka, California. The town was cut out of a heavily wooded territory, and the inhabitants were all connected to the lumber business, from forest to sawmill.

Gold was a melodrama. Wellman remembered the storyline: "The simple plot was big lumberman on trip to big city falls in love with New York actress who gives up career to become big lumberman's wife. Comes to live in God's country with him and can't take it. She leaves—he is heartbroken but carries on nobly—he still has his trees."

Shooting went well; it was on budget and on schedule until the last scene was filmed, leaving the "wrap" party as the final episode. Normally, when a picture has completed its shooting schedule, the company gathers together to celebrate its conclusion. This can be a happy, sad, or both a happy and sad occasion.

In 1914, Dustin Farnum was the star of Hollywood's first feature-length film and of William Wellman's directorial debut, *The Man Who Won*, in 1923. *Courtesy of the Academy of Motion Picture Arts and Sciences.*

When a Hollywood movie company invades a town—especially one filled with lumberjacks and their women—there are bound to be some resentments, several jealousies, and conflicts of one kind or another. Sometime during *Gold*'s production schedule, a slow burning fuse was lit in Eureka. It finally detonated during the wrap party in Dustin Farnum's suite at the hotel where the company stayed.

Often, silent film companies employed musicians to play background music behind the scenes being filmed. They believed that this music enhanced the dramatic elements of the picture. In this case, a fiddle, a cello, and an organ accompanied the production as well as the merriment at the wrap party.

Farnum was toasting his director, Durning; his assistant director, Wellman; and the camera crew, other crew members, actors, stunt men, and John Barleycorn, while the musicians played a marching song. Their spirits ran high!

A hard knock at the door ushered in a prop man who explained that one of the actors, whom nobody liked, was getting the hell beat out of him by a bunch of lumberjacks at the bar up the street. The fiddle, the cello, and the organ stopped playing; the celebrators stopped drinking. Farnum remarked that the actor probably deserved it, and continued with another toast. Durning jumped in with, "We may not like this actor, but he is a member of our company and deserves our support. Anyone who would like to join in follow me."

Durning left the room followed by the assistant director, the prop man, the stunt men, the actors, the camera crew, and the fiddle, cello, and organ.

Farnum was the only one left, standing with raised glass and looking around an empty room. "To the company!" He emptied his glass and threw it into the fireplace. He turned and ran after the rescue party.

Durning's cavalry numbered fourteen as they marched up the street. Among them were two former professional boxers, two ex-baseball players, one ex-pro football lineman, a couple of GIs, and a former WWI fighter pilot. Farnum caught up with the resolute group at the front of the pack.

In this typical small-town mountain café-bar, the actor in question was down on the sawdust-covered floor, covered with blood and screaming like a stuck pig. He was surrounded by the enemy—a dozen lumberjacks, all loaded and mean. They were teeing off on the actor individually.

Now, the cavalry arrived just in time and the donnybrook began. The loggers threw wild roundhouse punches, most of them fanning the air, while the movie boys used the lower and sometimes illegal blows below the belt. The headhunters were losing the battle royal to the lower-gut shooters.

Durning, using his height to good advantage, jabbed and moved, jabbed and moved, then crossed with hard rights and down went his lumberman. Wellman, fighting out of his usual crouch with great success, floored his man with many punches. Farnum mixed in a little judo and some karate kicks. The bar was being obliterated as the lumberjacks tried to take advantage of the furnishings. A fiddle met a splintered doom.

The town sheriff and his posse arrived with guns drawn. The sheriff fired two shots into the ceiling and the combatants froze.

Sheriff: That's quite enough, gentlemen. Stand and put your hands in the air. (*To deputies*) Get 'em up, move 'em out.

The six deputies went to work getting the men to their feet and herding them to the door. The troops filed by the sheriff, who noticed Durning and Farnum.

Sheriff: The director and the movie star. I'm surprised at you two getting involved in this.

Farnum: Just sticking up for one of our own.

Sheriff: Is your producer here as well?

Farnum: We left him at the hotel.

Sheriff: Good. Then I'll be able to contact him about the damages. Enjoy your night's stay in my hotel. (*To deputies*) Move 'em out.

The deputies herded the cavalry and Indians out the door.

Although they had been in regular phone touch, Wellman and Mother Celia had not been together for a long while. After several of Wellman's planned trips had collapsed—due to work or no work—she took the bull by the horns, boarded the "iron horse," and came west in the summer of 1922.

He met her at Los Angeles' Union Station and checked her into the Hollywood Hotel on Hollywood Boulevard. Their first dinner date took place at Musso and Frank's Restaurant, also on the "boulevard of broken dreams."

The restaurant was crowded and very noisy. Wellman secured a booth as far from the madding crowd as possible. Speaking loudly over the din and in rapid, excited delivery, he told her about his developing career. She could hardly get in a word edgewise. He talked about being elevated to assistant director and learning from eight different directors, including Bernie Durning. He spoke of his latest film, *The Fast Mail* (1922), a Western starring Charles "Buck" Jones and directed by Durning. Wellman was currently preparing his next Durning project, another Western, *Yosemite Trail* (1922), with Dustin Farnum as the lead. Both pictures were produced at Fox Studios.

Wellman explained to his mother that he felt forced to leave Goldwyn Studios because of Helene Chadwick—he couldn't stand working at the same studio any longer. Wellman stopped to take a long breath, and Mom took over. She said, "Now, Billy. Just because the marriage wasn't successful, doesn't mean you couldn't have worked together. You have to get along with people. You shouldn't have jumped into the marriage in the first place. Why buy the cow when you can get the milk for free?"

Wellman apologized but said that he wanted a family and thought this would work. Celia continued: "Billy, listen to your mother. Slow down. You're a very young man. Get settled in the pasture, and then look around for the cow."

Celia brought her son up to date on the rest of the family. Arthur was still struggling but doing okay as an investment banker. Brother Arch was now married and climbing the ladder of success in the wool industry. Arch's trips out west would have to wait another ten years. Arthur did not like to travel and never came to Los Angeles.

Since *Yosemite Trail* was several weeks away from shooting, Wellman was able to spend time with his mother, showing her the sights and sounds of Hollywood and Los Angeles. They visited the studios, Malibu and the Pacific Ocean, took a bus tour around town, and went out to the orange groves of San Fernando Valley, and then watched movies at Grauman's Chinese Theatre.

When *Trail* was close to its start date, Wellman put Celia back on the train, and she rode out of town. Before leaving, she vowed to come west every year for as long as she was able.

By May 1923, Wellman had completed eighteen films at Fox Studios. He was working on pre-production of his eighth picture with Bernie Durning. As usual, it was a Western, starring Buck Jones and Shirley Mason, called *The Eleventh Hour* (1923).

It was late afternoon when Wellman walked out the front entrance of the studio one day. He waved a goodbye to the gate cop, turned, and started up the street. All of a sudden he stopped cold. Leaning against a 1922 Rolls-Royce Silver Ghost touring car was Tommy Hitchcock, dressed in a silk sport coat and tie. Hitchcock shouted, "Wild Willy!"

Wellman, without a word, ran over and hugged his old buddy. They jumped all over each other, whooping and hollering and calling each other every swear word in the book.

Wellman would reminisce,

This was going to be a night of revived memories, exciting, unusual, sad . . . back to the wonderful, unbelievable, often times grief-stricken days, of the Lafayette Flying Corps. . . .

At dinner, in a little secluded cafe two guys who had seen and done many things, good and bad, in a short time, began asking questions. Tom started inquiring about the picture business in general, he was really interested in this odd dream world; my participation. . . .

I steered Tom away from Hollywood, back to the time we devoured a Rumpler; we relived the whole fantastic experience, when we at last reached the climax we were so excited, it was as if it had happened yesterday. We ordered a drink, drank silently, each of us wrapped up in our retrospection of many fast, successful flashes of dangerous time, we shared together.

I came to first, asked Tom the sixty-four dollar question, tell me how you made your escape, all I've heard are different versions, I would like to get it from the horse's mouth. Tom smiled, then told a remarkable story in such an unassuming way he might have been describing a game of backgammon.

"I was on patrol, I spotted five Albatross beneath me so I dove on them. I got one, they got my controls and me, politely speaking, in the thigh. I made a lousy landing, you could call it a crash-landing. That is all I remembered until waking up in a prison hospital. They had apparently finished patching me up, I came to feeling very disconsolate. This attitude remained buried in me through all the interrogations, examinations physical and mental, the badgering and some very unnecessary abuse. They finally realized that I was a young dumb cluck and left me alone—the food was as expected, bad, the medical treatments nil, but they provided me with an assortment of so-called bandages and dressings. I was my own practising physician, the one difficulty, the location of my wound, the thigh goes all around you, I became a double-jointed contortionist treating my awkwardly situated bullet hole. My great fear was infection, I was lucky or perhaps I was a brilliant dresser of shot-up thighs, maybe I had missed my calling, but what would I do with faulty female thighs? You can answer that better than I can, Bill."

You would get used to it, Tom, a thigh is a thigh, you would just ignore them, there are other subdivisions you might have a little more difficulty with, but after all you would be known as just Dr. Hitchcock of thigh fame, as long as you ignored the last four letters of your name, you would have no trouble at all, just a very dull career. . . .

"My sundry reason at this stage of my captivity was getting bored, bored to death. I started mousering around for a way to escape. I acted much weaker than I was, I did it so well, had you seen my performance, you would have put me under contract to act in one of your pictures. To cut out the dreariness, the loneliness, the helplessness, the frightful boredom, I want to skip to a train trip we took. We being a couple of brother flyer prisoners, Whitmore, McKee and Hitchcock, sounds like a team of dull commentators. We were being transferred to another prison camp far away from the closeness to the Swiss border. Whitmore and McKee had tried to escape a couple of times unsuccessfully.

"They both were sick, weak and shouldn't have been moved, they had a tough time walking. I stayed right along in step with them, we were three miserable half-dead looking Americans.

"Unfortunately they boarded us on a train in the middle of the day, which meant the whole afternoon would be spent piling up miles and miles away from the haven, the Black Forest which bordered on Switzerland. If you were lucky, looked enough like a tree, you had a chance of dodging the three border patrols and slipping into freedom.

"To toughen up things the train was filled to capacity with infantry. We were shoved, putting it politely, into a separate compartment; because of our weakened condition, had but one guard, a big hulking ugly monster, who spent most of the time glowering at us with the most loathsome expression on his face I have ever seen. God how he hated us. He had a gun, bayonet and a map that he kept looking at; he acted as if he didn't know what the hell he was looking for or at, probably trying to find our destination; by the charming looks he threw at us, I knew where he wished he could put us, with a pile of native soil keeping us warm.

"If I could get that map, oh, I forgot to tell you, the hospital Heinies at the first merry prison camp I arrived at, traded a lousy pair of puttees for my flying boots, they also filched my leather flying jacket, left nothing in return. I wasn't naked, but I sure wasn't overloaded with warm clothing.

"Come dinner time, we got a sumptuous meal, bread, cheese, water, not too much of either—it started to get dark, but the infantry didn't seem interested in going to sleep, mile by mile kept whizzing by, I was crazy, acting half dead waiting for my chance to pickpocket Mr. Ugly's map. Bit by bit it got quieter except for the welcome chorus of snoring in different tones, never in unison, a nightmare of discord.

"Finally Mr. Eyesore wrapped a blanket around his big ass and trundled off to sleepy time. I was not a professional pickpocket but this silly jerk had left his orders and the map under his head as a pillow. I tried sliding the map from under his noggin, no good, the second it started to move he awoke with a bellow of a bull, looked around sleepily, saw three sleeping, sick Americans, and fell off to dreamland once again. How the hell am I going to lick this problem, the miles were speeding by; I got a hunch. He smoked the foulest smelling cigarettes I have ever smelled, they were buried in a pack on the floor by his bunk, if I could just snake over, get one, crumble it up in a little bit of nothing but tobacco dust, rain it down on his ugly beak, it might bring on a seizure of God-given sneezes, you can't sneeze without raising your head, that would be all I needed. It worked, he damn near sneezed his brains out, I got the map, tore through two cars loaded with snoring Heinies, dove off the rear vestibule, went ass over teakettle down a steep grade, took off into the inviting darkness of a strange land. I had no idea where the hell I was, but I had to keep going as long as I could, until it got light enough for me to find a hiding place to study the map. It was a bumping, stumbling, falling, exhausting stroll in a moonless, pitch-dark unfriendly night.

"Dawn crept up through the darkness, I spotted a stack of hay in a field, very carefully crawled to it, unwound my puttees and wrapped them around my shivering body, burrowed into the hay, sneezed a couple of times and fell half starved asleep. When I awoke it was at dusk with enough light left for me to crawl to the outer edge of the hay pile, stick my hands with the map unfolded outside, peek at it with my head and body well covered by the hay. Bill, it wasn't as good as the map we have back in the pilotage. All those important miles gone by waiting for a jug head to go to sleep. C'est la guerre!

"I am going to end this melee of sorrow right now. For days it was a hide-and-seek of fear, hunger and complete exhaustion, boring in its never-ending repetition, with one beautiful unforgettable tragic experience, which will always remain mine alone, to treasure the rest of my life. I made it to Switzerland, I was free again—but very sad."

That was it, he never even told me her name.

Wellman felt sure that his pal had fallen in love. As had happened to Wellman, that first love was brief and devastating. Now both wartime buddies would share another incredible experience, another token of war.

Hitchcock talked about his life as a polo player, traveling around the world playing his beloved sport. Wellman had seen Hitchcock in action in newsreel footage before and after the war.

Watching Tom play polo was like seeing Dempsey deliver a k.o. punch, Ty Cobb stealing second with sharpened spikes, some idiot trying to stop Jim Brown, Pavlova dancing "The Swan." It was cruel, graceful wizardry, he played polo the way he attacked a Rumpler, all out, he was the best in the world.

Hitchcock Expected to Go Back Into Aerial Combat

Tommy Hitchcock
The New York Times, 1939

By The United Press.

LONDON, Nov. 22—Ten-goal Tommy Hitchcock is picking up in a Warhawk where he left off twenty-five years ago in a Nieuport. According to information received here today, Lieut. Col. Hitchcock, now air attaché to the United States Embassy, is believed to be slated for command of a new fighter group.

If he gets such an assignment, he will be one of the very few First World War American fighter pilots flying in the present conflict, but age may not prove a formidable barrier in his case. In the First World War he was rejected by the United States Army because of his age—17. However, he made his way into the famed Lafayette Escadrille and, in company with such men as William Wellman, Raoul Lufbery, Quentin Roosevelt, Charles Nordhoff and James Hall, made that squadron immortal in the history of aerial combat.

Wellman focused on his dream of becoming a director and making every kind of film—not just Westerns.

Hitchcock and Wellman talked deep into the late night. When they finished, they were all caught up. The A-Team would meet only one more time, ten years later. Again, they rolled back the years until they had said it all.

Wellman sadly remembered, "I never saw Tom again. He was killed in the Second World War preparing his own unit for action at the front. He was doing a power dive and never came out of it. Tom's dogged determination was too much for his age." Many years later, Wellman admitted that ever since Tommy Hitchcock had joined him at the front, he thought about him every day of his life.

Durning and Wellman were on location shooting _The Eleventh Hour._ "I had been with Bernie for eight pictures," Wellman recalled, "crammed full of excitement, laughs, the unexpected, and learning."

Wellman kept this clipping announcing Tommy Hitchcock's intention of re-enlisting in the Air Force for the rest of his life, long after his fellow flyer and best friend Hitchcock was killed in World War II. _Courtesy of the author._

He was a tough taskmaster, would excuse you a mistake, but never a repetitive one.

He was the big man, but when he was directing, you took everything else over; and if somebody didn't like it, that somebody was your responsibility, to be handled the way you saw fit, but that way had better be the way. Right or wrong, you were always right with him in front of anybody, from Charlie Bird who ran the studio right down, the whole parade, actors, extras, the troop, even the star; but when he got you alone, if you had been wrong, he let you have both barrels, loaded, and you never made that mistake again.

The thing that amazed me most was during all those pictures, under all kinds of stress and emotion, he never gave in to that sickness that was supposed to possess him. True, on a few occasions, he imbibed a little, but nothing that ever made him lose a single minute of work. The only drink he habitually overindulged in was chocolate ice-cream sodas. Three whoppers at a sitting and never bat an eye or add an inch to his waistline or a pound to his sit-down. Then the explosion.

The company had moved to San Diego, California. There was one week left on the schedule. Wellman's recall was vivid.

We were doing some air sequences on North Island, staying at the Grand Hotel. I was very happy, because I was in my world and Bernie's, and my nights were taken up with our own problems, the flying sequences, and I was answering the questions and Bernie was the pupil.

Wellman was worried about Durning's drinking. He never used to drink during production, but on this film he was. Wellman's bedside clock showed 2 a.m. when his phone rang one night. Bernie's slightly inebriated voice said, "Billy, this is Bernie. I need you."

Wellman dressed quickly and walked down the hallway to Bernie's suite. He knocked twice but there was no answer. He tried the door and it opened to a darkened living room. He noticed a light coming from the bedroom. On his way there, he passed a number of empty bottles of booze strewn around on tables, a couch, and the floor. He entered the bedroom and found Durning, fully dressed, but lying on top of the covers in bed. Durning's head was propped up by pillows, but his head was bowed. He spoke to Wellman without looking at him: "The time has come. I need you now. You are ready. I don't want to see or hear from you until the picture is wrapped up. Don't turn the light off on your way out. I don't want to be completely in the dark."

As Wellman left the room, he could hear Bernie snoring softly. Sol Wurtzel and Winnie Sheehan were in charge of production at Fox Studios. When they saw the final cut of *Eleventh Hour*, they told Durning that the picture was good, and the last act was great—his best work. Durning, who could have taken the credit, told them that he didn't do it. He explained that he had gone on one of his pilgrimages to the land of nod, and Wellman did it all. He told the heads of production to make Wellman a director. He also mentioned that Dustin Farnum was crazy about Wellman. It all worked.

Wellman's first assignment was *The Man Who Won* (1923), a Western starring Dustin Farnum.

5

The Director

William Wellman ran over to Bernard Durning's office to thank him and tell his mentor about his first directorial assignment. Bernie ignored the *thank you* by saying that Wellman had everything he needed to become a fine director—everything but good luck, and that must be acquired by hard work. Durning went on to stress the importance of getting along with the star, Farnum.

> With Dusty, you have that little gimmick, his toupee. Never, but never, allow it to be dislodged. When you hire your actors, their ability isn't as important as their allergy to that forelock, especially in fight scenes. One misdirected punch, one dusting off of Dusty's dustcloth, and you will be back assisting me and waiting for another battle of the Grand Hotel.

(Wellman) . . . For the first three or four days of the picture, I didn't see Bernie. Then one day, he came visiting, asked me how I was doing, if I needed any help. I told him no, that if, after two years with him, I couldn't handle a picture, then I got to get back in the air again. . . . He patted me on the back and left, a big smile on his face; he had given me the confidence of a pit bulldog and he liked it.

A few more days passed and no Bernie, when suddenly I saw him, way back, half hidden, just watching. I didn't let him know I had seen him, but it made me feel very happy. The master still cared.

We were going on location the next day, so I went over to his office to say good-bye to him. "I want to say good-bye to you, Bernie; we are leaving for Lone Pine in the morning."

"How long will you be gone?"

"About a week."

Publicity shot of director William Wellman. *Courtesy of the author.*

"I'm leaving for New York Monday."

"How long will you be gone?"

He didn't answer for a minute. Looking at him now, I could tell that he had changed; he didn't laugh anymore.

"Long time, Bill."

He meant longer than the picture, much longer.

Wellman never saw Bernie Durning again. He died from a disease he had kept secret: tuberculosis. Wellman was told on the location of the first film he directed, the one that Durning had made possible. Wellman was devastated.

From August 1923 to May 1924, Wellman directed seven Westerns at Fox Studios. Besides Farnum's *The Man Who Won* (1923), there were six starring Charles "Buck" Jones: *Second Hand Love* (1923), *Big Dan* (1923), *Cupid's Fireman* (1923), *Not a Drum Was Heard* (1924), *The Vagabond Trail* (1924), and *The Circus Cowboy* (1924).

Buck Jones was a hero and idol to millions of Americans. He starred in over a hundred movies.

He was born Charles Gebhart, December 4, 1889, in Vincennes, Indiana. Before becoming a stunt rider in Wild West shows, he was a member of the U.S. Cavalry. After a tour in the Ringling Brothers Circus, he became a film extra, doubling and doing stunts for Western film stars such as Tom Mix and William S. Hart.

In 1919, he played his first leading role in *The Last Straw* and quickly rose to the top of Fox Studios' star list. By 1936, his annual salary had risen to $143,000.

Being a real-life cowboy, he brought to the screen the image of a no-nononsense man of action with a strong sense of loyalty and justice for all.

"Jones' style was a compromise between the gaudy showmanship of Mix and the austere realism of Hart. . . . He also injected comedy and folksy humour, usually poking fun at himself rather than at a comic sidekick."

"After Tom Mix . . . Buck Jones was the best loved and most idolized of the series Western stars. Yet unlike Mix, to whom he was second-string at Fox in the twenties, he made a successful transition into talkies, achieving a twenty-five year career which was still progressing strongly when he died tragically in 1942 . . ."[1]

Wellman directed Charles "Buck" Jones in six Westerns for Fox Studios. *Courtesy of the Academy of Motion Picture Arts and Sciences.*

Wellman remarked about his friend,

He wasn't as big as Tom Mix mainly because he didn't have a horse as well-known as Tony, who shared popularity honors with his master. Buck did it all on his own. He was very popular and a wonderful guy. My whole experience directing Buck was, and still is, one of the happiest hours of picture making I ever had. He was an ace.

One odd story that some featherhead in the front office thought would be a big success and change for Buck, who was doing all right in westerns, was a nightmare called *Cupid's Fireman*. The title made you sick and after Buck and I had read it, we *were* sick. Buck squawked with great indignation in the front office and I complained to the story department and everybody, including the shoe shine boy, but a guy named Wurtzel (I don't know if the name is spelled correctly and I don't give a damn, it sounds the same, repulsive) was running the studio and he disagreed emphatically, so we had to make the picture.

One might wonder why I am spending so much time on a poop called *Cupid's Fireman*. The story I cannot remember, and since I have no scripts that date back to 1923, I can just remember the climax, because it reminds me of a terrible tragedy. Hoping my memory is correct, the big scene was the burning of a boarding house into which, well tricked with controlled fire on either side of the smoke-filled pathway through which Buck was to make three heroic rescues of a mother and her two children, plus a nine year old boy. With the aid of the trick department and unusual camera angles, Buck's acting and speed made it look real. The aftermath was Buck being decorated for bravery.

Years later there was a frightful fire at a very popular restaurant in Boston called the Coconut Grove. Many people were burned to death and the newspapers told of the heroism of one unknown man who made four plunges through a wall of fire and came out with three doomed people who still live to remember their horror, and who never knew the giant of guts was that saved them, all but one, the third, a kid whose movie star favorite was Buck Jones. With tears streaming down his face, he saw Buck go in a fourth time but never saw him come out.

Buck took a great leap in the dark.

Wellman's entrance into the rank of director had brought him the hard work that his mentor, Bernard Durning, spoke of, but the financial escalation was nowhere to be seen. As a contract director, his salary for the seven B Westerns stayed a constant $185 a week—no raises!

When Wellman left Goldwyn Studios for Fox, he moved to an apartment a few blocks from the studio. It was larger than his old place because he needed more space for his new roommate—a big chow dog. The apartment had a kitchen, a fairly large combination living room/bedroom, and a bathroom with shower. Chow slept in a large dog bed next to Wellman's pull-down. They were great buddies. The only problem was Chow's eating habits—he wanted to eat bigger portions than his master and more often, too.

In order to save some extra money for Chow's dining, Wellman made a deal with the landlord that covered six months at a time.

Wellman reminisced,

He was a hell of a dog and I was crazy about him, vice versa.

I had dinner in the cafe right across the street from the studio, run by two old gals who knew all about the art of simple cooking, inexpensive beer and once in a while on an occasional Saturday night, a little unlicensed firewater added to the menu. I had a comfortable bun on, and led by my seeing dog who sensed exactly what was up, we arrived in my small but very comfortable living quarters, sat us down and Chow, with the patience of Job, sat unblinking, listening to a barrage of drunken mishmash until finally I shut up and with a big sigh, Chow and I went to sleep. Chow on my bed, me in the rocking chair.

In the morning Chow awoke hale and scratching, I with an awful hangover. I split Chow's breakfast, he understood, ate and licked it clean off the floor. I mixed a beautiful bloody Mary—it did me so much good I mixed another, let Chow out for a short scratching at the door, let him in, lay down on the bed and went sound to sleep again.

I awoke late Sunday afternoon with nothing to do, so Chow and I went walking in the hills, Chow full of pep, me full of hatred that had been ripening in the last few Buck Jones pictures. My hatred was no raise in salary . . . I really got mad and explained the whole bloody business to Chow, there was nobody around except the squirrels who stopped their tree climbing the minute we came within ear shot. They didn't even move, just sat very quietly listening to a dumbwit talking business to a dog. They didn't know the importance of what I was talking about, nor did Chow, but Chow had one thing on them, he knew by the way I was speaking, the anger, the sincerity, the snarl, the indignation, that it was of great importance; that his master was as sore as hell and the old boy kept his tale wagging, hoping it had nothing to do with him. It did, his appetite.

Monday morning the great William Fox was arriving at the studio, and since nobody else would give me a break, I was going to see the big man if I had to sit in his outer office all day, which I did. Fox, knowing I was out there and guessing for what reason, kept me there, showing what an unreasonable bastard I was eventually to come face to face with.

Funny how flying could enter this problem but it did, and in a very understandable way. I was never afraid while flying fighting, some few times I couldn't breathe for awhile, but it passed and the fear, such as it was, changed to a frightful anger, topped by a desire to kill. That's a hell of a topper.

Being afraid of a man named Fox was as ridiculous as if I were going to have a fist fight with a nun.

It got very late. The secretary had tidied everything up, not even glancing at me after telling me a half a dozen times that Mr. Fox was too busy to see me. When suddenly God came out of his haven on his way home; as he passed me he said, "What do you want?" I answered with two words, "A raise." He answered back with two words, "You're fired," and went out into the hallway. I followed on his footsteps, reminding him that I had made seven pictures for the same salary. He didn't pay any attention to what I said, just repeated five deadly words, "You heard me, you're fired," and then I got in front of him, grabbed his necktie and twisted it tight, goddamned tight, and I saw the fear of a coward on his face, so I did the thing a face like that deserved, I spit on it. I went out of the studio for good, he went back to his office to cleanse his face of the only sincere tribute he had received for a long, long time.

Now I had an agent whose name I couldn't remember the next day. He said it would be easy to get a job after seven successful pictures, especially a few with Buck Jones like *Big Dan*, written by the Hattons and *Not a Drum Was Heard* written by Ben Ames Williams and Doty Hobart.

This easy to get a job went on for weeks, and the rumor was out that Wellman had hit the saliva bull's-eye and a lot of the brother producers had put the whammy on him. Chow and I began to lose weight. The lodgings were comfortable, the appetites just as ravenous, and the money was getting very low. Something had to be done and quickly, so I became a thief, not a full-fledged one, just enough of one to live and support my hungry roommate, until some producer took a distinct dislike to my spit-upon producer target. It will happen, they all hated each other, it was just a matter of a not too hungry time of patience.

So I got a job at a small grocery store as a delivery boy with a very old tired Maxwell delivery car. There was a reason for such a job, two guys, Chow and I, had to eat, no overeating just enough with what little I had left to keep us going, and not enough to be suspect. I became a very skillful pilferer, that sounds better than being an out and out thief. Of course our diets differed from delivery to delivery and Chow had to eat like a human being, which at times got pretty rugged for him, but he became so well adjusted that he downed fruit when necessary, and his fur coat shined like gold. My pilfering took place in four stages. #1, while filling out the orders; #2, while delivering said orders; #3, at homes where said orders were left; #4, when cleaning up the joint after the day was finished. The old boy always pitched in and helped, that was damn white of him. The best of the four was a toss up between #1 and #4. If he hadn't been such a nice guy, #4 would have been the favorite. The best days were of course Fridays and Saturdays when everyone, including me, was preparing for the weekend.

As an example of a good pilferer, one potato from a dozen to be delivered orders kept you in potatoes for quite a while. One pocketed can of salmon or tuna with rice or potatoes was good for a couple of days, and different broths with meat and potatoes on Saturday nights were fit for a king. I still had a little money left, and when I bought meat, dog bones were always included. Saturday nights were like Christmas dinners to Chow and me. For desserts, I pocketed gelatin in all flavors.

Milk was a problem but we beat it by watching where the milk wagon stopped when they had big deliveries and when the poor guy disappeared with both hands full of orders ready for distribution, a couple of quarts vanished but never in a hurry, just a normal bringing of milk to the wife and kids with the Sunday paper stuffed in Chow's big mouth, a very homely sight.

We always had fresh oranges and avocadoes until they came out of our ears. These we got by moonlight. With my small supply of money, I got an occasional helping of eggs, bread, coffee and sugar. These were the toughest to pilfer. They were too big and awkward to handle. Looking back, it really wasn't bad, better than jail slop, and a hell of an improvement over the Foreign Legion delicacies.

We were down to our last few dimes when the magic telephone rang. My agent had a hell of an important picture for me to make, a feature believe it or not, to be made in three and one half days and nights. . . . He didn't need a director, he needed a voodoo.

Wellman's producer was the infamous Harry Cohn. From Academy Award–winning filmmaker Frank Capra's book *The Name Above the Title* come these words:

Harry Cohn, an ex-streetcar conductor and former song plugger for Tin Pan Alley—who snarled out of the side of his mouth with the best of them—was hit by fillum fever. With his wife's money, and his older brother Jack and Joe Brandt as partners, Harry Cohn put together a small film company. C.B.C. (Cohn, Brandt, Cohn) Productions—with its un-unique trade mark of a Lady holding up a freedom torch.

Arriving in Hollywood, Harry stuck his camel's head under the tattered flags of a studio on Gower Street. Soon the camel was in, all others out. Unfurling a new sign, Columbia Pictures Studio, he pushed off into the foggy seas of "quickie" production . . . the Lady's torch was still above the waves—the rest of her was anxiously treading water. Lacking foresight, gagsters dubbed Harry Cohn's studios: *Columbia The "Germ" Of The Ocean.*

Harry Cohn was no aficionado of airy architecture and delicate traceries. His forte was men—hot-shot department heads who welcomed the challenge to make do with little or nothing. . . .

After Wellman directed *When Husbands Flirt* (1926), Columbia Studios head Harry Cohn, pictured here flanked by directors Frank Borzage and Frank Capra, engaged in an unsuccessful bidding war for the young director with future Paramount executive B. P. Schulberg. *Courtesy of the Academy of Motion Picture Arts and Sciences.*

Wellman's story of Harry Cohn and Chow continued:

Harry Cohn, on his way up, hiring me made me shy off a little, and the huge salary I got for preparation, writing, shooting, cutting, the works, made me realize he was definitely on the way up. Did I refuse it? Don't be foolish. I appeared in Mr. Cohn's office like magic and two pals were going to eat honestly again, not too soon, for Mr. Cohn was a very smart man. He said hello, I said hello. He gave me the story and the script to read and talk to him about my objections, if any, and also a few hoped-for funny additions, but no dough. I better not come up empty the day after tomorrow, so I got home in nothing flat and went to work. The story *When Husbands Flirt* was very good, written by Dorothy Arzner, so I started to pump up the script, try to get a few more laughs in it, which I did, and a few belly laughs. When Cohn read them and laughed, he called up some-body who brought up half my salary, $250. Cohn said, "You get the other half when everything is finished." That seemed fair, so I thanked him, that really surprised him, he smiled, so did I. We had apparently broken a Cohn record, two smiles in less than a minute.

I hadn't seen that much money for a lot of weeks so Chow and I had us a dinner, steak and some big bones I talked the butcher out of for Chow. We both over-ate and went to sleep very early. Chow fell asleep the minute he hit the sack. I didn't, something was holding me back, my con-science, not a guilty conscience, a pilferer's one, so I got up with pen and paper and tried to figure how much I owed my grocery crony.

I tried to arrive at a sum, adding up most of the foodstuffs I remem-bered pilfering. It was an impossible job without bookkeeping, which I did not keep, so I figured in the length of time I had been borrowing necessities it could come to about a hundred dollars. I couldn't let that amount fly out of my savings account until I had been paid in full by Mr. Cohn, so I decided to tell the old boy what I had been doing, give him fifty dollars and another fifty at the end of the picture. It is not an easy job to tell a helluva nice guy that you are a thief and have been keeping you and your dog alive at his expense. Try this someday, it is rugged, and unusual things might happen, such as being confined for an indefinite period as a guest of the city.

I expected him to let loose and bawl the hell out of me, instead of which, he told me very quietly what an unworthy rascal I had been. His language was not like mine, the four letter kind, it had an old-fashioned ring to it, like calling me a rascal. That apparently, in his manner of speech, meant a bad boy. If he had called me a dirty lousy thief or even a son of a bitch, I would have felt more at home, but a bad boy made me think I was little Lord Fauntleroy. He said he never had a son and I fitted what he had dreamed about for a long time. He knew what I had been doing and didn't have the slightest doubt that I would pay it back once I got going again.

I asked him if he thought $100 covered everything. He said it was far too much. I disagreed, gave him the fifty that I thought might be half the amount I owed him. He said, "I'll take the fifty to teach you a lesson." I told him everything he had said and done taught me an unforgettable les-son, but when I was paid for my whole job, he was going to take another fifty, and if he thought it was too much from a standpoint of paying for the food that I had pilfered, I would appreciate his buying a beautiful shawl that his lovely wife had always wanted. This got him, the fact that I had noticed what she wanted was enough for him to accept the fifty dollars, when I was paid, on finishing the picture. He was going to tell her she got it from me, because I was "just like the son we never could have." It all happened, with a little tear. He never let her know that I had been help-ing myself for weeks of their hard-earned groceries.

So many small people that you meet are so much bigger than the big people that you meet. All over the world.

In the winter of 1925, Wellman went to work at Columbia Studios on *When Husbands Flirt*. He remembered its uplifting theme.

Old man takes dose of castor oil, leaves home for office, things start to move; and we got six reels out of that; by borrowing long shots of big scenes in other pictures, by building corners of the sets and cutting our close shots into them, by rewriting to fit what we had or could steal, to give the picture production, by working so long and so hard that you could sleep standing up or sitting down, or lying on the floor or in your car with your feet sticking out. This was making them the rugged way and learning the tough way, but *learning* how to put a jigsaw puzzle together quickly, cheaply, efficiently, and presentably; and TV directors squawk because they only get five or six days to make their hourlong cartoons. I can even remember the hardworking cast—Tom Ricketts, Ethel Wales, Dorothy Revier, and Forrest Stanley.

During the days of pre-production, production, and post-production on *Flirt*, Wellman paid an elderly female tenant in his building to feed Chow and let him out once during the day. When Wellman returned home one evening, Chow was not waiting for him and was nowhere in sight. The tenant apologized, stating that when she let the dog out that day, Chow never came back.

Wellman searched high and low for his roommate. He asked everyone he came in contact with; and left notices at all the local stores, bulletin boards, telephone poles, and any place where somebody might see and read—Chow never returned. Wellman surmised that someone must have taken him a long, long way from home.

To celebrate the completion of *Flirt*, Wellman was invited to a dinner party at the Hollywood Hotel. A number of movie people were present there, including Jacques "Jack" Chapin. Chapin worked around Hollywood as a property man, stunt man, and assistant director. He and Wellman had met at Fox and become friends. They sat together at dinner, and between them sat Jack's sister, Margery. She was a former singer and dancer with the Ziegfeld Follies, but had no desire to be in the movies.

For the next several weeks, Bill and Margery became an item. After six months of courtship, they were married in a small church in Riverside, California, by a one-armed minister. Because of Wellman's lack of funds, he placed a thin gold ring—bought at a five and dime—on her slender finger, and their honeymoon consisted of a short weekend at the Riverside Inn.

Again, Wellman had kept his family out of his matrimonial endeavors. When he phoned home to tell Celia he had again bought the cow, she was quite disappointed. Grudgingly, she gave her son her blessing. Wellman promised to bring his new bride East when business improved.

When Husbands Flirt was, as they say, in the can and waiting for release. No other directing jobs came Wellman's way, so he took his agent's advice and signed on at MGM as an assistant director. Since he now had a wife to support, at least he would be able to bring home a paycheck.

Wellman first assisted Edmund Goulding—a New York stage director making his film debut—on *Sally, Irene And Mary* (1925). The film starred Constance Bennett and Joan Crawford. The story was based on a play by Edward Dowling and Cyrus Wood. Goulding liked Wellman and his work. When loca-

In 1926, former Ziegfeld Follies showgirl Margery Chapin became the third Mrs. William Wellman. *Courtesy of the author.*

tion was completed and the director returned to the studio, he recommended Wellman to the front office as a director. However, the only directing work he got was to "doctor" (uncredited) problem-plagued films like *The Way of a Girl* (1925), starring Eleanor Boardman, and *The Exquisite Sinner* (1926) with Conrad Nagel, Renee Adoree, and Paulette Duval. *Sinner* was directed by Josef von Sternberg from the Alden Brooks novel *Escape* (1924).

When Wellman was assigned *The Boob* (1926), starring Gertrude Olmstead, George K. Arthur, and Joan Crawford, he was replacing Robert Vignola—the same Robert Vignola he had taken over from on *Way of the Girl*. *The Boob*, however, turned out to be a full directing job with complete director's credit. MGM considered the film a bust, fired Wellman, and left it unreleased for almost a year. *Variety* (June 2, 1926) proclaimed, "In places where M-G-M means good pictures, this should never be shown."

Two months after *The Boob*'s release, *When Husbands Flirt* premiered and became an instant hit. *Variety* (July 21, 1926) stated, "Light and enjoyable farce with plenty of hoke and snappy subtitles. Comedy all the way and handled as comedy in a burlesque manner. Direction by William Wellman is good. Attractive title should bring them in and when in they will laugh. An 8th Avenue audience laughed heartily."

Wellman had directed eight features before *The Boob*. Unfortunately, only *Big Dan* has survived the test of time—the others have passed through that dark corridor leading to the world of lost films.

Flirt's box office success brought Wellman two important calls. The first, from Harry Cohn, offered a studio contract at $200 a week. The second caller was a clever and ambitious young producer on a fast track to fame and fortune.

Benjamin Percival Schulberg, who became known as B. P., was born on January 19, 1892, in Bridgeport, Connecticut. He attended the City College of New York, without graduating, before starting a career as a reporter on the *New York Mail* in April 1909. He left after two years to become the associate editor of *Film Reports*, a magazine for independent producers and exhibitors. He started writing scripts and in 1912 joined Rex Pictures Corporation in New York, where he worked both in publicity and screenwriting. Later that year, he accepted the same position at Famous Players Company under Adolph Zukor.

B. P. was responsible for the publicity campaign behind the very successful *Queen Elizabeth* feature. When Famous Players merged with Jesse Lasky Feature Play Company, Schulberg continued in the same capacity.

After World War I, he formed his own company and produced a series of low-budget features. With Clara Bow under contract, his publicity genius made her the "It" girl of the movies. In 1925, he rejoined Zukor and Lasky at Paramount's Hollywood studio as vice president in charge of production.

After seeing Wellman's *Flirt* and meeting with the youthful and ambitious director, B. P. engaged in a bidding war with Harry Cohn. Wellman's version of events is as follows:

B. P. Schulberg became the head of production at Paramount Studios in 1925. He brought rising star Clara Bow and young director William Wellman with him under contract. *Courtesy of the Academy of Motion Picture Arts and Sciences.*

B. P. Schulberg, who was then an independent producer, saw my three-day wonder and made me an offer; Cohn beat it and Schulberg bettered that. I signed with him at big money, $225 a week. I wasn't what you could call a high-paid director, but I was working and eating.

Schulberg pulled the deal of the year. He had a little dynamo under contract named Clara Bow, and with her he rode into Famous Players-Lasky as head of production. I went along as a questionable asset.

My first effort was a thing with a powerful title, *The Cat's Pajamas,* starring Betty Bronson, with Ricardo Cortez and Daddy Roberts. Roberts was the great character actor of that era. He died shortly after the picture, and I often wondered if he had seen the finished product. It could well have caused it. It was indescribably atrocious, and the powers-that-be took a look at the picture and accused Mr. Schulberg of false representation. He had not sold them a director, he had presented them with an idiot, and they demanded a rebate.

He had a sneaking hunch that my exit might well include him, so he fought like hell for one more chance for his young protégé. I'm sure he thought I was a bust; but this had to be a shot in the dark, so they reluctantly gave me another picture.

My defense had been a very honest one. The story called for the Peter Panish Miss Bronson to look and act like a woman of the world. She tried so hard, but all she succeeded in doing was to look like a little girl who had just wet her pants. They didn't need a director, they needed a magician.

My last chance was called *You Never Know Women.*

Schulberg boasted to Jesse L. Lasky, vice president of Paramount Pictures, that this film would prove Wellman's worth.

Wellman's wife, Margery, had worked on *Pajamas* as a script supervisor. At Wellman's side again in *Women*, production began in June 1926.

The picture was shot at Paramount's Vine Street studio in Hollywood. It is the story of a lady, played by Florence Vidor, with magic eyes. The original title was *Love–The Magician.* It concerned a romantic triangle set against the colorful background of the Russian theatrical troupe Chauve-Souris. It was released September 22, 1926 and became a commercial and critical success. *Variety* (July 28, 1926) had this to say about it: "Flawlessly acted, brilliantly directed and filled with novel situations . . .Wellman, at the megaphone, lifts himself into the ranks of the select directors by his handling of this story."

The Paramount brass were impressed, B. P. Schulberg was vindicated, and the "idiot protégé" Wellman was on a direct flight up that slippery Hollywood rope to the top.

By 1927, silent films—an art form inspired by music, transmitted through light, and inviting dreams in the dark—were at the pinnacle of their artistic and commercial success. Eight hundred feature films a year were being produced for an audience of 100 million people, who attended 25,000 movie theaters every week. The box office receipts amounted to $1–1.2 billion a year; 42,000 people were employed in Hollywood, and the American film industry accounted for 82 percent of the world's movies. The American studios were valued at about $65 million.

Jack Warner in *My First Hundred Years in Hollywood* remarked, "I believe—and the box-office returns will confirm it—that the most profitable pictures are those made by men who understand every nerve and muscle and vein that make up the remarkable body of a motion picture film."

A Hungarian-born furrier and a Jewish cornetist from San Francisco had built a Hollywood studio into the number-one ranking in the film industry: Paramount Pictures.

Adolph Zukor was born on January 7, 1873, in a small, wine-growing village in Risce, Hungary. Jesse L. Lasky was born seven years later in San Francisco, California. It would be another thirty-five years before the two would meet and join forces. Their paths to the top sprang from humble beginnings that hardly encouraged greatness.

Zukor's mother, Hannah, was a rabbi's daughter, and his father, Jacob, a simple storekeeper. A year after Adolph's birth, his father died from blood poisoning. Although Hannah remarried, she never recovered from Jacob's death and passed away when Adolph was but eight.

Even though Adolph had siblings and relatives, he grew up thinking of himself as an orphan and was treated accordingly. He loved reading and romanticizing dime novels of the American West. In Risce, on a five-foot, four-inch, hundred-pound frame, he felt destined to follow in his father's footsteps.

At fifteen, he dreamed of immigrating to America, but his age worked against him. However, he was able to persuade his uncle to intercede for him with the Orphans Bureau so that he could draw on his parents' estate to pay for his passage. In the autumn of 1888, with forty American dollars sewn into the lining of his vest, fifteen-year-old Adolph Zukor arrived in New York. In the beginning, he was fit only for apprenticing and worked for an upholsterer, then a furrier. He and a friend, Max Shosberg, moved to Chicago, where the fur business was just getting started. Adolph's earning ability was on the rise, and soon he became a full partner in the Novelty Fur Company. In 1897, he met and married Lottie Kaufmann.

By 1904, the fledgling film industry was taking off. "Moving pictures" were everywhere: in bars, music halls, amusement park arcades, kinetoscope parlors, and converted storefronts that became known as nickelodeons. Zukor began to realize the potential of movies, and he invested in the industry via penny arcades with peep shows and vaudeville. His biggest investment was in the Automatic One-Cent Vaudeville located in the heart of New York's "Broadway" on East Fourteenth Street. It featured rows of film-viewing machines as well as phonographs for those who preferred sound with their images.

The nickelodeon had become the first movie theater, and Zukor desperately wanted a place in that world. His fur-trade background made him aware of style and customer satisfaction, and he upgraded his Automatic One-Cent Vaudeville into a theater called Crystal Hall. The theater prominently displayed a glass staircase and fake iridescent waterfall.

Zukor opened another arcade and theater in Pittsburgh and, by 1910, owned his own nickelodeon chain. He merged with another ex-furrier, Marcus Loew, who had his own chain of theaters and, like Zukor, featured vaudeville as well as movies. They formed Loew's Consolidated Enterprises, the forerunner of Loew's Inc., which became the parent company of MGM. In 1912, Zukor sold his shares in Loew's for $35,000 to finance the purchase of a French-made film, *Queen Elizabeth*, starring Sarah Bernhardt. The film was already a hit abroad, and its American success convinced Adolph that there was an ever-expanding market for movies.

Ready to enter the production of films, Zukor put together the Famous Players in Famous Plays company. It was later shortened to Famous Players. They would be headquartered on West Twenty-Sixth Street in New York City.

Famous Players lived up to its name with films from James O'Neill—the father of Eugene O'Neill, considered by many to be America's greatest playwright—reprising the role that had made him famous, *The Count of Monte Cristo*; Mrs. Fiske in *Tess of the D'Urbervilles*; John Barrymore in *An American Citizen*; Lily Langtry in *His Neighbor's Wife*; and Mary Pickford, already a screen name, becoming "America's Sweetheart" in Zukor's *In the Bishop's Carriage* (1913), *Caprice* (1913), *Hearts Adrift* (1914), and *A Good Little Devil* (1914).

Zukor was not the only person interested in featuring famous players in movies. Jesse Lasky was another. Lasky had originally planned on being known as the world's greatest cornetist and was solo cornetist in the San José Juvenile Band before receiving a good dose of "gold fever." He took off for the Klondike but returned home without "the dust," joining his cornetist sister, Blanche, in a vaudeville act that led to his becoming an agent for vaudevillians.

Lasky built up a fortune of $100,000, which he lost in the disastrous collapse of his stage show, *Folies Bergere*. It couldn't compete with Ziegfeld's 1910 *Follies*. To repair his fortune, he developed an idea for an operetta, *California*, set in his native state. He met with Beatrice DeMille to seek her support in hiring her well-known playwright son, William. She explained he was already working on a new production with David Belasco and suggested her other son, Cecil.

Beatrice made the introduction and worked the meeting until Jesse and Cecil saw eye to eye. Their play became a moderate success. Jesse L. Lasky and Cecil B. DeMille became friends and partners. Jesse's sister Blanche, and Blanche's husband, a glove salesman named Samuel Goldfish, spent much time together.

Cecil, his wife Constance, and their baby barely made ends meet. They lived on the edge of poverty until mid-1912.

When Sam Goldfish realized he would never be a partner in the Elite Glove Company, he encouraged his brother-in-law to enter the movie business, from which both of them could prosper. Sam Goldfish changed his name to Samuel Goldwyn and gave them the title of their company: the Jesse L. Lasky Feature Play Company, with Lasky as president, DeMille as director-general, and Goldwyn as treasurer and general manager. Their first film, *The Squaw Man* (1914), directed by DeMille and starring Dustin Farnum, who had appeared in the successful 1901 revival of Edwin Milton Royles' play, was a bona fide hit.

Lasky and his Feature Play Company had pioneered the first feature-length movie (six reels) made in Hollywood. Zukor's Famous Players Company had produced the first feature in New York, *The Prisoner of Zenda*, starring James K. Hackett.

Although Lasky had never met Zukor, the day after the opening of *Squaw Man*, he received a congratulatory telegram from the president of Famous Players. When Lasky called Zukor to thank him personally, they set up a luncheon at Delmonico's, where executives of the era were rumored to close more deals than they did in their offices. The meeting was a complete success. They truly liked each other and had much in common beyond the similarity in company names.

At the same time Lasky was cranking out one picture after another in Hollywood, Zukor was doing the same in New York. Their success was driving the same highway, and when Jesse visited New York, Delmonico's was the usual meeting place for the two megaproducers. However, Famous Players was making more pictures, and its assets were considerably greater. Both men realized that together they could produce more ambitious films of higher quality.

On July 19, 1916, Famous Players and the Jesse Lasky Feature Play Company merged to form Famous Players-Lasky with Zukor as president and Lasky as vice president in charge of production. They split the company's stock 50/50.

By this time, DeMille had wanted to form his own company where he would be better suited to develop his own projects, which had been too expensive for Lasky's budgets. DeMille, the master showman, wanted to make all the decisions of producer and director. Jesse and Adolph were pleased to sign Cecil as one of their directors.

In the merger, there was also no room for Goldwyn, whom Zukor had grown to distrust, having realized that Sam's interest was more in the moviemaking than management. Zukor brought this up, asking Lasky to keep Goldwyn or lose Zukor. It was a difficult decision to make, yet Jesse realized that with Adolph's courage, style, and leadership, their company had a grand future. Lasky also knew that with Sam's high-powered personality, he would not take a back seat to Zukor. Another consideration was that Goldwyn was no longer family after his divorce from Blanche. Regardless, neither Zukor nor Lasky wanted an ugly separation. Lasky and his associates met and considered a proper buyout proposal. The value of Sam's stock was estimated at $900,000. The money would have to be borrowed from bankers. Goldwyn accepted the deal and went on to form his own company, the Goldwyn Pictures Corporation, and later Metro-Goldwyn-Mayer (MGM).

For a time, Famous Players-Lasky operated as a holding company for its subsidiaries, but on December 29, 1917, Famous Players-Lasky consolidated its subsidiaries (Famous Players, Feature Play, Oliver Morosco Photoplay, Bosworth, Cardinal, Paramount Pictures Corp., Artcraft, and George M. Cohan Film Corp.) into its fold. Lasky would be in charge of the studios and the production of their films, while Zukor would devote his genius to the financial end and building a worldwide network of film exchanges and theaters.

In 1920, Famous Players-Lasky opened a second studio in London and a third in Astoria, Queens. The New York studio allowed them to continue to star stage actors in their movies. Between 1920 and 1927, they made 127 silent films there with such stars as Gloria Swanson, Rudolph Valentino, and W. C. Fields. During this same period, Paramount Hollywood produced 671 movies.

During the 1920s, Famous Players-Lasky's annual profits rose from $5.2 million at the beginning of the decade to $15.5 million at the end. The com-

Jesse L. Lasky, vice president of Paramount Studios, pictured here with studio president Adolph Zukor, championed the story of *Wings* but wanted a more experienced director to helm the war film. *Courtesy of the Academy of Motion Picture Arts and Sciences.*

pany owned over a thousand theaters that played their smash hits *The Sheik* (1921), *Blood and Sand* (1922), *The Ten Commandments* (1923), *The Covered Wagon* (1923), *Beau Geste* (1926), and many others.

The consolidation of Famous Players-Lasky was not enough for Adolph Zukor, and he conceived the idea of combining production, distribution, and exhibition under one banner. In 1927, the company was renamed Paramount-Famous-Lasky, and later Paramount Pictures Corporation.

Adolph Zukor and Jesse Lasky were the first "moguls" of the film industry; together they built the nation's largest movie company.

Jesse Lasky was not content to rest on his or Paramount's laurels. It was time to produce the year's big road show picture. During his search for the right property, New York publisher George Palmer Putnam, who later married Amelia Earhart, introduced Jesse to John Monk Saunders, a good-looking graduate of the University of Washington and a Rhodes scholar who had been a pilot in World War I.

Saunders outlined his story of a young lad's dream of flight—leaving home and loved ones, enlisting in the Air Corps, and becoming a World War I fighter pilot. It was a story filled with action, romance, camaraderie, patriotism, tragedy, hope, and love. The story was called *Wings*. Lasky immediately recognized the dramatic possibilities and production grandeur. There had been a long period in which war films were thought to be box-office poison, but the enormous success of *The Big Parade* (1925) and *What Price Glory* (1926) had fueled new interest in the subject matter. Lasky believed the public was now eager to see stories about the Great War, and the story of that war fought in the air had never been told.

Lasky bought the story and gave Saunders a contract as a writer to adapt his novel for the screen. Saunders would also be the technical adviser during filming and would receive a percentage of the film's profits. It was a daring move to hire a student just out of Oxford University with no screenwriting or movie experience to author Paramount's major road show film of the year. However, Lasky planned to attach the best possible talent the studio had to offer.

Top scribes Hope Loring and Louis D. Lighton were hired to write the screenplay with Saunders. Julian Johnson would handle the titles. Lasky considered Buddy Lighton and his wife, Hope Loring, Paramount's best writing team. One of their credits was the milestone achievement *It* (1927), which skyrocketed Clara Bow to stardom.

The story of *Wings* eventually became a love triangle between small-town rivals Jack Powell and David Armstrong, both in love with Sylvia Lewis. Mary Preston, Jack's tomboy friend next door, has always loved him. War breaks out and Jack and David enlist, train at the same camp, and become fighter pilots. After a fisticuffs, they become friends and are sent to the front together. During combat, David is shot down and presumed dead. In a fit of revenge, Jack flies off after the enemy. Although wounded, David steals a German plane and attempts to return to his base. Thinking David is the enemy, Jack shoots down David's plane. In an emotional moment, David dies in his best friend's arms. The war ends and Jack returns home a decorated hero. He apologizes to David's mother, father, and Sylvia, then realizes his true love is Mary.

In order to do justice to such a picture, great expense would be necessary. After Lasky proposed the project to Zukor and the New York bankers, their answer came back a definite negative—they were not willing to pay that price for *Wings* or any movie. They thought it was pure insanity.

Millions sunk into a film about airplanes? Moving specks in the sky? The public couldn't be expected to show interest in something they could hardly see. How could they tell the good guys from the bad guys? Insert close-ups of the markings on the wings? Goggles made all pilots look alike—Hun, Yank, or Limey. How could you root for men you couldn't recognize? Worse, Lasky wanted to get sound effects into the silent film. Sound effects . . .! Hadn't many exhibitors protested that sound in films would keep the audience awake? People, they said, went to movies to rest, relax, and yes—in many cases get some sleep!²

Fearing his project was going to be dropped, a desperate Saunders suggested to Lasky that the federal government might be encouraged to put up some of the necessary funds, or at least provide troops, equipment, and military facilities. Lasky didn't want his pet project to go away either, and so he agreed and sent Saunders to Washington.

Lucien K. Hubbard, a screenwriter-turned-producer, was set to be *Wings'* producer. He was also an experienced editor and would handle that job under Paramount's editor-in-chief, E. Lloyd Sheldon.

Hubbard was sent to Washington to support Saunders. Word came back positive for *Wings*. After all, no wars were being fought, and the U.S. Army was available. The War Department agreed to support the production, but only on several conditions: Paramount would be liable for any damage done to government property during filming, each military man would be insured for $10,000, and the film company would have to provide legitimate training for any of the troops who worked on it. Lasky again pleaded his case to Zukor and the bankers; however skeptical, they agreed, and Paramount began preproduction aspects.

It was Jesse Lasky's belief that the main reason Paramount was the number-one-ranked studio was that he had the finest stable of directors under contract: Cecil B. DeMille, Victor Fleming, Allan Dwan, Gregory LaCava, Eddie Sutherland, Clarence Badger, and Malcolm St. Clair, to name just a few of the fine veteran filmmakers.

Lasky believed in the power of the director, saying, "A director, to be successful, must combine efficiency with artistry, blending the two by the exercise of judgment and finesse, and knowing instinctively when to cease exercising one quality and when to begin employing the other. He should at once possess the qualifications of a dramatist, of an actor; should be a good executive and have a sympathetic understanding of human nature."³ Lasky believed that the Paramount directors should have the authority to make their films, but, of course, under his guidance and certain constraints of his studio executives.

During a casting meeting between Lasky and Schulberg concerning the candidates for director of Paramount's most important film of the year, Jesse was extolling the virtues of his experienced staff of filmmakers when B. P. suggested the young man who had been under contract to him when Schulberg came to Paramount: his protégé William Wellman. Lasky was somewhat appalled at this suggestion. B. P. went on to explain that because of the complexity and unique qualities of *Wings*, only a man with a background in war could fully understand it. Wellman had seen it all; he had lived it. He'd fought the enemy on the ground and in the air. He'd seen the horror and the honor of war. He'd won medals and lost comrades. He had been wounded, and he was the only director under contract with frontline battle experience.

Jesse Lasky with Western star William S. Hart, Mary Pickford, and Cecil B. DeMille in 1925. *Courtesy of the Academy of Motion Picture Arts and Sciences.*

Lasky quieted Schulberg, explaining that he appreciated Wellman's background and he liked his work on *You Never Know Women*, but he believed him still too raw and untested. For a picture of this magnitude, he didn't want a director of B Westerns and pictures like *The Cat's Pajamas* and *The Boob*! Schulberg countered by telling his boss that he had a good feeling about this young director, who was always on schedule and under budget. An unconvinced studio head listened to one more plea about meeting with Wellman before making the final decision.

The brash young director sat down with Lasky. "I've directed eleven pictures. I took the scripts I was given and made the best pictures I could. Nobody at this studio could have done better. You said you liked *You Never Know Women.*"

Lasky jumped in. "We all did. But one quality film doesn't put you ahead of the fine veteran directors at my studio."

Wellman shot back. "My war record does. I flew support for 'Black Jack' Pershing and his Rainbow Division when they went over the top. I know what those battles are about. You're worried about the damn budget. I never go over budget. This is a great story. I'll make it the best goddamn picture this studio's ever had!"

Before seriously considering Wellman, Lasky questioned Schulberg again. "What makes you think you can control this headstrong Wellman?" B. P.'s answer was clear. "He's my boy. I brought him here. I can control him."

Since Wellman's marriage to Margery Chapin in April 1925, he had reeled off four pictures in succession: *When Husbands Flirt*, *The Boob*, *The Cat's Pajamas*, and *You Never Know Women*. Even though he had hired Margery as his script girl on the first two films, there was little time for their relationship away from work. Both director and script girl had wanted to start a family, but two things had gotten in the way—the constant work and Margery's inability to become pregnant. Her doctor told them that she might not ever get pregnant. So, after *The Boob*, on March 25, 1926, Margery adopted a two-year-old daughter, Gloria, and stayed home with her. Wellman had wanted Margery to be patient so they could keep trying to have a child of their own. He promised her a vacation together after *Women*, but she would not wait.

In July, Mr. and Mrs. Wellman took that vacation at the Arrowhead Hot Springs Hotel in San Bernardino, California. Wellman was still smarting over the adoption business, and the couple was being pulled apart.

Wellman's spirits were lifted when the call came from Paramount announcing his casting as the director of *Wings*. He cut short the vacation and beelined back to Hollywood.

6

The Picture

Before William Wellman arrived on the scene, pre-production had been going on for months. Producers had been signed, writers were developing the screenplay, the cinematographer had been set, and casting of the leading players was moving forward at a fast clip—the *Wings* company was in full gear . . . but without a director.

Clara Bow was the first actor cast. This, of course, would mean a rewrite in the story to improve her role. However, Clara was a film superstar, and the studio wanted the biggest names available as insurance against the huge financial risk.

Bow had been born in Brooklyn, New York, on August 15, 1905. Her ancestry was English, Scotch, and French. She came from an impoverished home and a highly dysfunctional family, run by a domineering, cunning, self-serving mother.

At seventeen, Bow was 5 feet, 3½ inches tall with bobbed, flaming red hair and big brown eyes; she was 110 pounds of dynamite. She won first prize in a *Fame and Fortune* fan magazine beauty contest. She received an evening gown, silver trophy, and a screen test, which led to a screen contract. When her mother found out about the contest and her chosen career, she snuck into her daughter's bedroom and tried to slit her throat with a butcher knife. Clara awoke in time to defend herself and leave her deplorable family behind.

With her screen contract tucked under her arm, she attempted a debut in Metro Studios' *Beyond the Rainbow* (1922). She was so upset at being cut out of the picture that she quit showbiz until a phone call from director Elmer Clifton, who had seen her photos, convinced her to try again. This time, she landed a small part as a stowaway in Clifton's *Down to the Sea in Ships* (1922). Bow's role called for her to be attacked, beaten, wrestled around, and subjected to all sorts of physical types of action.

Clifton liked her work so much that he built up the part. *Ships* led to a

The poster for *Wings. Courtesy of the author.*

score of films and, eventually, a contract with B. P. Schulberg and Paramount Studios. After the film *It* (1927)—"it" meaning sex appeal—she became the "It" girl and a full-blown movie star. Clara Bow definitely had *It*—she represented the Roaring Twenties and was the model flapper of the Jazz Age.

The studio had also announced marquee players Neil Hamilton and Charles Farrell as male leads. Hamilton's rise to stardom began with D. W. Griffith's *White Rose* (1923), and his recent starring role in Paramount's highly successful *Beau Geste* (1926) placed him on top. Farrell's heat had come from the studios' big-budgeted *Old Ironsides* (1926).

Producer Lucien Hubbard wanted to sign Charles "Buddy" Rogers, a newcomer in Hollywood, instead of Farrell. The production team and studio executives continued to battle over casting. Now Ralph Forbes, another star from *Beau Geste*, was chosen for the Farrell/Rogers role, with Hamilton still holding onto his part. Rogers was so upset at being left out that he went to Lasky and asked out of his new contract. Lasky explained the star system to the newcomer and its need for this big budget film. Lasky added that he had already cast Buddy in another film.

When Wellman made his appearance at Paramount, he didn't appreciate all these decisions without his input. He jumped into the mix and threw out both Forbes and Hamilton, casting Buddy Rogers and another non-star, Richard Arlen.

Wellman had met Rogers on the Paramount lot and thought him perfect for the role of Jack Powell, the surviving hero of the movie. Rogers reminded Wellman of his buddies from the war. Charles Rogers had been born August 13, 1904, in Olathe, Kansas. He grew up loving music and wanted to be a band-leader. He could play piano, accordion, drums, trumpet, and trombone—and did so in dance bands both in high school and at the University of Kansas. His father, publisher of a weekly newspaper, saw an ad by Paramount Pictures for an open audition for actors. He urged his handsome son to send photographs and a resume. Paramount answered quickly, and Buddy, as he was called, was sent off to New York and the much-publicized acting school at Astoria.

Soon he was cast in the feature *Fascinating Youth* (1926). His next role was with W. C. Fields in Gregory LaCava's *So's Your Old Man* (1926). Both films were produced at Paramount's New York studio. Rogers was 6 feet, 1 inch tall and 175 pounds, with brown eyes and black hair. Wellman's friend and assistant director on *Wings*, Charles Barton, had suggested Arlen, but Wellman didn't want another unknown in one of the leads. He was already under pressure from Lasky and the studio executives for dismissing their stars in favor of the unknown Rogers.

While Wellman was out of town scouting locations, Barton secretly tested Arlen. When Wellman returned and looked at Arlen's test, he shouted, "Jesus Christ! Who's that good-looking son of a bitch?" When Barton came clean, Wellman went from mad to glad in a moment's change.

Richard Arlen was born Cornelius Mattimore on September 1, 1899, in Charlottesville, Virginia. He climbed the ladder from extra to a bit part in *Ladies Must Lie* (1921), then to a supporting role in *Vengeance of the Deep* (1923). Then came a big break in *Volcano* (1926), but after only eight days in production, he was fired. He became despondent for a time before persevering through other supporting roles until *Wings*. Arlen was 5 feet, 10 inches tall and 150 pounds, with brown hair and blue eyes.

Wellman was happy with his three leading actors, but Paramount was not so excited about having only one star, Clara Bow, in their big picture of the year. The studio's resentment toward Wellman was on the rise. In Lasky's book *I Blow My Own Horn*, he said, "We not only gambled on an untried writer and an unknown director, but parlayed the risk by starring a novice actor, Buddy Rogers, fresh out of our talent school."

With the lead roles cast, Wellman was hard at work filling the many supporting players. There were fifteen roles to cast from the studio; the rest of the small parts, including pilots seen on screen, would be filled by location locals, service personnel, and stunt flyers.

During all this casting fever, Wellman was looking for a very special actor to play a small but important role, Cadet White. This character had but one scene, then would be killed during a training flight. His death would set the tone for the two leading characters, played by Rogers and Arlen, to understand the dangers of training and the tragedy of war—things that Wellman had learned and wanted punctuated.

The actor playing Cadet White would have to be able to make an immediate and lasting impression. His only help would come from the on-screen words: "I've got to go up and do a flock of eights before chow" and "Luck or no luck, when your time comes, you're going to get it."

Wellman had met a tall, gangly, shy actor who had had only one acting role and was down on his luck. Wellman liked him and thought he was perfect for Cadet White. In that critical role, the director cast Frank James Cooper, who became Gary Cooper.

"Coop," as he was often called, was born in Helena, Montana on May 7, 1901. The son of English parents, he lived on a ranch until age twelve, when he was sent to England until he finished high school. After returning to Helena, he lived the life of a cowboy for two years before an automobile accident nearly ended his life. After recovery, he entered Grinnell College in Grinnell,

Buddy Rogers, Clara Bow, and Richard Arlen pose for a publicity shot for *Wings*. *Courtesy of the author.*

Gary Cooper's small role in *Wings* made him a star. Wellman would also direct Cooper in his first leading role in *Legion of the Condemned* (1928), another flying picture. *Courtesy of the author.*

Iowa, as an art student. He was 6 feet, 3 inches tall and 175 pounds, with brown hair and light blue eyes. He became entranced with an attractive, strong-willed student named Doris Virden. She became his sweetheart, and they talked of marriage after he had established himself as an illustrator. Helena being a small town, Doris pushed her boyfriend to leave and go to California to make it in the big city. Even though he loved home, family, the ranch life, and working as a cartoonist in Helena, Coop packed his bags and, with a $200 bankroll, left for the dream of success in Los Angeles.

Unfortunately, the city editors did not like his work, and he was reduced to toiling as a drapery salesman and house-to-house portrait photographer. Doris and Coop wrote often; she was constantly filling him with confidence, but these jobs did not succeed either, and he was down to his last dime. Months went by and, thinking himself a failure, he stopped writing Doris.

In desperation, he went to the Hollywood studios and signed up as an extra in Westerns. This was logical because he loved and missed the cowboy life, and could certainly ride a horse and do other related chores.

When he began to get work, his pay was only $5 a day, but he could survive on it. After a number of extra jobs and a little money in his pocket, he paid $65 for his own screen test—with his own mother cranking the camera. The test was short and sweet. In it, he rode up to a camera, made a flashy dismount, looked at the camera for a brief moment, then ambled into a saloon.

Director Henry King was preparing a Western, _The Winning of Barbara Worth_ (1926), starring Ronald Colman and Vilma Banky. King wanted to take ten riders to the Nevada location and had already chosen nine. He spotted a tall, cowboy-looking gent sitting outside a casting director's office at the studio. King asked the casting director about the man and looked at his test. The director liked what he saw and hired the cowboy for his first acting role, paying him $50 a week.

All excited, Coop started writing Doris again, but discovered that she had given up on him and married a local druggist. With the loss of his beloved and so much failure in his career, _Worth_ was a very significant event to him. Primarily, it gave him the confidence to continue on—and only a short time later, along came Wellman.

After Cooper became a star, Fay Wray, one of his co-stars, received a long letter from Doris explaining that she had felt awful about losing him and desperately wanted him back. They never reunited, and Doris died of throat cancer in 1934.

When Wellman came onboard the _Wings_ Express, he was far behind the Paramount team—but he picked up steam in a hurry. In addition to the rigors of casting the actors, he became totally immersed in every aspect of the film production process: writing, producers and production staff, assistant directors, photography, editors, script supervisors, extras, Air Corps and Army personnel, stunts and stunt men, costuming and makeup, property, music, set design and construction, location, travel and transportation, and so on.

The producers, Lucien K. Hubbard and B. P. Schulberg, were involved as well and had been for over four months. There were times when they worked in tandem with the director, but on other occasions battles took place as to who had the last word. Even though he was the new kid on the block, Wellman wasn't going to take a back seat to any producer or studio executive. He believed that this was his film, his big opportunity, and he wasn't going to do anything or let anything happen that wasn't in the best interests of _Wings_.

The producers accepted the fact that this twenty-nine-year-old, undertested director was captain of their ship. They were going to try to please him, but also expected that their more experienced voices would be heard and even accepted. Hubbard and Schulberg took care of the business and financial ends, which included the budget. It was their job to keep that budget in line and not go over. All Wellman cared about was that he had enough money to get the production values he needed. One of the major budgetary stumbling blocks to come would arise from the fact that since no aerial warfare on this scale had ever been photographed, the costs were only guesstimates.

Before 1926, there had been some aerial warfare work in films; however, flying footage was gathered from independent sources, government financed films, and with the use of miniatures. Actors were not seen in actual flight. When an actor or stunt pilot was seen in the air, that footage was shot on the ground to simulate in flight.

Wellman believed that the story and screenplay were of the utmost importance. John Saunders was an extremely helpful ally, as he and Wellman spoke the same flyer's lingo. Before and during production, Wellman interjected the script with many ingredients that he had experienced during his days in France and at the front.

Throughout his lifetime, Wellman declared that the cameraman was his right arm. He had many meetings with Harry Perry, topnotch director of photography, concerning story values and how to get them onto the screen. The aerial photography alone would be a new dimension in filmmaking. Perry and Wellman hired the best men available, some with flight experience. Before the end of production, there would be thirteen cameramen, including Perry.

One can imagine that with all this intense pre-production, Wellman had little time for Margery and Gloria. Of course, Margery was not going to be a script girl or anything else on this picture. Hopefully, both mother and child would be able to spend some time on the location.

High on the list of locations was San Antonio, Texas—"the next Hollywood," "the new Hollywood," "the next Los Angeles." These were the catch phrases being bandied around in the early days of moving pictures.

When the picture business was entrenched in New York and New Jersey, film pioneers needed a better climate and picturesque landscapes to be able to film year-round. Some filmmakers went to Florida, others to California. Much of the film community believed that Texas and San Antonio were the right places. "Remember the Alamo!" led the Texans to victory over Mexico in 1836 in their war for independence. The Lone Star State—because of a single star on its flag—joined the Union on December 29, 1845, as the twenty-eighth state. Flags of six nations flew over it: Spain, France, Mexico, the Republic of Texas, the Confederate States of America, and the United States.

Moviemakers were inspired and energized by the mystique of the Alamo. They felt their imaginations soar by the rich history of the colorful men who developed Texas: Spanish adventurers, French explorers, Comanche Indians, Texas rangers, Franciscan missionaries, cattle barons, homesteaders, miners, lumberjacks, and oil drillers. The state offered a wide variety of attractive scenery with great natural resources. There were beautiful countrysides, mountains, rivers and lakes, wildlife, unique architecture, and, of course, pleasing weather. The city of San Antonio could resemble anything from the eighteenth to the twenty-fifth centuries.

Beginning in 1910, Gaston Méliès and his Star Film Company said goodbye to New York, settling in the Texas city on a twenty-acre parcel. It was the first movie studio in San Antonio. They called it the Star Film Ranch. On the ranch was a large, two-story farmhouse and a large barn. Star Films was a repertory company. The high-priority members lived at a famous hotel, Hot

Wells, while the rest of the flock stayed with local families. The company would be responsible for producing over seventy of the more than 110 films made prior to 1926.

In the 1920s, the film capitals were New York, Los Angeles, and San Antonio. San Antonio was experiencing its golden age of film with bigger and better filmmakers and films coming to shoot. The year 1925 brought King Vidor and _The Big Parade_. Vidor picked San Antonio to film some of the most important scenes in his picture.

Wellman remembered _Parade_ as _the_ picture of the year. He said, "I saw it twenty-two times until I knew every cut and, I thought, every reason for it. I lay in bed and tried to figure out how I could have topped King Vidor in his direction. I had no success."

Wellman made numerous trips back and forth from Hollywood to San Antonio. Many weeks were required for the construction and landscape design needed to transform parts of Texas into France. A French village and countryside were created, as well as World War I airfields and battlefields.

By the time September 1926 rolled around, the _Wings_ company had been a mainstay in the community for a long time. After six months of pre-production, with the full support of the War Department and $16 million worth of government manpower and equipment, and a production budget of $2 million—the most expensive budget of all-time!—the _Wings_ Express blasted off from Paramount Studios. With the clickety-clack of the wheels, chug-chug of the engine, the squeal of brakes, a great hiss of steam, and a high-powered whistle blast, it landed in San Antonio, Texas.

Wellman later wrote,

We stayed at the Saint Anthony Hotel and were there for nine months. I know that was the correct time because the elevator operators were girls and they all became pregnant. They were replaced by old men, and the company's hunting grounds were barren. Victor Fleming was making _The Rough Riders_ at the same time and was staying at the same hotel. San Antonio became the Armageddon of a magnificent sexual Donnybrook. The town was lousy with movie people, and if you think that contributes to a state of tranquility, you don't know your motion picture ABCs. To recount all that happens when a company of well over two hundred are taken away from their homes and families, and dumped into a strange locale? It's rough on the company and rough on the locale.

The fires that start burning are burning in every neighborhood in the country. The only difference being that we who lit the match are in the movies. We are monkeys in a weird cage. There is something unique about us, and only we know what it is. Maybe the closest to us is a doctor. His business is human beings, sick ones. Our business is the same, only our beings are not suffering, they are acting suffering or acting happiness, success or failure, excitement or boredom, life or death—everything that can happen to a human being, every thought they possess the actor echoes, the writer writes, the director directs, the cameraman photographs, and every other department has a share in.

Day in and day out, year after year, you are crying or you are laughing, you are terse or relaxed, your emotions are turned on and off like a spigot, and you must be careful not to become so callused that when the real thing happens it hasn't been robbed of its vitality. A motion picture company lives hard and plays hard, and they better or they will all go nuts.

Clara Bow was a superstar wherever she went—in Hollywood, in New York, in London, in San Antonio. She was single, stunning, vivacious, captivating, seductive, and crazy about men. From 1925 until 1930, she was "everybody's dreamboat." She received 20,000 fan letters a week. In San Antonio, she was mobbed everywhere she appeared—in the hotel, out on the town, at the locations. A dozen local men had to be hired as extra security to help the company control the gathering crowds.

All the young actors from *Wings* and *The Rough Riders* fell in love with her. The long list included *Wings*' writer, John Saunders, and *Rough Riders*' director, Victor Fleming. Bow was the Queen Bee of Texas.

One might think the courtship for her caused a domino effect of conflicts and jealousies, but it didn't. Wellman recalled, "She took care of it how, I will never know. She kept Gary Cooper, Rogers, Arlen, Mack (Charles Mack, a *Rough Riders*' star), and a few names I can't remember, plus a couple of pursuit pilots from Selfridge Field and a panting writer, all in line. They were handled like chessmen, never running into one another, never suspecting that there was any other man in the whole world that meant a thing to this gorgeous little sexpot."

Even Clara tired of this show of suitors because at one point, she announced her engagement to Victor Fleming. This hanky-panky of passion was overshadowed by a growing hatred between the two services, the Army and the Air Corps.

Wings would be shot at Kelly Field, Camp Stanley, and other San Antonio locations. Flyers came from Selfridge Field, Michigan; Crissy Field, California; Langley Field, Virginia; and Brooks Field, San Antonio. Balloon officers, crews, and equipment were imported from Scott Field, Illinois. Artillery, tanks, troops, wire, and high explosives came from Fort Sam Houston, Texas.

From the get-go, Wellman got along with the Air Corps and their officers; the Army was another matter. Wellman explained, "We had the army too, thousands of them, infantry, artillery, the works, and in command a general who had two monumental hatreds: fliers and movie people."

He met me, the director, and immediately disliked me. This has happened to me many times before, but never so quickly. I hardly drew a breath and I was in the doghouse, for three hatreds: I was an ex-flier turned motion-picture director and I was only twenty-nine years old, and apparently anybody under forty was to him ungrown.

We had a couple of very hot vendettas, and I could get nowhere with the old boy until I reminded him that whether he liked it or not, he was working for Paramount Pictures and that I, despite my age, was the director of the Paramount Picture called *Wings* and brought a copy of the orders from the War Department as a convincer. It convinced. The old boy was still in the army.

Years later, when Wellman wrote about the making of *Wings*—from his hiring, through the huge production, the battles with the studio, the king-size opening, the awards, and the aftermath—he was surprised to discover that often he remembered the less-important things more vividly than some of the major experiences; for instance, on the night of his arrival, the dinner party at the Saint Anthony Hotel.

The great director was to come face-to-face with the assembled military who had been ordered by the War Department to place themselves at his disposal. The generals and their wives, the colonels and their wives, the majors and their wives, the unending brass and their never-ending wives, all curious and anxious to meet this mature genius of the art of motion pictures who was to guide Wings into immortality and in I walked.

I was tucked in between John Saunders, the writer, on my right and Lucien Hubbard, the supervisor, on my left. Mr. Biggest General, seeing us enter, had started to stand, and all the other officers at the tables, in true army fashion, followed suit. When Mr. Biggest General saw me and realized that I was the only one of the three that he had not met and must be the director, he quickly sat down, as did the others, some fully erect, some caught halfway up as if in a crouch, others who had just moved their feet. They all sat down noisily and looked at this gossoon with the long hair, as if the world had just played a dirty trick on them.

I wasn't mad and I wasn't embarrassed. I just felt as if I had suddenly been embalmed.

I was led to the slaughter of introductions. First the big man. He had to rise, rather reluctantly, to shake my hand and introduce me to his wife, to the other wives and their husband-generals, all of which was accomplished with a minimum of handshakes and a maximum of curt bows. I was as welcome as a psychiatric trauma, and I had to do something to off-set this wave of resentment that was slowly enveloping me.

The introductions over and everyone seated, Mr[.] Biggest General reached for his fruit cocktail, as did everyone else. This was the time. I bowed my head and mouthed a silent grace. It caught everybody by sur-prise. Saunders damn near slid under the table, Hubbard stared at me unbelievingly, and the fruit cocktails remained untouched. I held it long enough for all to see, finished my prayer, and started on my dinner as if nothing had happened, but I saw that it had hit home with a few of the ladies. Some kept looking at me for an added moment, two or three whis-pered to their husbands. At least I had some of them going in a different direction.

I turned to Mrs[.] Biggest General and told her things that I wanted relayed to the big man via pillowtalk. I said that I hoped they all would forgive me my age, implying that age cannot be counted in years but in what those years had lived. I spoke of flying pals gone, of Pershing and Teddy Roosevelt and Tommy Hitchcock, and how badly I needed help in this the biggest, most important, and most expensive flying picture the entire motion-picture industry had ever attempted.

She was lovely and seemed most interested, and I felt sure I was acquiring a valuable ally.

The dinner was over, the welcoming speeches of the three top gener-als, that of the infantry, the air corps, and the head man of the whole she-bang, and it was my turn, the sacrilegious grace invoker.

I started right out by telling them that the correct thing to say would be that I was very happy and honoured to be here. That is the correct way. The truthful way is that I am not happy and not honoured to be here, but since there seems to be great doubt of my ability because of my age, I would like to defend myself on this point-at-issue by telling you how old I really am and then perhaps you will re-evaluate this whole situation, and I will be viewed in a more flattering light.

I was born on 29 February 1896, leap year, which makes me seven years old. For one so young I have lived a tremendously interesting life. I have been married, not once but twice, I have flown at the front with some success, I have been in two armies, including the Foreign Legion, I have made moving pictures, and I know Clara Bow. I was also invited to break bread with the officers, high and low, of the services that have been ordered by the War Department to take part in a motion picture called *Wings*.

Perhaps the most prosperous producing company in the motion-picture business is the Paramount Pictures Corporation. The idiots that have been so successful in the development of a multimillion-dollar industry have appointed a seven-year-old to guide the destiny of this, their most important project. Quite naturally, one so young must be considered in the category of genius and because of his infancy must be given unending help and encouragement. I stand before you as that young prodigy and in all humility request the decency and the support that is due him; and I sat down.

It was very quiet. Then Mrs[.] Biggest General started to applaud, vigorously, the old boy took it up, vigorously, and then everybody in the room, including the waiters, vigorously. It was thunder, and it was honesty, and the little old gal took my hand and squeezed it and she said, "Mr[.] Genius, I want to ask you one question: Were you really saying grace, or better still, can you say grace?" I looked her straight in the eye and said no.

There was a lovely understanding smile on her face as she said, "You are an amazing young man, and I like you." She turned and left. I stood, watching her go, the wife and strength of a big man, and I wondered if amazing was the right word. Maybe it should have been phoney.

After two months of shooting, Wellman decided to throw away everything they had filmed. The flying scenes didn't look real. Jesse Lasky later wrote, "The company entrained to Texas—and sat there. Wellman stubbornly refused to start shooting until there were clouds in the sky. There were days on end of perfect sunshine, and our $200-a-week director wouldn't turn a camera, while overhead mounted at thousands of dollars a day. I confess that we were about ready to yank him off the picture and replace him with someone who would be more amenable."[1]

Wellman wrote, "Say you can't shoot a dogfight without clouds to a guy who doesn't know anything about flying and he thinks you're nuts. He'll say, 'Why can't you?' It's unattractive. Number two, you get no sense of speed, because there's nothing there that's parallel. You need something solid behind the planes. The clouds give you that, but against a blue sky, it's like a lot of goddam flies! And photographically, it's terrible."

Wellman was starting to lose patience with executive interference. He no longer wanted to discuss these problems via long-distance phone calls with Lasky or Schulberg. He explained the situation to Hubbard, the supervising producer and link to the studio, letting him handle the jawing. Even though he was on the location, Lucien knew little about flying and, considering the continuing loss of money, had difficulty understanding Wellman's point of view. However, Hubbard stuck by his director and begged the studio executives to be patient and understanding . . . at least for awhile.

Since no aerial photography on or near this scale had been done previously, a new book would have to be written. Both hand-cranked and battery-run cameras were standard for the era. Cranking by hand was preferred because the operator could control the speed of the action by cranking slower or faster. The motorized camera filmed at the same speed.

During the early attempts at *Wings* photography, the operators tried to

Wellman, second from left, worked closely with officers at Brooks and Kelly airfields in Texas to film the first staged aerial battles, which are depicted in *Wings*. From left: Brooks airfield Commanding Officer Major J. E. Cheney, Wellman, Brigadier General Frank P. Lahm, author John Monk Saunders, Kelly airfield Commanding Officer Major F. M. Andrews, and producer Lucien Hubbard. *Courtesy of the author.*

hand-hold and crank the cameras while flying alongside the picture planes. There was too much movement of camera and plane. Even bolting the cameras down did not solve the problems.

Both the camera plane and picture plane moved in opposition to one another—the flimsy crafts vibrated, wobbled, and shook with the wind, moving backward and forward, up and down, and side to side, resulting in a shot that was unsteady, unclear, and uncomfortable to the eye of the audience.

E. Burton Steene saved the day! Wellman recalled, "Burton Steene was the number one aerial photographer of the 20s and I grabbed him for *Wings*, the luckiest grab I ever made. He had a camera with an Akeley head, which means it had gears, a pan handle and a frightening whine to it as Burton panned up or down or from side to side. For 1926, it was unbelievable and Burton was so expert at it, he shot ninety percent of all the air scenes in *Wings*."

Because stunt pilots, not the actors, were flying the picture planes, the cameramen couldn't get close or the cameras would identify them instead of Buddy Rogers and Richard Arlen. Therefore, no close-ups! Wellman tried shooting close-ups on the ground, faking the fact that they weren't in the air, but it looked completely unreal.

Wellman himself took to the skies to view the complex problems. He and Harry Perry discussed all the possibilities and made a number of decisions:

- Camera mounts would be created and fastened or strapped to the fuse-lages of the planes.
- Platforms and up to one-hundred-foot towers would be constructed from the ground to photograph the low-flying aircraft and the ground warfare.
- Thirteen camera operators would film the aerial sequences.
- There would be no trickery in the filming of actors flying—Buddy Rogers and Richard Arlen would learn to fly. Motor-driven cameras would be mounted on the front of two-cockpit planes or behind the rear cockpit; once airborne, the safety pilot would duck down or hide behind a large headrest, and the actors would turn on the cameras and pilot the planes.

In *Wings*, Wellman and his cameraman, Harry Perry, advanced the technology for filming aerial warfare. *Courtesy of the author.*

Wellman confers with Perry. *Courtesy of the author.*

Arlen had had some flying experience; Rogers, none. They were given the best flight instructors available, but only received a few hours' training. Rogers remembered, "I was the photographer, the director, the actor, everything . . . for five hundred feet." Arlen fared quite well with his flying, but Rogers, Wellman recalled, "was a tough son of a bitch. He hated flying, which made him deathly sick. He logged over ninety-eight hours in the picture and every time he came down, he vomited. That's a man with guts. I love him."

Paramount did not understand either the waste or Wellman's passion for realism. They were also afraid that he was going to kill the stars.

During the delays due to waiting for clouds and weather, as dull gray skies had taken over the clear blue ones, Wellman's special effects cameramen, mainly Harry Perry, tried to trick clouds where no clouds existed. Perry placed white cotton balls on thin pieces of thread in front of the camera lens. It didn't work. When the camera moved, so did the cotton clouds. They even sent up skywriters in an attempt to create imitation clouds. Nothing they tried worked.

As a diversion during the downtime, the crew played tackle football on the concrete runways. Buddy Rogers and Dick Arlen joined the games. As he had done in high school, Wellman played quarterback against the Army and Air Corps teams. Both Wellman and Bill Clothier, a cameraman who played center, boasted that the movie company always won. Now, the studio believed that if Wellman didn't kill their stars during flying, he would certainly break their arms and legs.

While waiting for better weather and their new technology for filming aerial sequences, Wellman was shooting everything else possible. When not directing the film, he and Hubbard were settling problems and politics with the Army and Air Corps. Impatient troops were treated to barrels of beer, movies, dinners, and dances. There were crew problems as well. The unit manager was skimming money off the top. When sets were built, he would purchase lumber and sell it back to the studio at a higher price. There were constant firings and hirings. Charles Barton, Wellman's friend and assistant property man, was promoted three times; and when the crooked unit manager was fired, he was promoted again, ending up as first assistant director.

Government officials began to side with the studio against Wellman. After all, the War Department hadn't placed their servicemen at Paramount's disposal to drink beer and play football. *Wings* and Wellman were fast losing their support system.

With all this turmoil going on (and Wellman no longer talking to the studio), Lucien Hubbard on location and B. P. Schulberg in the studio were caught between a rock and a hard place. They understood some of Wellman's concerns, but not all of the waste and downtime. While Hubbard was working to keep the production running, Lasky in Hollywood and Zukor in New York were urging Schulberg to keep his promise to control the headstrong, twenty-nine-year-old director. Wellman needed studio support, but he made it crys-

After taking flying lessons, star Richard Arlen flies while shooting one of the aerial scenes from *Wings. Courtesy of the author.*

Assistant director Charlie Barton stands ready to employ signal flags, which were used to direct the stunt pilots' maneuvers. *Courtesy of the author.*

tal clear that this was his picture now and, whatever the cost, he would do what he thought best for *Wings*.

Gary Cooper was another thorn in Paramount's side. He had only one scene and Wellman kept putting off shooting it. This allowed the financially strapped newcomer to stay on Paramount's salary. Wellman later wrote,

---

Cooper's big scene was in a tent, so I had the tent lugged everywhere the company shot scenes. It travelled all over San Antonio, was unloaded and put up in the morning, taken down and reloaded when work was finished. This was a travelling tent, an emergency set to be used when all else failed or at my discretion. My discretion was influenced by a growing fondness for this awkward, lovable guy. He was broke, needed a break, and the longer his engagement on *Wings*, the more important his part looked to those back in Hollywood.

Time eventually ran out. On the night before Coop's big scene, Wellman called him to his suite for a rehearsal. "It was simple," the director noted, "because he was very natural and very good."

Cooper's character, Cadet White, is the veteran flyer rooming with Rogers and Arlen, playing the new recruits. Cadet White always carried a talisman

Fittingly, Wellman appears to thumb his nose on the set of *Wings*. In the midst of the costly, complex, and often contentious shoot, Wellman stopped speaking to Paramount executives about production problems. *Courtesy of the author.*

when he flew. On this particular flight, he forgets his good luck piece and is killed. The rookies don't realize his mistake until too late. When White reaches the tent entrance, he turns back, throws a salute to the admiring recruits, smiles and departs. Wellman recounted,

---

This sounds very simple, but it is not. To be remembered, Coop not only must salute and smile, but he must have something unusual about him, that indescribable thing called motion-picture personality, to make it that effective that quickly. Don't ask me what it is or how you get it, because I don't think you can get it. If you have it, it came to you, and you're lucky as hell. . . . Cooper had it.

The next day, the scene was shot. Wellman, as usual, took two takes only—printing the first and saving the second for protection against problems from the camera, processing, etc. "I yelled cut, print it, and Coop's face dropped," Wellman remembered.

Wellman believed Cooper's negative reaction was due to the fact that he was finished in *Wings*. The next day he would be on his way back to Hollywood. His tent was reloaded for good.

Wellman recalled,

That night just before dinner, I was taking a shower, and there was a knock on the door. I yelled come in and went out with a towel around me, and there was Coop. I thought he came up to say goodbye, but he just stood there sort of embarrassed and didn't say a word. As a matter of fact, Coop didn't talk much anyway, so I said, what can I do for you, Coop? He piddled around some more and finally it came out; it was almost like a faltering recitation: "Mr. Wellman"—he always called me Mr. Wellman—"you know I appreciate everything you have done for me, and I'll never forget it, and, and, and I haven't any right to ask this but, but, but couldn't I do that scene over again?" I asked him why and he said, "Because I just, just think I could do it better," and he breathed a sigh of relief. He had gotten it off his chest.

I didn't want to hurt Coop's feelings, but I told him quite frankly that I was the director and was supposed to know my business, and I thought he had done it beautifully, and asked him just what there was about it he didn't like.

And then he told me, "Well, you know right in the middle of the scene, I, I picked my nose and, and."

"Just a minute, Coop. You keep right on picking your nose, and you will pick yourself into a fortune—and just one more thing, always back away from the problems, from the heavy, and, above all, from the girl. Make them pursue you. Never, but never be the aggressor."

He stood there for a hushed minute and then gave me that goddamned funny little smile and said, "Thanks, Mr. Wellman, for everything."

He knew I was right, I knew I was right, and you know I was right. For a seven-year-old, I was gazing into the crystal ball of the future.

Wellman's wife and adopted daughter were able to make several trips down to San Antonio. With all the work, excitement, conflicts, and distractions of every kind, it was next to impossible for the family to spend much time together.

In trying to make amends, Wellman put both of them in the movie—Margery as a French peasant and Gloria as her daughter. They lived in the farmhouse that served as the final resting place for the dying David Armstrong, played by Richard Arlen. While David died in the arms of his best friend, played by Buddy Rogers, Margery, and Gloria watched the very emotional, climactic death scene.

As sometimes happens in the film world, stars Rogers and Arlen, rivals before becoming friends in *Wings*, were rivals and not pals in real life. They respected and tolerated each other. The turning point of their movie friendship happened during the fisticuffs in the training camp sequence. Before the fight scene took place, Arlen told his director that he knew how to box and he didn't think Rogers did. So, Arlen said, Wellman should tell Rogers to be very careful. The director followed the actor's orders.

When Wellman yelled "action!" and the combat began, choreography soon disappeared from view. Buddy Rogers, admittedly not a fighter, beat the living hell out of Richard Arlen simply on guts alone—just the way it was supposed to be in the script. Richard Arlen and Buddy Rogers continued to be rivals and not the best of friends.

The *Wings* company had seventeen stunt men on the payroll. The picture was loaded with a variety of stunts: fistfights, boxing matches, and pratfalls; battle scenes crowded with running, walking, standing, and sitting soldiers being shot, gassed, burned, and blown up; parachute leaps from observation balloons; various kinds of vehicle wrecks and collisions; and any number of plane smashups into houses, trees, rivers, and the good old ground.

Airplane crashes were a new department in the film-stunt world. Who better to explain the concept to the stuntmen than Wild Bill Wellman, whose resume was filled with plane fragmentations? The only difference was that Wellman's crackups were not scheduled. This director would not think of asking a stunt man to do something that he wouldn't do. So, he filled the gas tank of a German plane, with only a small amount of petrol to avoid setting

Richard Arlen and Buddy Rogers enact the climactic death scene in *Wings*. *Courtesy of the author.*

himself on fire, strapped himself into the cockpit, took off, flew around the field once or twice, and crashed into the ground, rolling over several revolutions.

The pilot unstrapped himself and strolled over to the amazed stunt performers with, "That's how you do it! And always remember to duck your head when you hit ground. The goddamn plane will roll over on its own."

During filming, the only stuntman to get seriously injured was the legendary Dick Grace—considered to be the greatest of the silent-era stunt men. He performed incredible crashes in *Wings* and injured himself doing a less-dangerous one. He was required only to land his plane at a slow speed and turn it over. In doing so, he snapped his head back and broke his neck. The crew took him to the hospital, where a large cast was placed around his neck.

Grace was told to keep it on for a year. Six weeks later, Wellman walked into the dance hall at the Saint Anthony Hotel and saw Grace on the dance floor, dancing up a storm. He had gotten a hammer, broken the cast, and gone dancing. He never wore it again.

Bad weather was causing further delays in shooting the climactic battle scene—the re-creation of the famous battle of Saint-Mihiel. Plus, the Air Corps and the Army were losing patience, and Paramount Studios wanted to fire its young, under-tested, headstrong director, William Wellman. But who would be his replacement? Who would be able to get it all together? Who would even understand the project? How much more money would be lost in the turnaround? The studio brass sent the three major financiers from New York to the filming location with the power to discharge the director, if they so desired.

It just so happened that the "three wise men" arrived on the location the day that Wellman was hoping to film that climactic sequence.

Wellman wrote,

It was all there. Hills in the background, first-line, second-line, third-line and communication trenches, all down to depth, all done in precise army fashion. I didn't need all of them that perfectly, but when you play with the army, that is the way you get them. It seemed a shame that we couldn't transplant some of our enemy here and fight out our differences. It looked exactly like Saint-Mihiel.

We had been rehearsing with 3,500 army personnel and sixty-five-odd pilots for ten days. Camera positions on one-hundred-foot parallels erected at the apex of a triangle and at various distances down either side. Seventeen first cameramen and crews plus positions for twenty-eight eyemos electrically controlled. It was a gigantic undertaking, and the only element we couldn't control was the weather. That is what I thought.

Wellman and producer Lucien Hubbard confer from the 100-foot platform they had built to survey and film the picture's aerial and ground warfare scenes. *Courtesy of the author.*

I had positioned myself on the seventy-five-foot level of the main parallel at the apex of the triangle and had an organlike board with push buttons that controlled and positioned the creeping barrage that preceded the advancing wave of doughboys. This I had practised until I could do it in my sleep. I insisted on being alone so that nothing would disconcert me when the big time came.

The day had been set and arrived. Everything was ready, everything but the weather. We needed sunshine, bright sunshine, because in those days we did not have the fast film of today. We were in the lap of the gods.

As if more suspense was needed for this little drama, the Air Corps had presented the *Wings* company with an ultimatum. During the filming of aerial sequences to this date, there had been two accidental crashes by Air Corps pilots. Neither flyer was seriously injured, but the planes were demolished. The ultimatum stated that if there was one more wreck, the military body would immediately withdraw its pilots and planes.

"The whole damned picture would go down the drain," Wellman remarked.

You can imagine my position and the condition of my not-to-be-trusted stomach. I was sick, couldn't keep cooked cereal down. I was on the threshold of being a seven-year-old has-been.

As a topper to this spider web of trouble, the three imposing financial giants of the Paramount Pictures incorporated were expected in momentarily. The railroad siding had been lengthened so that they would arrive within a hundred yards of the battle of Saint-Mihiel. The three great magicians of the buck were, in order of importance, Otto Kahn, Sir William Wiseman, and a gentleman who owned among other things a leading cigarette company, a William Stralem.

All morning long we waited, everything in readiness. The barrage to gouge its creeping devastation and noise, the troops to plough through God knows what, and the cameras to record the countless number of rehearsed bits of battle business. The planes on the runways ready to take off and circle to my right of the battlefield, to swoop down on their strafing assignments, and the camera planes at different altitudes to photograph the air view of the maze of confusion of a battle.

I had been a sky-gazer for a long time and for good reason: at the front, just before taking off on a shooting-up-an-enemy-airfield assignment, to try to figure out how long the low overcast might remain. To get over the objective just as it started to break up and take advantage of the mousetrap holes to dive through, do a little fast shooting, and zoom up into the protection of the blanket of safety. Shooting exteriors on a Western, when sunshine was needed, and a wagon train was stretched out in the long distance waiting to be called in.

The big three arrived, and I saw Lucien Hubbard, God bless him, take over and explain what was supposed to happen, at a moment when talk wasn't as necessary as prayer, or as easy.

Then it came, a little streak of flimsy brightness fighting its way through the cloud layer. It faded in and out like a faltering heartbeat. There it was, my Holy Grail. I felt like Sir Galahad, only I wasn't a Knight of the Round Table, and I wasn't noble and pure. I was just a lousy moving-picture director with a hell of a problem on his hands, and one bad decision or a false move or a push of the wrong button and somebody might get hurt, badly.

I ordered the planes in the air. It didn't take long for them to arrive overhead, in the right formations, at the correct altitudes, and in the chosen positions, circling like soaring hawks waiting to pounce.

I know that Hubbard thought I had gone crazy. The look of anguish on that poor man's upturned face.

One of the aides, a captain of the infantry, came tearing up to the bottom of the parallel. He forced his way through Hubbard and the moneymen and yelled up at me:

"Wellman, what are you doing?"

"What the hell do you think I'm doing? I'm getting ready to shoot the scene."

"But you need the sun."

"That's right. You get your big ass back and get ready!"

I looked up, and by God my little rift was widening, and the sun was just beginning to shine through.

Five minutes. That's all I needed. We had timed the rehearsals and the scene took exactly five minutes: a lifetime.

I yelled for everybody to get ready. I took my position with my fingers on the board, readying myself to play the loudest, most exciting cacophonic solo of bedlam that has ever been wrapped up in five minutes.

I yelled, "Camera." They heard my voice in the lobby of the Saint Anthony Hotel fifty miles away.

The first barrage going off was the signal for all the action to start, on the ground and from the air. I pushed my number-one button, and the first barrage blasted. Chee-rist, it goddamn near blew me off the parallel, and all hell broke loose, advancing infantry, diving planes, falling men. I kept the barrage creeping just ahead of the first wave. I couldn't watch anything else. I didn't know what the hell was happening around me, just what was going on directly in front of me, and it was majestic.

I was up to button number eight, nine, ten, the sun was still out and strong. If it would shine for only one more minute, we were in, eleven, twelve, only six more to go, and some son of a bitch spoke to me. I pushed the wrong button, and a couple of bodies flew through the air. They weren't dummies.

I didn't take my eye off any more of the buttons, just kept playing the right tune, with no more sour notes, and watching some crazy pursuit pilot knocking the helmets off the advancing waves of doughboys. The bastard was going nuts, he was slowing us down, screwing up the whole carefully planned advance, and then I saw him crash, and his plane rolled over and over, and I was almost glad.

I yelled to somebody who was standing behind me, keeping one eye on the few remaining buttons, the other on the action—

"Get down off this parallel, you goddamned idiot, or I'll break every bone in your body."

The sun was getting dim—two more buttons to go—seventeen, eighteen, and it blacked out, and the scene was over, and I was limp.

Cheers broke out. Everybody was running around hugging each other. Cameramen were yelling up to me, how sensational it was. What wonderful shots they had gotten. Generals were clustered around my parallel chattering like magpies, and I was watching the ambulances picking their way to my big mistake.

I started the long climb down. Lucien grabbed me in a big bear hug, somebody was pumping my hand. I broke loose and started to run to the ambulance. I got there, all out of breath. Nobody was killed, but two were badly hurt. How bad? Don't know. One is still unconscious. Oh goddamn— I started for the crack-up, slowly and alone. When I got there, the plane was demolished, but the pilot was leaning against an ambulance with a bandage around his head. He was dazed, but not from the crash, and I suddenly realized that in all my planning I had forgotten one terribly important factor, the human element. This pilot had flown at the front. He had been decorated. He had flown missions just like this one. For five minutes it was not 1926 to him; it was 1918. He just stuck his hand out and said, "I'm sorry. C'est la guerre."

Noted historian and author Frank Thompson, in his book *Texas Hollywood* (2002), discovered a report that said an Air Corps pilot had been killed during the filming of *Wings*. Cadet Charles M. Wiseley was listed as killed in the line of duty. He was buried with full military honors on October 26, 1926. His parents received $10,000 from Paramount Pictures. Wellman never acknowledged this occurrence, and this author doubts he ever knew of it.

Wellman continued the story.

Alone at last. Maybe this isn't home, but this suite will do for a few belts and a shower and a "to hell with everything and everybody" for a few no-decision hours. I locked the door, told the operator not to ring the room if the Pope wanted to speak to me.

Scenes from the re-creation of the Battle of Saint-Mihiel in *Wings*. *Courtesy of the author.*

My first drink was a mischief-maker, it encouraged a second, which introduced me to number three. The goddamned drinks became push buttons, and the creeping barrage was the roar in my head.

The five minutes was apparently a huge success. The army was raving about it, the air corps paid no attention to the crack-up, and we were still shooting a picture. Hubbard was in happy land, the three wise men from the east duly impressed, and the two casualties were going to recover.

The only screwed-up one was the wrong-button-pushing director who was pinning on a loner and was getting to feel sorry for himself, which is almost as insufferable as being a reformed drunk.

Even in his cups, Wellman knew why the New York bankers were there—he was way over budget and refused to shoot the major dogfight until clouds appeared. Wellman also knew that he was a dirty name around the executive offices at the studio. He had stopped talking to Paramount executives, and when the studio sent one of their own to force him to shoot no matter what the conditions, he challenged the man with a choice: a trip home or a trip to the hospital. The executive accepted the former.

Wellman cast himself as an extra and lies "dead" in the foreground in this scene depicting the Battle of Saint-Mihiel. *Courtesy of the author.*

Wellman wondered how much nastier it would become when the money-lenders sounded their judgments. He believed his chances of not being fired were 50/50. The principal actors were long gone from the location and waiting to complete the interior scenes at the studio. The only major sequence remaining to be shot was the big dogfight, and Wellman figured he was the only one who knew how to stage it.

"So help me, for a lousy $250 a week," he thought, "I was going to get it right."

I was going to give Paramount the ride of their life. Mr. Wrong-Button Pusher was drunk and blazing, and the hate hangover was going to outlast the alcoholic one.

A muddled train of thought choo-chooed through my befuddled brain. The button I missed was number thirteen. I counted and recounted just as I remembered doing during the actual scene, and the son of a bitch who spoke to me did it after the twelfth button. Thirteen has always been an unlucky number for me. On the Friday the thirteenths that have come up during my life, I have never left the house, been careful how I walked downstairs, took the phone off the hook, sat down, gingerly, nursed my way through the gruesome twenty-four hours, and always uttered a prayer of relief on the dawn of the fourteenth.

As a matter of fact, why blame it on the thirteenth button? All my life, I have been coasting along under full sail and doing pretty well, when for no good reason I push the wrong button, and then pain. Already I have pushed wrong matrimonial buttons, wrong business buttons, wrong friendship buttons, and wrong sexual buttons. I am habitually a sometime wrong-button pusher, and I'm loaded and alone and dirty, so to hell with it. I'm going to take me a shower and maybe I can hot-and-cold myself into not being a button pusher and become a pussy pusher, at least nobody will get hurt, not even the little pussycat.

Never has anybody enjoyed the shower as I did. Each bubble of water, hot or cold, seemed to snap me out of my button-pushing complex. I staggered into the shower, but strode out of it almost a sober man. It had cleansed me of the last few dreadful hours, and I was once more nothing but hungry. The button pushing was forgotten, and the pussy pushing but a moment of alcoholic daydreaming.

There was a loud knocking at the door. Bathrobed and slightly tipsy, I answered it. I opened the door, and there they stood: the unholy three.

I asked them in and poured them a drink. I did not take one myself. They sat down, all but Mr. Kahn. He started to pace the room, and I knew I was in for it, but what a hell of a way to go out. I had just shown them five minutes of unbroken madness, and I don't think they will ever forget it as long as they lived.

I sat down and waited for the ultimatum. It came fast and concise.

Mr. Kahn: "Wellman, we like you"—I goddamned near passed out—"and furthermore you stay here as long as you think is necessary to get what you believe is best for the picture. We have complete confidence in you, and the picture is in your young capable hands." I excused myself and went into the bathroom to vomit.

I did a good job, kneeling on the floor gazing into the relief bowl, when there was a very polite knock on the door and I heard Mr. Kahn asking: "You all right, Wellman?"

"Yes, sir, all right and getting sober," and he continued: "I was that goddamned idiot who opened his big mouth at the wrong time. I am terribly sorry and I apologize." I heard them go out and the door close. I lay down, on the floor and cried.

A few moments later, Wellman's suite door opened and the bathrobed director went running down the hallway shouting, "Charlie! Charlie!" A door at the end of the hall opened and Charlie Barton, Wellman's assistant, stuck his drunken head out as Wellman arrived at his door. "Charlie, we're going on. We're going on, Charlie." Wellman turned and, as he ran back up the hallway, Barton gulped out a yell, "Yippee! Yippee!"

For the next period of filming, Wellman shot close-ups, special business, and pieces of action to cut into the Saint-Mihiel sequence. Most of the Army and some of the Air Corps were released. Many of the soldiers who stayed had become veterans of the cinema wars. They not only played doughboys for the allies in *Wings*, but changed uniforms to portray Huns on the German side. Some even had charged up San Juan Hill in that famous scene from the *Rough Riders* saga.

Since the departure of the Paramount financiers, the atmosphere around the company was much more relaxed. Wellman was a great deal more comfortable. He put crew members, flyers, stunt men and himself into the picture. Wellman played a doughboy who is shot while advancing on a pill-box. After taking a round of machine gun fire, he twirls and falls to the ground. When Roger's plane attacks the enemy, Wellman's doughboy looks to the sky and utters, "Atta boy, them buzzards are some good after all."

Now, it was time to shoot that major air combat. Billowy cumulus clouds floated across bright blue skies, and Wellman filmed a breathtaking dogfight that still holds up today as a magnificent piece of aerial artistry.

Wellman's final night at the Saint Anthony was highlighted by a small dinner party with his pilots—those from Brooks Field, San Antonio; and Selfridge Field, Michigan.

Wellman and his aeronautical team, all of whom were World War I combat pilots or veteran stunt flyers. From left, Captain Frank Tommick, British Ace Captain S. C. Campbell, Wellman, stunt flyer Dick Grace, French Ace and Director of Aeronautics Ted Parsons, technical assistant Norman McLeod, and *Wings* author John Monk Saunders. *Courtesy of the author.*

Wellman reminisced,

Contrary to what you might expect, there was but little drinking, no speeches, just a bunch of guys getting together to say goodbye.

When dinner was over and the coffee was on, someone passed me a silver platter. A simple silver platter, with the lone letter "W" inscribed in the center. Around it, in their own handwriting, their nicknames. They were in no particular alignment, just sort of spotted here and there: Pop, Bill T., Bill P., Ris, Bill I., Burdie, Van, Whick, Robbie, Si, Barry, John I., Carl J., KH, Rod, George, Buck.

They were the best, and they are mine to treasure the rest of my life.

"My homecoming could hardly be called triumphant," Wellman remembered.

There was a very noticeable lack of enthusiasm at the studio and in my own home at the sight or sound of me. The domestic one, so help me, is like an unsolved jigsaw puzzle. . . . If I went through hours and hours of research, asking friends if they remembered when such and such happened. If I dug into stored-away boxes of cancelled cheques and spent long hours interrogating my business manager, turned the safety-deposit box upside-down reading papers of divorce and settlement, maybe I could piece this matrimonial disaster together and get the true picture of the whole best-forgotten mess.

To hell with it. . . . She fell out of love with me. I had been so busy, so completely wrapped up in my work when I found out, I didn't care. The lawyers were retained and whatever there was that jingled, most of it would go their way.

Meanwhile, at my other nook of comfort, the studio, two acts of God had taken place. Number one: they didn't take up my option and I was off salary, but still working. I hadn't been barred from the studio; they still needed me in the cutting room. Number two: I signed with a new young agent, Myron Selznick.

When I told him my story, he said he had a couple of keeps for me to do—keep working and keep my mouth shut—that he would take it from here and then, asked me if I needed any money. I told him no, and he said if you do, let me know. I became the second client of the agent who became the commander-in-chief of them all.

Myron Selznick wore a vendetta like a watch—he inspected it often. His father, Lewis J. Selznick, had been one of the pioneering leaders in New York's film industry from 1912 to 1922. L. J., as he was sometimes called, was a rough, tough, Russian Jew. He was one of eighteen children and learned to fend for himself at an early age. He emigrated from czarist Russia to England at twelve and worked in a factory until he could earn passage to America.

In Pittsburgh, he worked as a jeweler's apprentice and eventually owned his own store and later a successful chain of stores and a national bank. By age twenty-four, he was married and soon boasted three sons.

L. J.'s high-powered ideas and headstrong approach took him to New York and the film industry, where he formed his own production company and produced many films. His sometimes-unethical business practices provided him enemies such as Carl Laemmle, Adolph Zukor, L. B. Mayer, and others. By 1923, his empire was bankrupt and no one would hire him. He spent his remaining years in California supported by his two sons, David O. and Myron.

Myron, a successful producer in New York, came to Hollywood before David did. He found Tinseltown a tough nut to crack. Because no one would hire him to make movies, he became an agent. In 1927, agents occupied one of the lowest positions in the film industry. These facts and his vendetta powered his energies to succeed and avenge his father's name. Nothing gave him greater pleasure than to wreak financial damage on the men who would not hire him and had helped to ruin his father.

While Selznick was planning his attack on Paramount, Wellman continued working and finishing _Wings_. He shot the final scenes at Paramount's Vine Street studio and local spots. The biggest interior scene yet to shoot was the Folies Bergere nightclub. Wellman was trying to figure out a different way to film a group of actors, including Arlen and Rogers, sitting at a table getting drunk. Then Clara Bow was to join the celebrators.

The huge room was filled with five hundred dress extras; costumes ranged from soldiers of many nations to ladies of the evening. It was Paris at night in full tilt. Wellman thought how wonderful it would be if the camera could move from one end of the room to the other, just skimming over the tops of the busy tables—one continuous motion.

Wellman's agent Myron Selznick (older brother of legendary producer David O. Selznick) was instrumental in guiding Wellman's early career, particularly in the wake of his unfair treatment at Paramount after the huge success of _Wings. Courtesy of the Academy of Motion Picture Arts and Sciences._

An overhead track was constructed with a platform for the camera crew; and, for the first time, in *Wings*, the camera "dollied" from one end of the room to the other without stopping, without a cut. Burton Steene was on that platform during this movie innovation. He had shot dogfights, stunt crashes, troops under fire, hand to hand fighting in the big battle scenes, even pan shots of the lovely "It" girl, Clara Bow.

Wellman remembered,

God knows what I would have done without him. Personally he was one of the quietest, unassuming men I have ever known. I used to kid him about the dangerous profession he chose; to me he looked more like a fakey, sorrowful undertaker with a glint in his eye . . . He was on the dangerous end of the photographic stick, the aerial end, if he had any nerves I had yet to see them. His eagle sharp eyes belonged behind a rifle.

During the final days of shooting, Wellman wanted another long dolly movement. This one was to take place outside near the studio. Clara Bow and Buddy Rogers would be walking along the sidewalk on a tree-lined street.

Wellman wrote,

There were several little bits of separation such as Bow leaving Rogers just long enough to pick a daisy, a few more that separated the two and I wanted the camera to pan on each of the little bits of business, so I had Burton and his magical Akeley do the job. The scene started with the camera on a four-wheel dolly.

We had rehearsed it successfully. Then we took it, a very long dolly shot and I was riding along just behind Burton, peeking over his shoulder at the action when suddenly Burton fell backwards, I caught him before he fell off the dolly, his fall whipped the Akeley off Bow and Rogers and with a death grip on his pan handle, the gear head whining, the camera was photographing the rich blue sky, with beautiful clouds in artistic little clusters. Burton had a heart attack from which he did not recover. The next night when I ran the rushes, the fatalistic whining of the gear-headed Akeley had stopped and its last still photograph was Burton Steene's most beautiful, a sky so soft and ethereal, it had a face like heaven.

Many critics believe Wellman to be the forerunner of the wide screen. "I got the screwy idea for a wide screen on the take-off of the dawn patrol," he wrote. "A brilliant man, the head of the special-effects department, Roy T. Pomeroy, made it work." The process, called Magnascope, was invented by Lorenzo del Riccio and sold to Paramount in 1926. Basically, it enlarged the picture, giving the wide screen appearance.

Wellman and Pomeroy worked on other innovations as well; namely, sound effects. *Wings* was the first film to add sound effects to a silent picture. Pomeroy, who had parted the Red Sea for Cecil B. DeMille, added the roar of the planes' engines, the firing of guns, even the scream of a German killed in a dogfight. All these effects were synchronized from turntables behind the screen.

In the final black and white and tinted print, red-orange flames were seen coming from the burning airplanes. These flames were colored by hand, frame by frame, in the special effects art department.

Wellman was now finished with *Wings*, and Selznick was ready for his vendetta.

The fifth and final Mrs. William Wellman, Dorothy "Dottie" Coonan, was a Busby Berkeley dancer. *Courtesy of the author.*

7

Judgments

Paramount Pictures was ready to preview *Wings* to get an audience response. "Despite good preview reactions," Wellman wrote, "the powers-to-be were still dubious. One bet me $100 that *Wings* wouldn't play for more than three weeks on Broadway." Considering Paramount's huge cost of this first-time air epic, many studio executives believed that the picture was doomed to fail.

Wellman wrote,

After a very successful preview in New York (to which I was not invited), the front office began to suspect that they might have a pretty fair picture on their hands, so I was called into the head man's cave [Lasky]. He greeted me as if I had just turned up from the dead. It was so insincere that I got mad wondering if he really thought I was dumb enough to swallow it. I guess he did, because he never stopped his inane barrage of hollow-sounding lickspittle. He made excuses for our differences of opinion. Lauded me for my tenacity, which he pronounced tenisity. Complimented me on the excitement and beauty of the dogfight and ended by telling me I was to direct the first Gary Cooper starring vehicle, a flying picture, right up my alley, titled *The Legion of the Condemned*, which was my own story. I had tried to sell them on doing it before I started *Wings*, with no success whatsoever, and he had forgotten all about it.

When he finally ran out of breath and came to a welcome stop, I said nothing. This took what little wind was left out of his sails, and he asked me very apologetically, "Aren't you happy?" I said, "No." Then I gave him the twelve-inch prod. I told him I had been working here for nothing the

Dorothy Coonan as seen in *Gold Diggers of 1933*, the film on which she met Wellman. *Courtesy of the author.*

last six weeks, since they had not seen fit to take up my option. He said that was ridiculous, probably some clerical oversight, and called the business manager of the studio.

He had one of the first interoffice communication boxes on his desk. You could get other people on the gadget, but you couldn't cut off their voices.

Wellman waited patiently as Lasky switched on the talk box. When the business manager came on the line, Lasky asked about this Wellman option business. The manager, not knowing Wellman was in the room, reminded the studio head that he had said, "to hell with Wellman. Paramount Pictures is fed up with the son of a bitch director of B Westerns."

Lasky, of course, apologized to Wellman, saying that it was just a fit of temper and meant nothing.

Then the sales talk took a new turn. Now I was obligated to Paramount. He recalled the Bronson picture but never said a word about *You Never Know Women*. He told me what I had meant to him, that I was like a son, yeah, but he didn't say what kind of a son. It got boring as hell, and I finally said two words that he, being a big gambler, knew well, "No dice," and started out of his nest.

At the door, I turned and told him who my agent was. A freshman named Myron Selznick and that he was in the outer office and would be tickled to death to talk over my remarkable talent with him, bowed low and retired.

I winked at Myron, he smiled back, and the intercom came alive: "Send Selznick in." (He forgot the Mr.; it was a bad mistake.) Myron got up, stretched, yawned, and told the secretary to tell God that he will call him in the morning, that he has an appointment for Mr. Wellman (emphasized the Mr.); we are late now. The nervy little bastard.

When we got out in the corridor, I said to Myron: "Jesus, do you think you did the right thing?" and Myron's answer was typical. "If he wants you now, when he and that other nincompoop [Schulberg] get through their dogfight, he will want you more; and when I finish talking to New York [Zukor and the moneymen], he had better."

Myron came in the next afternoon, and all I got out of it was a $1,000-a-week raise, a seven-year contract, at the end of which I was getting paid in figures I couldn't count, and the first picture was my own, *The Legion of the Condemned*, starring Gary Cooper. Mr. Selznick had established himself at Paramount.

"The picture suffered another major affliction on the very day of its New York premiere," Lasky later wrote about *Wings*.

> It represented a record outlay of $2,000,000 gambled on unknown quantities from the theme to the writer to the director to the star. Some of the business heads were still smarting over the disappointing reception of the costly *Old Ironsides*, which had dealt with war. Worry and suspense over what the public reaction would be to our new road show, which also dealt with war, reduced them to distraction. One of them thought this episode should be in a different place; another favored cutting out that scene entirely and tightening a whole sequence. They went through the entire picture finding big and little faults they were sure were going to affect its chances of success.[1]

Released three months after Charles Lindbergh's famed transatlantic flight, *Wings* premiered on August 12, 1927, at the Criterion Theatre in New York—its director was not invited to attend.

At a top ticket price of $2, the picture played there for sixty-three weeks before moving to the Rialto Theatre. The New York first-run exhibition lasted for two solid years. Each performance was accompanied by an orchestra. Before its national run was completed, the picture was re-released on January 5, 1929, with a sound effects track and synchronized musical score.

While millions of Americans packed into movie houses, rave reviews filled the pages of magazines and newspapers. *Wings* was a colossal hit. Adolph Zukor, Jesse L. Lasky, B. P. Schulberg, the New York bankers, and all of Paramount Pictures were ecstatic—all save one: William Wellman was suffering over his matrimonial miscue, his opening night snub, and the somber atmosphere surrounding him at the studio.

October 6, 1927, marked a monumental date on the calendar of motion picture history. When Al Jolson took a knee and sang "Mammy" to audiences around the world in *The Jazz Singer*, it turned a blossoming fad into a full-blown revolution, ticking down the doomsday clock for the silent era. Many sound musical shorts had been produced, but never a feature film that brought together dialog, musical numbers, and a synchronized score.

Movies could now make big noise. Audiences could hear bursts of gunfire; the tap-tap-tap of dancing feet; and the clash of swords, music, and the spoken word. For several years to come, the box office marquees bannered, "All Talking—All Singing—All Dancing!"

More and bigger studios were built as young, ambitious, enthusiastic, and professional craftsmen—both in front and behind the cameras—began rolling out hundreds of films: crime and social dramas, musicals, adventure stories, comedies, mysteries, and war films. It was the birth of the high-octane glamour factories of Hollywood.

When Paramount joined the sound craze, Jesse Lasky called a meeting of his contract directors. Extra chairs had been brought into Lasky's conference room, and all the available directors were sitting in them. Adolph Zukor had flown in from New York with several of the bankers. Zukor sat next to B. P. Schulberg, and Lasky presided over the meeting. An uneasiness filled the room, and many of the directors fidgeted in their chairs.

Lasky pontificated for some time before getting to the point. "You are the finest contract directors in all of Hollywood. However, pictures are going to talk. It's the wave of the future. We have hired the best stage directors in New York. They will work with you to help you understand dialogue. They will share credits."

From the back of the room, a voice interrupted: "Mr. Lasky." Wellman stood as he said, "I have bad news for you, good for me. I have a seven year contract with this studio. It has nothing to say or do about any lousy stage director coming in and making half my pictures. Furthermore, I won't accept one of them on my set unless they are a better man than I am." Wellman turned and left a stunned group of executives and a silent bunch of contract directors, still fidgeting.

Although stage directors did come, including George Cukor, who became an Academy Award—winner, none ever worked with Wellman. Buoyed by his new contract and the continuing success of *Wings*, he poured himself into his work. He directed eight films in the next two and a half years, including *Legion of the Condemned* (1928), starring Fay Wray and Gary Cooper; *Ladies of the Mob* (1928), with *Wings'* stars Clara Bow and Richard Arlen; *Beggars of Life* (1928), starring Wallace Beery, Louise Brooks, and Richard Arlen. Gravel-voiced Beery spoke the first words in a Wellman picture. The only other words heard were uttered by Beery as he sang "Hark the Bells." Unfortunately, only the silent version of *Beggars* exists.

In *Beggars*, Beery plays a tramp and was supposed to sing while standing in a group of hobos. Wellman wanted him to walk down a dirt road, singing and carrying a barrel of moonshine, before making his entrance at the hobo camp.

Unlike the days of silent films, when cameras could be moved with the actors, sound was causing scenes to be more static. Microphones had to be

Fay Wray and Gary Cooper in Wellman's *Legion of the Condemned* (1928). *Courtesy of the author.*

Louise Brooks and *Wings* star Richard Arlen in Wellman's *Beggars of Life* (1928). *Courtesy of the author.*

steady and stationary. Wellman hated this unnatural, non-movement of his actors; so, against the advice of his sound man and the standard of the day, he grabbed a broom, hung a microphone on it, and walked along with Beery, just out of camera range. This event was the first time the microphone moved with the camera in pictures.

Wellman cast Beery again in *Chinatown Nights* (1929), also starring Florence Vidor. Then came *The Man I Love* (1929), starring Richard Arlen and Mary Brian. Wellman's first all-talking picture, *Woman Trap* (1929), headlined Hal Skelly, Chester Morris, and Evelyn Brent; *Dangerous Paradise* (1930) starred Nancy Carroll and Richard Arlen; *Young Eagles* (1930) showcased Jean Arthur and Charles "Buddy" Rogers. It's interesting to note Wellman's loyalty to his *Wings* stars, casting them in five of the films plus Gary Cooper's first starring role in *Legion*.

Unfortunately, only *Legion*, from John Monk Saunders and Wellman's original story, was a project Wellman brought to the table. The others were assignments—contractual obligations that Wellman believed were nothing short of B picture material. The rift between Wellman and Schulberg, begun during the making of *Wings*, was now widening. Since Schulberg was the head of production, it was his job to develop and assign directors to scripts. It seemed to Wellman that the best projects were going to other directors and he was getting the leftovers.

Although Wellman much appreciated Schulberg's support in helping him get the *Wings* directing job, the quality of scripts and his studio treatment proved that B. P. had turned away from him. When Wellman brought projects to Schulberg, they were never put into production. Even *Legion of the Condemned*, which Wellman developed, turned out to be a "cheater"—a picture made to cash in on the success of *Wings*. Schulberg okayed a very low budget and told Wellman to use, in place of original film, as much of the *Wings* footage already shot. The studio even called *Legion* "the sequel to *Wings*"—which it was not.

As time passed, Wellman's frustration grew stronger. Even though he disliked the material he was assigned, he did his best to improve the scripts and make good films.

Harkening back to his days with Bernie Durning, he was taught that when he began a studio production, it became his picture. He even added "Produced and Directed by" to his titles. He supported his company members in every way. He did not allow interference from executives or producers.

Wellman was a prankster. He loved practical jokes and often played gags on his cast and crew, but if a studio executive came on his set, there was no fun intended. Several things were bound to happen. Wellman would take an air rifle or slingshot and shoot out the overhead lights of the sound stage, or he would just stop work and sit down in his director's chair until the man left. On other occasions, he would address the individual and offer two choices. One,

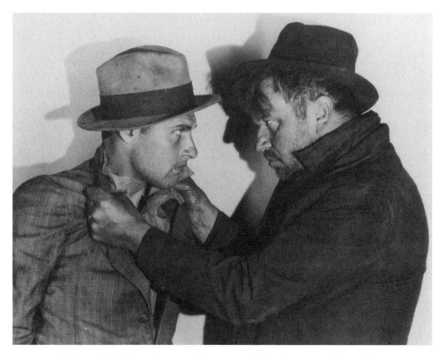

Arlen and Wallace Beery in *Beggars of Life. Courtesy of the author.*

Wellman douses Carole Lombard and Frederic March behind the scenes of _Nothing Sacred_ (1937). _Courtesy of the author._

to walk off the sound stage on his own two legs or two, to be dragged out feet first. At least one Paramount executive and one producer of note refused both alternatives and were punched in the nose. They staggered off the sound stage.

As a helpful payback to his agent, Wellman hired Myron Selznick's brother, David O. Selznick, as a producer on _Chinatown Nights_ and _The Man I Love_. This relationship between director and producer would account for two classic films of the future: the original _A Star Is Born_ and _Nothing Sacred_ (both from 1937). With pictures like _Gone with the Wind_ (1939), _Rebecca_ (1940), _Since You Went Away_ (1944), and _Spellbound_ (1945), Selznick would become one of the greatest producers in history.

Both Jesse Lasky and B. P. Schulberg had asked Wellman to get an automobile more commensurate with his position as a Paramount contract director. Wellman was driving a used, 1920s Essex Roadster, with much of its paint missing, rather than the high-class vehicles being driven by the other contract directors. Wellman's reason was, "I had no automobile yet, nor the money to purchase one. I was waiting until the amount was large enough for me to go into a dealer, pick my car, and pay cash for it. This was a habit of mine that has never been broken."

Wellman and a friend had been out on a double-date. The friend was driving with Wellman in the back seat. Both men had desirable beauties next to them. Instead of paying attention to the road, they were entranced by the pulchritude close by. Neither the driver nor the backseat friend noticed the host of red, lighted lanterns signaling a torn-up street dead ahead. The only injury from the crash was a wounded Essex.

The friend never liked the car in the first place. It had been a gift from a protective father and was too small for the six-foot, six-inch son. The friend gave the remains to his buddy; Wellman had enough money to fix it and surely enjoyed its ride.

Wellman remembered,

True, it was not in the class moneywise with the cars the other stars, producers and directors had, but I wouldn't have swapped it for any one of them. If anybody or any dame was ashamed to ride in my car, to hell with them. One director named von Sternberg made a disparaging remark about it and got a good kick in the ass, with a promise to beat his brains out if he said anything more uncomplimentary about my Essex. He didn't.

Fredric March and Janet Gaynor in the original *A Star Is Born* (1937), for which Wellman was honored with an Oscar for Best Original Story. *Courtesy of the author.*

To thank his agent Myron Selznick, Wellman hired Myron's brother, David O. Selznick (seen here), as producer on two of his Paramount films. *Courtesy of the author.*

During production on *Legion*, even Wellman's agent was called to the mat by Lasky and Schulberg for allowing his client to drive this low-class vehicle. Just as Wellman had said to the executives, he told Myron, "It's none of their goddamn business what I drive!"

Wellman decided to do something about this Essex business. He told the plane painters that when they finished their work on the airships for *Legion*, to paint his car camouflage green and brown—just like his World War I fighter planes.

Wellman recalled,

To top off the great job of camouflaging, they painted in black, a skull and crossbones on a front end unit which you could open or close according to the weather, closed when cold, opened when hot. It helped to keep the motor cool or warm . . . the artist had painted an eye on the skull and fast opening or closing gave it the effect of winking at you, always good for a laugh from those who saw it. My humble Essex became famous, especially with the girls.

Wellman decided to show off his newly designed auto in front of the studio's "biggies." He chose to do it in front of their dining room entrance. When they all came out, he was waiting with a big wink. "I gave it the gas and purred by them all, looking in my mirror saw everyone of them watching me as I sped away. Only one was talking, fast and furious, the big Napoleon [Lasky], all but one had poker faces, the nice guy from New York was smiling."

Wellman made phone calls and set meetings with his agent to discuss his unhappiness at the studio. May 16, 1929, would bring even more melancholy his way. It was Academy Award night.

The Blossom Room of the Hollywood Roosevelt Hotel was adorned with 270 elegantly attired guests, paying five dollars apiece for the first-class bill of fare. The feast was highlighted by Lobster Eugenie; filet of sole au beurre; jumbo squab; and, with a dash of homespun spirit, Los Angeles Salad. Dancing followed the sumptuous dining experience. When Louis B. Mayer, MGM's mogul, thought there had been enough frivolity, he silenced the orchestra and got down to the real bread and butter of the evening.

The Academy Awards were L. B. Mayer's creation. In the beginning, it was not about the glamour, the entertainment, the food, or even the industry paying homage to its members. It was a way of uniting the power brokers to

The director of the first Best Picture was not invited to the 1929 Awards Presentation at the Hollywood Roosevelt Hotel. Paramount's studio executives attended the event and received the statuette later named Oscar. *Courtesy of the Academy of Motion Picture Arts and Sciences.*

diminish the strength of the labor unions. When that couldn't happen, the new Academy would serve as its own censor before the government tried to intervene. Already activist groups like concerned mothers, clergymen, and rabble-rousers from other walks of life were upset about the violence and titillating aspects of the day's movies.

Mayer, his buddies, and other studio heads were looking for a way to control their own business and bring class and publicity to their organization by rewarding the best of the best. A golden statuette became the answer. L. B. hired his studio's art director, Cedric Gibbons, to design the piece: a gold-plated, athletic figure fourteen inches tall and weighing seven pounds. The figure is plunging a sword into a reel of film containing five notches denoting the branches of the Academy: producers, directors, writers, actors, and technicians. The term *Oscar* came a few years later.

There were 230 members joining the Academy at $100 for the privilege.

Films released between August 1, 1927, and July 31, 1928, were eligible for nomination by a board of judges chaired by L. B. Mayer. Three months before the actual event, *Wings* was rumored to be the Best Picture winner. William Wellman was not nominated for Best Director and was also not on the invitation list for the presentation.

It was ironic that the man who helped Wellman begin his movie career, Douglas Fairbanks, was the host of the evening. He presented the coveted Best Picture statuette, called Best Production for this year only, to Adolph Zukor, the president of Paramount. The film that Wellman had given so much of himself and fought so hard for received the industry's highest award, and he was not allowed to participate.

The Best Production category was defined as "the most outstanding motion picture considering all the elements that contribute to a picture's greatness."[2] *Wings* became the first Best Picture.

Fairbanks handed out all the awards in less than five minutes. The winners walked to the podium, received their statuettes, made no speeches, and then sat at the head table. Losing nominees were given honorable-mention certificates. They included Paramount-Famous Lasky's *The Last Command*, for which German-born Emil Jannings won Best Actor; Paramount's *The Way of All Flesh*, another Best Actor nomination for Jannings; Paramount's *The Racket*, produced by Howard Hughes; and Fox's *Seventh Heaven*. The star of *Seventh Heaven*, Janet Gaynor, won Best Actress. She was also nominated for two other films, Fox's *Sunrise* and *Street Angel*. *Heaven*'s Frank Borzage won Best Director, and the film's writer, Benjamin Glazer, received one of the Best Writing statuettes.

For the first year only, there was a second Best Production category that stated, "the most artistic, unique, and/or original motion picture without reference to cost or magnitude."[3] This award went to William Fox's melodrama *Sunrise*. Honorable-mention certificates were awarded to Paramount's *Chang* and MGM's *The Crowd*, directed by King Vidor. *Crowd* told the realistic but depressing story of the hard-luck life of an urban couple. Vidor's film

After leaving Paramount, Wellman went to work for Darryl F. Zanuck at Warner Brothers, where he directed such classics as *The Public Enemy* (1931), with James Cagney. *Courtesy of the author.*

was considered the favorite for the artistic prize, but L. B. and friends deemed it too downbeat and not in the best interests of film audiences.

When the awards portion of the evening began, producer Darryl F. Zanuck gave the only speech after picking up a special award for the first talkie, *The Jazz Singer*. Its star, Al Jolson, ended the evening with a song and the first big laughs in Oscar history when he said, "I notice they gave *The Jazz Singer* a statuette. But they didn't give me one. I could use one; they look heavy and I need a paperweight,"[4] and "For the life of me I can't see what Jack Warner [head of Warner Brothers, which produced *Jazz*] can do with one of these awards. It can't say yes."[5]

What did Wellman do the night of the awards? Did he host his own party? Did he go to another Academy Award party? Did he accept his agent's invitation to join a small dinner party? None of the above. The director of the Academy Award winner for Best Picture went home with an old friend, Jack Daniels, and got very drunk.

William Wellman's Academy snub has taken on some historic proportions since *Wings*. For the next seventy-seven Academy Award presentations—

including 2005—there have been only two times when the director of the Best Picture winner did not receive a Best Director nomination. Edmund Goulding was so dishonored for MGM's _Grand Hotel_ in 1932, as was Bruce Beresford for his _Driving Miss Daisy_ in 1989. One wonders how it is possible for a film to be so honored as the Best Picture of the year and yet not even a nomination for the artist who painted the picture.

Wellman returned to the studio that had orchestrated the snubbing and completed two more weak-storied pictures, _Dangerous Paradise_ (1930) and _Young Eagles_ (1930). For his endeavors, he received another bad script, then called his agent to say that he had had enough. He was finished with Paramount Pictures. Myron told him not to do anything foolish, just to wait for him to call back. A few days later, Myron contacted his client with exciting news. He had made an appointment for Wellman to meet a very interested producer: Darryl F. Zanuck at Warner Brothers.

Wellman's buddy, Charlie Barton, was sleeping comfortably in his apartment bed. The bedside clock was ticking out 4 a.m. when the telephone rang. Barton fumbled the pickup before gaining some control. Wellman was calling with a very specific command: "Meet me at the Sunset Ranch in twenty min-

Wellman and assistant director pal, Charlie Barton, enjoying a good joke. _Courtesy of the author._

utes. Bring a shovel." The Sunset Ranch was not only a horse ranch but a well-used movie location in the San Fernando Valley. Both Barton and Wellman had worked there on numerous films.

The light from the moon splayed onto two shovels digging into horse manure. The two men worked feverishly to fill the bed of Wellman's rented pickup truck with fresh, organic fertilizer. No conversation took place until a large pile was made and the two laborers were back in the truck and on their way to Paramount.

When Wellman's vehicle arrived at the drive-through gate, the gate was closed and the security guard inside his small shelter. Barton leaped from the cab and ran over to the guardhouse to keep the man occupied. Wellman backed the truck up to the doorway of a first-floor office next to the gate. The office belonged to B. P. Schulberg.

At this early hour, the office was closed. Wellman thrust the key, which he had pilfered a few days before, into the lock and opened the door. He began the transfer of manure from shovel to Schulberg. In less than fifteen minutes, a large pile covered the studio executive's desk. After a final shovel full of horse shit, Wellman planted a script on top of the mountain. A note on the front page stated, "Here's what I think of your lousy script!"

Sunrise at Paramount Studios found Wellman backing out of Schulberg's office, keying the door locked, flipping the shovel onto his shoulder like a rifle in resting position, and then marching over to his truck. After dropping the weapon into the truck bed, he whistled for Barton and got into the cab. When he started the engine, Barton trotted over and the two Paramount employees left the studio.

This incident marked the final separation between William Wellman and Paramount Pictures, as well as the termination of his seven-year contract after only two-plus years. The exact story surrounding the breakup is not known, but one thing seems clear—both parties were not willing to continue their association. This author believes that the end came via mutual agreement—the contract was torn up, as they say, and no more money changed hands as a result.

What had transpired between Wellman and Paramount from 1925 to 1930 was of great shared benefit. The ten films directed by William A. Wellman brought fine profits to the studio; and one great picture, *Wings*, would stand as a virtuoso for all time.

In the words of noted film historian and filmmaker John Andrew Gallagher, "*Wings*' impact on popular culture was comparable to that of George Lucas's *Star Wars* trilogy. *Wings* is a masterpiece of the silent cinema and Wellman's first great work, a legendary World War One aviation epic with dazzling cinematography and stunts, documentary-like realism, dynamic direction, and a warm, engaging cast. It stands as a pioneering achievement and a prototypical adventure movie, retaining its potency ever since its release."

When Jesse L. Lasky set out to find his road show picture of 1927, it's hard to imagine that he could have dreamed for more than he got. In his own words, "We needn't have worried quite so much about whether it would make the grade. It turned out to be the last great silent picture and won the first Academy Award ever given for best production."[6]

Wings took the careers of Buddy Rogers and Richard Arlen through the roof, and Clara Bow, already the "It" girl, into the heavens. How amazing to think that in just one scene, Gary Cooper made such an impression that Paramount, their distributors, and fans around the globe wanted his star to shine above them all. Jesse Lasky gave him a five-year contract and a growing list of starring pictures.

Wings jump-started a whole new film genre. For the next six years, movie screens overflowed with stories of the chivalrous knights of the skies.

There was Wellman's own *Legion of the Condemned* (1928) and *Young Eagles* (1930); *Lilac Time* (1928), starring Colleen Moore and Gary Cooper; Howard Hawks's *The Dawn Patrol* (1930) with Douglas Fairbanks Jr., Richard Barthelmess, and Neil Hamilton; Howard Hughes's *Hell's Angels* (1930), starring Jean Harlow, James Hall, and Ben Lyon; *Sky Devils* (1932), with Spencer Tracy, William (Hopalong Cassidy) Boyd, and Ann Dvorak; John Ford's *Airmail* (1932), with Pat O'Brien, Ralph Bellamy, and Gloria Stuart; and *The Eagle and the Hawk* (1933), starring Fredric March, Cary Grant, and Carole Lombard.

Some of the other titles include *Air Circus* (1928), *Air Mail Pilot* (1928), *Air Patrol* (1928), *Sky Hawk* (1930), *Air Police* (1931), *Sky Raiders* (1931), *Men of the Sky* (1931), and *Air Eagles* (1931). None of these or any of the other air pictures of that time reached the artistry, technique, or excellence of their parent, *Wings*.

When Howard Hughes began preparing *Hell's Angels* in 1927, he watched *Wings* repeatedly before setting up a meeting with Wellman, hoping to entice him into directing the picture. Wellman had never met the youthful filmmaker and was not interested in another air epic after *Wings* and his next project, *Legion of the Condemned*.

The two mavericks got along well, but Hughes could not change Wellman's mind. Wellman respected Hughes, the aviator, and wanted to help the young filmmaker. He offered advice and two lists containing the names of both the eighteen cameramen and thirteen stunt pilots from *Wings*. Hughes, in turn, hired many of the men from both lists who had helped create the technology for aerial photography and warfare for the movies.

Even in today's era, films like the highly successful *Top Gun* (1986), starring Tom Cruise, owe much to *Wings*. In the award-winning documentary *Wild Bill Hollywood Maverick* (1996), Tony Scott, *Gun's* director, alluded to *Wings* in his film's preparation. In *Aviator* (2004), it appeared that Martin Scorsese did the same.

In March 1930, Wellman drove off the Paramount lot in Hollywood in his camouflaged Essex Roadster and traveled over the hill to the Warner Brothers studio in Burbank. He met with Jack Warner, the head of the studio, and Darryl Zanuck, who with Hal Wallis produced the studio's pictures. Wellman signed a two-year contract: $2,500 per week for the first twenty-two weeks;

$2,750 per week for the next forty weeks; and $3,000 per week for the remainder. This contract would be extended for another two years with continuing salary increases up to $5,000 a week.

The money was better than at Paramount, but what pleased Wellman most were the stories he was assigned and the number of pictures he was allowed to make. From 1930 to 1934, he would direct twenty films under his Warner Brothers contract, compared to Paramount's ten films in a similar time period. In addition to the assigned pictures, he was given choices and projects of his own making. On one occasion, he was instrumental in bringing *Beer and Blood* to Zanuck's table. This story was re-titled *The Public Enemy* (1931); after Wellman switched the second lead to the leading role, it made a star of James Cagney and became a screen classic.

In a film career spanning forty-four years, Wellman directed seventy-six motion pictures. He worked uncredited on at least a dozen others. His films received thirty-two Academy Award nominations, with seven Oscars.

In 1937, *A Star Is Born*, from Wellman and Robert Carson's original story, received six Academy Award nominations: Best Picture; Best Actor (Fredric

Robert Carson and Wellman hold their Oscars for writing the original story for *A Star Is Born* (1937). *Courtesy of the author.*

Wellman escorts his mother Celia, his wife Dottie (behind and to the left of Celia), Mrs. Andy Devine (behind Wellman's right shoulder), and Andy Devine (behind Wellman's left shoulder) to the premiere of *A Star Is Born* in 1937. *Courtesy of the author.*

March); Best Actress (Janet Gaynor); Best Screenplay (Alan Campbell, Robert Carson, and Dorothy Parker); Best Original Story (Wellman and Carson); and Best Director. Although Wellman would never win a Best Director Oscar, he was presented an Academy Award for writing the original story for *Star*. A Special Oscar was given to his right arm, W. Howard Greene, for color cinematography. *Star* was the first dramatic feature with a contemporary setting shot in color (Technicolor).

Wellman's father, Arthur, was a great fan of his son's pictures. He saw each of them at least twice. Unfortunately, he passed away in the summer of 1936, before seeing his son win the Academy Award.

Another fan, Mother Celia, continued her trips to Hollywood well into her eighties. She died on June 11, 1967—at ninety-seven years, ten months. Celia was never present at any of her son's weddings. There would be five in all. The last one finally hit the jackpot. Wellman was married to Dorothy "Dottie" Coonan, a Busby Berkeley dancer and author's mother, for forty-two years—until Wellman's death from cancer on December 9, 1975.

Wellman had always planned to repay the generosity of his brother and parents for helping to support him during the war. When he joined the U.S.

Air Service as an instructor at Rockwell Field, he began to send money home. When he became a contract director at Fox Studios in 1923, he sent checks to all three with more regularity.

As time went by, Brother Arch became a highly successful businessman, founding the Wellman Company. He made his fortune in the wool and oil industries. Arch asked his brother to stop sending money. After all, Wellman lived in Los Angeles, and Arch and their parents in Boston.

Arch stayed responsible for the full support of his mother and father. Wellman, however, continued his ritual of sending regular checks to his mother for the rest of her life. Although Wellman and his brother had great respect and admiration for each other, they never became close friends. Arthur Ogden Wellman passed on March 4, 1987.

William A. Wellman's life shelves were certainly crowded with his achievements in the film industry. But, due to his maverick style, those shelves were not filled with trophies and awards. Anyone who really knew him realized

Wellman directs his future bride, Dorothy Coonan, on the set of *Wild Boys of the Road* (1933). *Courtesy of the author.*

The Wellmans, *from left to right,* front: Kitty, Pat, Bill, Maggie (in Bill's lap), Cissy, and Mike; standing: Bill Jr. (author), Dottie, and Tim. *Courtesy of the author.*

that he didn't care about self-gratification and accolades; he cared about his three great loves: his wife, Dottie, and family; making all kinds of movies; and his island in the sky.

Wild Bill's adventures in a foreign land, the comradeship of barracks life, the beauty of flight, the threat of peril in the skies, the gain and loss of friends—these always played a major and continuing role in his life. He would never cease to celebrate his life as a pilot in World War I.

Throughout his film career, Wellman would continually return to the skies for stories of flight, planes and the men who flew them. His attitudes about loyalty, friendship, and the bonds between men under duress would come to characterize every film he would ever direct.

The movie *Wings* embodies more of the values he stood for than any other picture he directed, and it stands as a testament to who he was as a man.

William Wellman directed his last film in 1958. This photo was taken in 1970, five years before his death. *Courtesy of the author.*

Notes

CHAPTER 2

1. James Norman Hall and Charles Bernard Nordhoff, eds., *The Lafayette Flying Corps* (Boston, New York: Houghton Mifflin Company, 1920), 2:317–323, 340, appendix.

CHAPTER 3

1. William A. Wellman, *Go, Get 'Em!* (Boston: The Page Company, 1918), 282–283.
2. John Durant and Alice Durant, *Pictorial History of American Presidents* (New York: A. S. Barnes and Company, 1955), 206.
3. Vrilles are spinning nosedives. Tournants are effected by giving the control stick a swift jerk to one side and back, causing the plane to roll completely over. A Russian mountain can be achieved by diving with the motor going full speed, shutting off the engine, and straightening the plane parallel to the ground; then you push forward on the control stick, which elevates the rear ailerons, start the motor, and pull back on the control stick, shooting the plane upward in roller coaster fashion.
4. Hall and Nordhoff, *The Lafayette Flying Corps*, vol. II, 47.

CHAPTER 4

1. Samantha Hart, *Hollywood Walk of Fame* (LCF, CA: Cry Baby Books & Entertainment, 1987, 2000), 111, 112.

CHAPTER 5

1. Michael Parkinson and Clyde Jeavons, *A Pictorial History of Westerns* (London: Hamlyn, 1972), 113.
2. Jesse Lasky Jr., *Whatever Happened to Hollywood?* (New York: Funk & Wagnalls, 1973, 1975), 23.
3. Kevin Brownlow, *The Parade's Gone By* (New York: Alfred A. Knopf, 1968), 68, 70.

CHAPTER 6

1. Jesse L. Lasky, *I Blow My Own Horn* (New York: Doubleday & Co., 1957), 208.

CHAPTER 7

1. Jesse L. Lasky, *I Blow My Own Horn*, 210.
2. David Sheward, *The Show Business Awards* (New York: Billboard Books, 1997), 6.
3. Gail Kinn and Jim Piazza, *The Complete History of Oscar* (New York: Black Dog & Leventhal Publishers, 2002), 11.
4. David Sheward, *The Show Business Awards*, 6.
5. Kinn and Piazza, *The Complete History of Oscar*, 11.
6. Jesse L. Lasky, *I Blow My Own Horn*, 210.

Bibliography

Alicoate, John W. *Film Daily Year Book*. 10th ed. New York: Film Daily, 1928.

Brownlow, Kevin. *Mary Pickford Rediscovered*. New York: Harry N. Abrams, 1999.

———. *The Parade's Gone By*. New York: Alfred A. Knopf, 1968.

———. *The War, the West, the Wilderness*. New York: Alfred A. Knopf, 1978.

Capra, Frank. *The Name above the Title*. New York: MacMillan, 1971.

Dick, Bernard F. *Engulfed: The Death of Paramount Pictures*. Lexington, KY: University Press of Kentucky, 2001.

Durant, John and Alice. *Pictorial History of American Presidents*. New York: A. S. Barnes and Co., 1955.

Eames, John Douglas. *The Paramount Story*. New York: Crown Publishers, 1985.

Eyman, Scott. *The Speed of Sound*. Baltimore and London: Johns Hopkins University Press, 1997.

Griffin, Richard, and Arthur Mayer. *The Movies*. New York: Bonanza, 1957.

Hall, James N., and Charles B. Nordhoff. *The Lafayette Flying Corps*, vols. I and II. Boston, New York: Houghton Mifflin Company, 1920.

Hart, Samantha. *Hollywood Walk of Fame*. LCF, CA: Cry Baby Books, 1987, 2000.

Higham, Charles. *Cecil B. DeMille*. New York: Charles Scribner's Sons, 1973.

Jeavons, Clyde. *A Pictorial History of War Films*. Secaucus, NJ: Citadel, 1974.

Kinn, Gail, and Jim Piazza. *The Complete History of Oscar*. New York: Black Dog & Leventhal Publishing, 2002.

Lasky, Jesse L. *I Blow My Own Horn*. New York: Doubleday & Co., 1957.

Lasky, Jesse, Jr. *Whatever Happened to Hollywood?* New York: Funk & Wagnalls, 1973, 1975.

Marquis, Albert N. *Who's Who in America*, vol. 15. Chicago: Marquis Who's Who, 1928, 1929.

Paramount Produced Properties and Releases. Los Angeles: AMPAS, 1920–1927.

Parish, James R. *The Paramount Pretties*. New York: Random House, 1972.

Parkinson, Michael, and Clyde Jeavons. *A Pictorial History of Westerns*. London: Hamlyn, 1972.

Sheward, David. *The Show Business Awards*. New York: Billboard Books, 1997.

Thomas, Bob. *Selznick*. New York: Doubleday & Co., 1970.

Thompson, Frank. *Texas Hollywood*. San Antonio, TX: Maverick Publishing Co., 2002.

——. *Lost Films*. New York: Citadel, 1996.

Variety Film Reviews. Los Angeles: *Variety*, vol. 3. 1926–1929.

Whitehouse, Arch. *Legion of the Lafayette*. Garden City, NY: Doubleday & Co., 1962.

Wingart, Earl W., ed. *Biographies of Paramount Players*. 1930–1931. New York: Paramount Publicity, 1931.

WELLMAN SOURCES

The memoirs of William Wellman. Unpublished.

Personal audiotapes of William Wellman. Unpublished.

Wellman family history. Unpublished.

Wellman, William A. *A Short Time for Insanity*. New York: Hawthorn Books, 1974.

Wellman, William A. *Go, Get 'Em!* With introduction and notes by Eliot Harlow Robinson. Boston: The Page Co., 1918.

Wellman, William A. *Growing Old Disgracefully*. Unpublished: 1975.

Wellman, William A. *Wrong Head on the Pillow*. Not completed: 1975.

Filmography

THE FOLLOWING FILMS CREDIT DIRECTION TO WELLMAN

The Man Who Won (1923, Fox). Presented by William Fox. Produced and directed by William A. Wellman. Screenplay: Ewart Adamson. Based on the novel *The Twins of Suffering Creek*, by Ridgwell Cullum (Philadelphia: George W. Jacobs & Co., 1912). Photography: Joseph H. August. With Dustin Farnum, Jacqueline Gadsden, and Lloyd Whitlock.

Second Hand Love (1923, Fox). Presented by William Fox. Produced and directed by William A. Wellman. Screenplay: Charles Kenyon. Story: Shannon Fife. Photography: Dan Short. With Charles "Buck" Jones, Ruth Dwyer, Charles Coleman, and Harvey Clark.

Big Dan (1923, Fox). Presented by William Fox. Produced and directed by William A. Wellman. Story and screenplay: Frederick and Fanny Hatton. Photography: Joseph H. August. With Charles "Buck" Jones, Marian Nixon, Ben Hendricks, Charles Coleman, and Lydia Yeamans.

Cupid's Fireman (1923, Fox). Presented by William Fox. Produced and directed by William A. Wellman. Screenplay: Eugene B. Lewis. Based on the story *Andy M'Gee's Chorus Girl* (New York: Van Bibber & Others, 1892) by Richard Harding Davis. Photography: Joseph H. August. With Charles "Buck" Jones, Marian Nixon, Brooks Benedict, Eileen O'Malley, and Lucy Beaumont.

Not a Drum Was Heard (1924, Fox). Presented by William Fox. Produced and directed by William A. Wellman. Screenplay: Doty Hobart. Based on a story by Ben Ames Williams. Photography: Joseph H. August. With Charles "Buck" Jones, Betty Bouton, Frank Campeau, and Rhody Hathaway.

The Vagabond Trail (1924, Fox). Presented by William Fox. Produced and directed by William A. Wellman. Screenplay: Doty Hobart. Based on the novel *Donnegan* (New York: Chelsea House, 1923) by George Owen Baxter. Photography: Joseph H. August. With Charles "Buck" Jones, Marian Nixon, Charles Coleman, L. C. Shumway, and Virginia Warwick.

The Circus Cowboy (1924, Fox). Presented by William Fox. Produced and directed by William A. Wellman. Screenplay: Doty Hobart. Story: Louis Sherwin. Photography:

Joseph Brotherton. With Charles "Buck" Jones, Marian Nixon, Jack McDonald, Ray Hallor, and Marguerite Clayton.

When Husbands Flirt (1925, Columbia). Presented by Harry Cohn. Directed by William A. Wellman. Story and screenplay: Paul Gangelin and Dorothy Arzner. Photography: Sam Landers. With Dorothy Revier, Forrest Stanley, Thomas Ricketts, Ethel Wales, Maude Wayne, and Frank Weed.

The Boob (1926, Metro-Goldwyn-Mayer). Directed by William A. Wellman. Original screen story, *Don Quixote Jr.*, by George Scarborough and Annette Westbay (May 14, 1925). Screenplay: Kenneth B. Clarke. Treatment: Agnes Christine Johnston. Photography: William B. Daniels. Editor: Ben Lewis. Art direction: Cedric Gibbons and Ben Carre. With Gertrude Olmstead, George K. Arthur, Charles Murray, and Joan Crawford.

The Cat's Pajamas (1926, Famous Players-Lasky/Paramount). Presented by Adolph Zukor and Jesse L. Lasky. Associate producers: B. P. Schulberg and Hector Turnbull. Directed by William A. Wellman. Screenplay: Hope Loring and Louis D. Lighton. Story: Ernest Vajda. Photography: Victor Milner. Art direction: Hans Dreier. Props: Charles Barton. Makeup: James Collins. With Betty Bronson, Ricardo Cortez, Arlette Marchal, Theodore Roberts, Tom Ricketts, and Gordon Griffith.

You Never Know Women (1926, Famous Players-Lasky/Paramount). Presented by Adolph Zukor and Jesse L. Lasky. Associate producers: B. P. Schulberg and Hector Turnbull. Directed by William A. Wellman. Screenplay: Benjamin Glazer. Story: Ernest Vajda. Photography: Victor Milner. Art direction: Hans Dreier. Props: Charles Barton. Makeup: James Collins. With Florence Vidor, Lowell Sherman, Clive Brook, El Brendel, Roy Stewart, and Sidney Bracy.

Wings (1927, Paramount/Famous Lasky). Presented by Adolph Zukor and Jesse L. Lasky. Produced by Lucien Hubbard. Associate producer: B. P. Schulberg. Directed by William A. Wellman. Screenplay: Hope Loring and Louis D. Lighton. Story and novelization: John Monk Saunders. Titles: Julian Johnson. Photography: Harry Perry. Engineering effects: Roy Pomeroy. Editor: Lucien Hubbard. Editor-in-chief: E. Lloyd Sheldon. Art direction: Lawrence Hitt, Hans Dreier. With Clara Bow, Charles "Buddy" Rogers, Richard Arlen, Jobyna Ralston, and Gary Cooper.

Legion of the Condemned (1928, Paramount/Famous Lasky). Presented by Adolph Zukor and Jesse L. Lasky. Produced and directed by William A. Wellman. Associate producer: E. Lloyd Sheldon. Screenplay: John Monk Saunders and Jean de Limur. Based on an original story by William A. Wellman and John Monk Saunders, and novelized by Eustace Hale Ball. Titles: George Marion. Photography: Henry Gerrard. Editor: Alyson Schaeffer. Editor-in-chief: E. Lloyd Sheldon. Art direction: Hans Dreier and Laurence Hitt. With Fay Wray, Gary Cooper, Barry Norton, Lane Chandler, Francis MacDonald, and Albert Conti.

Ladies of the Mob (1928, Paramount/Famous Lasky). Presented by Adolph Zukor and Jesse L. Lasky. Produced and directed by William A. Wellman. Screenplay: John Farrow. Adaptation: Oliver Garrett. Based on a story by Ernest Booth in *The American Mercury* (December 1927). Titles: George Marion. Photography: Henry Gerrard. Editorial supervisor: E. Lloyd Sheldon. Editor: Alyson Schaefer and Edgar Adams. Art direction: Hans Dreier. Costumes: Travis Banton and Edith Head. Makeup: James Collins. With Clara Bow, Richard Arlen, Helen Lynch, Mary Alden, and Carl Gerrard.

Beggars of Life (1928, Paramount/Famous Lasky). Presented by Adolph Zukor and Jesse L. Lasky. Produced and directed by William A. Wellman. Associate producer: Benjamin Glazer. Screenplay: Benjamin Glazer and Jim Tully. Based on the novel by Jim Tully. Titles: Julian Johnson. Photography: Henry Gerrard. Editor: Alyson Schaefer. Art direction: Hans Dreier. Assistant director: Charles Barton. Costumes: Travis Banton and Edith Head. Makeup: James Collins. With Wallace Beery, Louise Brooks, Richard Arlen, and Edgar "Blue" Washington.

Chinatown Nights (1929, Paramount). Based on Samuel Ornitz's story "Tong War." Associate producer: David O. Selznick. With Wallace Beery, Florence Vidor, Warner Oland, Jack McHugh, Jack Oakie, Tetsu Komai, Frank Chew, Mrs. Wing, Peter Morrison, and Freeman Wood.

The Man I Love (1929, Paramount). Based on a story by Herman J. Mankiewicz. Titles: Joseph L. Mankiewicz. Associate producer: David O. Selznick. With Richard Arlen, Olga Baclanova, Mary Brian, Harry Green, Jack Oakie, Pat O'Malley, and Leslie Fenton.

Woman Trap (1929, Paramount). Based on the playlet *Brothers*, by Edwin Burke. With Hal Skelly, Chester Morris, Evelyn Brent, William B. Davidson, Effie Ellsler, Gary Oliver, Leslie Fenton, Charles Giblyn, Joseph Mankiewicz, and Wilson Hammell.

Dangerous Paradise (1930, Paramount). Based on incidents from a novel by Joseph Conrad. With Nancy Carroll, Richard Arlen, Warner Oland, Gustav von Seyffertitz, Francis MacDonald, George Kotsonaros, Dorothea Woolbert, Clarence H. Wilson, Evelyn Selbie, Willie Fung, Wong Wing, and Lillian Worth.

Young Eagles (1930, Paramount). Based on Elliott White Spring's stories "The One Who Was Clever" and "Sky-High." With Charles Rogers, Jean Arthur, Paul Lukas, Stuart Erwin, Frank Ross, Jack Luden, Freeman Wood, Gordon de Main, George Irving, and Stanley Blystone.

Maybe It's Love (1930, Warner Brothers). Screenplay: Joseph Jackson and Mark Canfield, from the story "College Widows," by George Ade. With Joan Bennett, Joe E. Brown, James Hall, Laura Lee, Anders Randolf, Sumner Getchell, George Irving, George Bickel, Howard Jones, Bill Banker, and Russell Saunders.

Other Men's Women (1931, Warner Brothers). Screenplay: Maude Fulton and William K. Wells. With Grant Withers, Regis Toomey, Mary Astor, James Cagney, Joan Blondell, Fred Kohler, J. Farrell MacDonald, Lillian Worth, and Walter Long.

The Public Enemy (1931, Warner Brothers). Screenplay: Kubec Glasmon and John Bright. With Edward Woods, James Cagney, Donald Cook, Joan Blondell, Jean Harlow, Beryl Mercer, Ben Hendricks Jr., Robert Emmett O'Connor, Leslie Fenton, Murray Kinnell, and Mae Clarke.

Night Nurse (1931, Warner Brothers). Story: Dora Marcy. Adaptation: Oliver H. P. Garrett. Dialog: Oliver H. P. Garrett and Charles Kenyon. With Barbara Stanwyck, Ben Lyon, Joan Blondell, Clark Gable, Charles Winninger, Charlotte Merriam, Vera Lewis, Blanche Frederici, Edward Nugent, and Ralf Harolde.

Star Witness (1931, Warner Brothers). Screenplay: Lucien Hubbard. With Walter Huston, Charles "Chic" Sale, Dickie Moore, Grant Mitchell, Frances Starr, Ralph Ince, Sally Blane, Edward J. Nugent, Tom Dugan, Robert Elliott, Noel Madison, George Ernest, and Russell Hopton.

Safe in Hell (1931, Warner Brothers). Story: Houston Branch. Adaptation and dialog: Maude Fulton. With Dorothy Mackaill, Donald Cook, John Wray, Ralf Harolde, Ivan Simpson, and Victor Varconi.

The Hatchet Man (1932, Warner Brothers). Screenplay: J. Grubb Alexander, based on the play *The Honorable Mr. Wong*, by Achmed Abdullah and David Belasco. With Edward G. Robinson, Loretta Young, Dudley Digges, Leslie Fenton, Edmund

Breese, Tully Marshall, Noel Madison, Blanche Frederici, J. Carroll Naish, Toshia Mori, Charles Middleton, Ralph Ince, Otto Yamaoka, Evelyn Selbie, Allyn Warren, Eddie Piel, Willie Fung, and Anna Chang.

So Big (1932, Warner Brothers). Screenplay: J. Grubb Alexander and Robert Lord, based on the novel by Edna Ferber. With Barbara Stanwyck, George Brent, Dickie Moore, Guy Kibbee, and Bette Davis.

Love Is a Racket (1932, Warner Brothers). Screenplay: Rian James and Courtenay Terrett. With Douglas Fairbanks Jr., Ann Dvorak, Lee Tracy, Frances Dee, Lyle Talbot, Warren Hymer, William Burress, and George Raft.

The Purchase Price (1932, Warner Brothers). Screenplay: Robert Lord, based on the story by Arthur Stringer. With Barbara Stanwyck, George Brent, Lyle Talbot, David Landau, Leila Bennett, Murray Kinnell, Crawford Kent, and Hardie Albright.

The Conquerors (1932, RKO). Based on a story by Howard Estabrook. With Richard Dix, Ann Harding, Edna May Oliver, Guy Kibbee, Julie Haydon, Donald Cook, Harry Holman, Richard Gallagher, and Walter Walker.

Frisco Jenny (1933, Warner Brothers). Screenplay: Wilson Mizner and Robert Lord. With Ruth Chatterton, Donald Cook, James Murray, Louis Calhem, Hallam Cooley, Pat O'Malley, Robert Warwick, Harold Huber, and Helen Jerome Eddy.

Central Airport (1933, Warner Brothers). Screenplay: Rian James and James Seymour, from the story by Jack Moffitt. With Richard Barthelmess, Sally Eilers, Tom Brown, Glenda Farrell, Harold Huber, Grant Mitchell, James Murray, Claire McDowell, Willard Robertson, Arthur Vinton, Charles Seldon, and John Wayne.

Lilly Turner (1933, Warner Brothers). Screenplay: Gene Markey and Kathryn Scola, from the play by Philip Dunning and George Abbott. Produced by Hal Wallis. With Ruth Chatterton, George Brent, Frank McHugh, Guy Kibbee, Gordon Westcott, Ruth Donnelly, Marjorie Gateston, Robert Barrat, Arthur Vinton, Grant Mitchell, Margaret Seddon, Hobart Cavanaugh, Catherine Ward, Lucille Ward, and Mae Busch.

Midnight Mary (1933, MGM). Based on a story by Anita Loos. With Loretta Young, Ricardo Cortez, Franchot Tone, Andy Devine, Una Merkel, Frank Conroy, Warren Hymer, and Ivan Simpson.

Heroes for Sale (1933, Warner Brothers). Screenplay: Robert Lord and Wilson Mizner. Produced by Hal Wallis. With Richard Barthelmess, Aline MacMahon, Loretta Young, Gordon Westcott, Berton Churchill, Robert Barrat, Grant Mitchell, Charles Grapewin, Robert McWade, George Pat Collins, James Murray, Edwin Maxwell, Margaret Seddon, and Arthur Vinton.

Wild Boys of the Road (1933, Warner Brothers). Screenplay: Earl Baldwin, based on a story by Daniel Ahearn. Produced by Robert Presnell. With Frankie Darro, Dorothy Coonan, Rochelle Hudson, Edwin Phillips, Ann Hovey, Arthur Hohl, Grant Mitchell, Claire McDowell, Sterling Holloway, Charles Grapewin, Robert Barrat, Ward Bond, Adrian Morris, Shirley Dunsted, Minna Gombell, and Willard Robertson.

College Coach (1933, Warner Brothers). Screenplay: Niven Busch and Manuel Seff. Produced by Robert Lord. With Dick Powell, Ann Dvorak, Pat O'Brien, Arthur Byron, Lyle Talbot, Hugh Herbert, Arthur Hohl, Philip Faversham, Charles C. Wilson, Guinn Williams, Nat Pendleton, Philip Reed, Donald Meek, Berton Churchill, Harry Beresford, Herman Bing, Joe Sauers, and John Wayne.

Looking for Trouble (1934, 20th Century-Fox, United Artists). Based on a story by J. R. Bren. With Spencer Tracy, Constance Cummings, Jack Oakie, Morgan Conway, Arline Judge, Judith Wood, Paul Harvey, Joseph Sauers, Franklyn Ardell, and Paul Porcasi.

Stingaree (1934, RKO). Based on stories by E. W. Hornung. With Irene Dunne, Richard Dix, Mary Boland, Conway Tearle, Andy Devine, Henry Stephenson, Una O'Connor, George Barraud, Reginald Owen, and Snub Pollard.

The President Vanishes (1934, Paramount). Screenplay: Lynn Starling, from the novel by an anonymous author. Produced by Walter Wanger. With Arthur Byron, Janet Beecher, Paul Kelly, Peggy Conklin, Rosalind Russell, Sidney Blackmer, Douglas Wood, Walter Kingsford, De Witt Jennings, Charles Grapewin, Charles Richman, Jason Robards, Paul Harvey, Robert McWade, Edward Arnold, Osgood Perkins, Edward Ellis, Andy Devine, and Harry Woods.

Call of the Wild (1935, 20th Century-Fox). Screenplay: Gene Fowler and Leonard Brackins, based on the novel by Jack London. Produced by Darryl F. Zanuck. Presented by Joseph Schenk. With Clark Gable, Loretta Young, Jack Oakie, Frank Conroy, Reginald Owen, Sidney Tyler, Katherine DeMille, Lalo Encinas, Charles Stevens, James Burke, and Duke Green.

The Robin Hood of El Dorado (1936, MGM). Screenplay: William A. Wellman, Joseph Calleia, and Melvin Levy, based on the biography by Walter Noble Burns. Produced by John W. Considine Jr. With Warner Baxter, Ann Loring, Bruce Cabot, Margo, J. Carroll Naish, Soledad Jimenez, Carlos de Valdez, Eric Linden, Edgar Kennedy, Charles Trowbridge, Harvey Stephens, Ralph Remley, George Regas Howard, and Harry Woods.

Small Town Girl (1936, MGM). Screenplay: John Lee Mahin and Edith Fitzgerald, based on the novel by Ben Ames Williams. Produced by Hunt Stromberg. With Janet Gaynor, Robert Taylor, Binnie Barnes, Lewis Stone, Andy Devine, Elizabeth Patterson, Frank Craven, James Stewart, Douglas Fowley, Isabel Jewell, Charles Grapewin, Nella Waller, Robert Greig, Edgar Kennedy, and Willie Fung.

A Star Is Born (1937, United Artists). Screenplay: Dorothy Parker, Alan Campbell, and Robert Carson (with Ring Lardner Jr. and Budd Schulberg uncredited), based on a story by William A. Wellman and Robert Carson. Produced by David O. Selznick. With Janet Gaynor, Fredric March, Adolphe Menjou, Andy Devine, May Robson, and Lionel Stander.

Nothing Sacred (1937, United Artists). Screenplay: Ben Hecht (with Ring Lardner Jr. and George Oppenheimer uncredited), from the story "Letter to the Editor," by James A. Street. Produced by David O. Selznick. With Carole Lombard, Fredric March, Charles Winninger, Walter Connolly, Sig Ruman, Frank Fay, Maxie Rosenblum, Margaret Hamilton, Troy Brown, Hattie McDaniel, Olin Howland, George Chandler, Clair Du Brey, John Qualen, and Charles Richman.

Men with Wings (1938, Paramount). Screenplay: Robert Carson. Produced by William A. Wellman. With Fred MacMurray, Ray Milland, Louise Campbell, Andy Devine, Lynne Overman, Porter Hall, Walter Abel, Kitty Kelly, James Burke, Willard Robertson, Virginia Weidler, Donald O'Connor, Billy Cook, Dorothy Tennant, Juanita Quigley, and Marilyn Knowlden.

Beau Geste (1939, Paramount). Screenplay: Robert Carson, based on a novel by Percival Christopher Wren. Produced by William A. Wellman. With Gary Cooper, Ray Milland, Robert Preston, Brian Donlevy, Susan Hayward, J. Carroll Naish, Donald O'Connor, James Stevenson, Harry Woods, James Burke, Albert Dekker, and Broderick Crawford.

The Light That Failed (1939, Paramount). Screenplay: Robert Carson, based on the novel by Rudyard Kipling. Produced by William A. Wellman. With Ronald Colman, Walter Huston, Muriel Angelus, Ida Lupino, Dudley Digges, Ernest Cossart, Ferike

Boras, Pedro de Cordoba, Colin Tapley, Fay Helm, Ronald Sinclair, Sarita Wooton, Halliwell Hobbes, Charles Irwin, Francis MacDonald, George Regas, and Wilfred Roberts.

Reaching for the Sun (1941, Paramount). Screenplay: W. L. River, based on a story by Wessel Smitter. Produced by William A. Wellman. With Joel McCrea, Ellen Drew, Eddie Bracken, Albert Dekker, Billy Gilbert, George Chandler, Bodil Ann Rosing, James Burke, Charles D. Brown, and Regis Toomey.

Roxie Hart (1942, 20th Century-Fox). Screenplay: Nunnally Johnson, based on the play *Chicago*, by Maurine Watkins. Produced by Nunnally Johnson. With Ginger Rogers, Adolphe Menjou, George Montgomery, Lynne Overman, Nigel Bruce, Phil Silvers, Sara Allgood, William Frawley, Spring Byington, Helene Reynolds, George Chandler, George Lessey, Iris Adrian, and Milton Parsons.

The Great Man's Lady (1942, Paramount). Screenplay: W. L. River. Original story by Adela Rogers St. John and Seena Owen, based on a short story by Vifia Delmar. Produced by William A. Wellman. With Barbara Stanwyck, Joel McCrea, Brian Donlevy, Katherine Stevens, Thurston Hall, Lloyd Corrigan, Lillian Yarbo, Damian O'Flynn, Charles Lane, George Chandler, Anna Q. Nilsson, George P. Huntley, Milton Parsons, Etta McDaniel, Mary Treen, and Helen Lynd.

Thunder Birds (1942, 20th Century-Fox). Screenplay: Lamar Trotti, from an original story by Melville Crossman. Produced by Lamar Trotti. With Gene Tierney, Preston Foster, John Sutton, Jack Holt, Dame May Whitty, George Barbier, Richard Haydn, Reginald Denny, Ted North, Janis Carter, Archie Got, Lawrence Ung, Montague Shaw, Nana Bryant, Iris Adrian, Viola Moore, Connie Leon, Walter Tetley, Billy McGuire, and Richard Woodruff.

The Ox-Bow Incident (1943, 20th Century-Fox). Screenplay: Lamar Trotti, from a novel by Walter Van Tilburg Clark. Produced by Lamar Trotti. With Henry Fonda, Dana Andrews, Mary Beth Hughes, Anthony Quinn, William Eythe, Henry Morgan, Jane Darwell, Matt Briggs, Harry Davenport, Frank Conroy, Marc Lawrence, Paul Hurst, Victor Kilian, Chris-Pin Martin, Frank Orth, Ted North, Dick Rich, Francis Ford, Rondo Hatton, and Leigh Whippen.

Lady of Burlesque (1943, United Artists). Screenplay: James Gunn, based on the novel *The G String Murder*, by Gypsy Rose Lee. Produced by Hunt Stromberg. With Barbara Stanwyck, Michael O'Shea, J. Edward Bromberg, Iris Adrian, Gloria Dickson, Victoria Faust, Stephanie Bachelor, Charles Dingle, Marion Martin, Eddie Gordon, Frank Fenton, Pinky Lee, and Frank Conroy.

Buffalo Bill (1944, 20th Century-Fox). Screenplay: Aeneas MacKenzie, Clements Ripley, and Cecile Kramer, based on a story by Frank Winch. Produced by Harry A. Sherman. With Joel McCrea, Maureen O'Hara, Linda Darnell, Thomas Mitchell, Edgar Buchanan, Anthony Quinn, Moroni Olsen, Frank Fenton, Matt Briggs, George Lessey, Frank Orth, George Chandler, Chief Many Treaties, Nick Thompson, Chief Thundercloud, and Sidney Blackmer.

This Man's Navy (1945, MGM). Story and screenplay: Borden Chase, based on an idea by Commander Herman E. Holland, USN, retired. Produced by Samuel Marx. With Wallace Beery, Tom Drake, James Gleason, Jan Clayton, Selena Royle, Noah Beery Sr., Henry O'Neill, Steve Brodie, George Chandler, Donald Curtis, Arthur Walsh, Will Fowler, and Richard Crockett.

Story Of G. I. Joe (1945, United Artists). Screenplay: Leopold Atlas, Guy Endore, and Philip Stevenson, based on Ernie Pyle's books *Here Is Your War* and *Brave Men*. Produced by Lester Cowan. With Burgess Meredith, Robert Mitchum, Freddie

Steele, Wally Cassell, Jimmy Lloyd, Jack Reilly, Bill Murphy, and combat veterans of the campaigns in Africa, Sicily, and mainland Italy.

Gallant Journey (1946, Columbia). Screenplay: Byron Morgan and William A. Wellman. Produced by William A. Wellman. With Glenn Ford, Janet Blair, Charles Kemper, Jimmy Lloyd, Henry Travers, Arthur Shields, Willard Robertson, Selena Royle, Robert DeHaven, and Charles Ruggles.

Magic Town (1947, RKO). Screenplay: Robert Riskin, based on a story by Robert Riskin and Joseph Krumgold. Produced by Robert Riskin. With James Stewart, Jane Wyman, Kent Smith, Ned Sparks, Wallace Ford, Regis Toomey, Ann Doran, Donald Meek, E. J. Ballentine, Ann Shoemaker, Mickey Kuhn, Howard Freeman, Harry Holman, Mary Currier, Mickey Roth, Frank Fenton, George Irving, Selmer Jackson, Robert Dudley, and Julia Dean.

The Iron Curtain (1948, 20th Century-Fox). Screenplay: Milton Krims, based on the personal story of Igor Gouzenko. Produced by Sol C. Siegel. With Dana Andrews, Gene Tierney, June Havoc, Berry Kroeger, Edna Best, Stefan Schnabel, Nicholas Joy, Eduard Franz, Frederick Tozere, Noel Cravat, Christopher Robin Olsen, Peter Whitney, Leslie Barrie, Mauritz Hugo, John Shay, Victor Wood, and John Ridgeley.

Yellow Sky (1949, 20th Century-Fox). Screenplay: Lamar Trotti, based on a story by W. R. Burnett. Produced by Lamar Trotti. With Gregory Peck, Anne Baxter, Richard Widmark, Robert Arthur, John Russell, Henry Morgan, James Barton, Charles Kemper, Robert Adler, Harry Carter, Victor Kilian, Paul Hurst, Hank Worden, Jay Silverheels, and William Gould.

Battleground (1949, MGM). Screenplay: Robert Pirosh. Produced by Dore Schary. With Van Johnson, Ricardo Montalban, John Hodiak, George Murphy, Marshall Thompson, Jerome Courtland, Don Taylor, Bruce Cowling, James Whitmore, Douglas Fowley, Leon Ames, Guy Anderson, Thomas E. Breen, Denise Darcel, Richard Jaeckel, Jim Arness, Scotty Beckett, and Brett King.

The Happy Years (1950, MGM). Screenplay: Harry Ruskin. Based on *The Lawrenceville School Stories*, by Owen Johnson. Produced by Carey Wilson. With Dean Stockwell, Darryl Hickman, Scotty Beckett, Leon Ames, Margalo Gilmore, Leo G. Carroll, Elinor Donahue, Dwayne Hickman, Robert Wagner, Timothy Wellman.

The Next Voice You Hear (1950, MGM). Screenplay by Charles Schnee, based on a story by George Sumner Albee. Produced by Dore Schary. With James Whitmore, Nancy Davis, Gary Gray, Lillian Bronson, Art Smith, Tom D'Andrea, and Jeff Corey.

Across the Wide Missouri (1951, MGM). Screenplay: Talbot Jennings, based on a story by Talbot Jennings and Frank Cavett, and a book by Bernard de Voto. Produced by Robert Sisk. With Clark Gable, Ricardo Montalban, John Hodiak, Adolphe Menjou, Maria Elena Marques, J. Carroll Naish, Jack Holt, Alan Napier, George Chandler, Richard Anderson, Henri Letondal, Douglas Fowley, Louis Nicoletti, Ben Watson, Russell Simpson, and Frankie Darro.

Westward the Women (1952, MGM). Screenplay: Charles Schnee, based on a story by Frank Capra. Produced by Dore Schary. With Robert Taylor, Denise Darcel, Henry Nakamura, Lenore Lonergan, Marilyn Erskine, Hope Emerson, Julie Bishop, John McIntire, Renata Vanni, and Beverly Dennis.

It's a Big Country (1952, MGM). Screenplay: William Ludwig, Helen Deutsch, Ray Chordes, Isobel Tennant, Allen Pinkin, Dorothy Kingsley, Dore Schary, and George Wells. Directed by Richard Thorpe, John Sturges, Charles Vidor, Don Weis, Clarence Brown, William A. Wellman, and Don Hartman. With Ethel Barrymore, Keefe Brasselle, Gary Cooper, Nancy Davis, Van Johnson, Gene Kelly, Janet Leigh, Majorie Main, Fredric March, George Murphy, William Powell, S. Z. Sakall, Lewis Stone, James Whitmore, Keenan Wynn, Leon Ames, Angela Clarke, Bobby Hyatt, and Sharon McManus.

My Man and I (1952, MGM). Screenplay: John Fante and Jack Leonard. Produced by Stephen Ames. With Shelley Winters, Ricardo Montalban, Wendell Corey, Claire Trevor, José Torvay, Jack Elam, Pascual García Peña, George Chandler, Juan Torena, and Carlos Conde.

Island in the Sky (1953, Warner Brothers). Screenplay: Ernest K. Gann, based on his novel. A Wayne-Fellows Production. With John Wayne, Lloyd Nolan, Walter Abel, James Arness, Andy Devine, Allyn Joslyn, James Lydon, Harry Carey Jr., Hal Baylor, Sean McClory, and Wally Cassell.

The High and the Mighty (1954, Warner Brothers). Screenplay: Ernest K. Gann, based on his novel. A Wayne-Fellows Production. With John Wayne, Claire Trevor, Laraine Day, Robert Stack, Jan Sterling, Phil Harris, Robert Newton, David Brian, Paul Kelly, Sidney Blackmer, Julie Bishop, Pedro Gonzalez-Gonzalez, John Howard, Wally Brown, William Campbell, Ann Doran, John Qualen, Paul Fix, George Chandler, Joy Kim, Michael Wellman, Douglas Fowley, Walter Reed, and Regis Toomey.

Track of the Cat (1954, Warner Brothers). Screenplay: A. Bezzerides, based on a novel by Walter Van Tilburg Clark. A Wayne-Fellows Production. With Robert Mitchum, Teresa Wright, Diana Lynn, Tab Hunter, Beulah Bondi, Philip Tonge, William Hopper, and Carl Switzer.

Blood Alley (1955, Warner Brothers). Screenplay: A. S. Fleischman, based on his novel. A Batjac Production. With John Wayne, Lauren Bacall, Paul Fix, Joy Kim, Mike Mazurki, Henry Nakamura, Berry Kroeger, W. T. Chang, George Chan, Anita Ekberg, and Victor Sen Yung.

Goodbye, My Lady (1956, Warner Brothers). Screenplay: Albert Sidney Fleischman. From the novel by James Street. A Batjac Production. Executive producer: John Wayne. Produced and directed by William A. Wellman. With Walter Brennan, Phil Harris, Brandon de Wilde, Sidney Poitier, William Hopper, George Chandler. Narration: William A. Wellman. Featured song: "When Your Boy Becomes a Man"; music by Don Powell, sung by Howard Keel (uncredited).

Darby's Rangers (1958, Warner Brothers). Screenplay: Guy Trosper, based on a book by Major James Altieri. Produced by Martin Rackin. With James Garner, Etchika Choureau, Jack Warden, Edward Byrnes, Venetia Stevenson, Torin Thatcher, Peter Brown, Joan Elan, Corey Allen, Stuart Whitman, Murray Hamilton, Bill Wellman Jr., Andrea King, and Adam Williams.

Lafayette Escadrille (1958, Warner Brothers). Screenplay: A. S. Fleischman, based on a story by William A. Wellman. Produced by William A. Wellman. With Tab Hunter, Etchika Choureau, Bill Wellman Jr., Jody McCrea, Dennis Devine, Marcel Dalio, David Janssen, Paul Fix, Veola Vonn, Will Hutchins, Clint Eastwood, Bob Hover, Tom Laughlin, Brett Halsey, Henry Nakamura, Maurice Marsac, Raymond Bailey, and George Nardelli. William A. Wellman (narration).

THE FOLLOWING ARE WELLMAN FILMS
WITH UNCREDITED DIRECTION

The Eleventh Hour (1923, Fox). Presented by William Fox. Directed by Bernard J. Durning. Screenplay: Louis Sherwin. Photography: Dan Short. Assistant director: William A. Wellman. Cast: Shirley Mason, Charles "Buck" Jones, Richard Tucker, Alan Hale, and Walter McGrail.

The Way of a Girl (1925, MGM). Presented by Louis B. Mayer. Directed by Robert G. Vignola. Screenplay: Albert Shelby LeVino. Based on the story "Summoned," in *Ainslee's* (February 1923), by Katherine Newlin Burt. Photography: John Arnold. Art direction: Cedric Gibbons. Assistant director: John Carle. Cast: Eleanor Boardman, Matt Moore, William Russell, Matthew Betz, and Charles K. French.

The Exquisite Sinner (1926, MGM). Presented by Louis B. Mayer. Directed by Josef von Sternberg. Screenplay: Josef von Sternberg and Alice Miller. Based on the novel *Escape* (1924), by Alden Brooks. Titles: Joe Farnham. Photography: Max Fabian. Editor: John W. English. Art direction: Cedric Gibbons, Joseph Wright. Assistant director: Robert Florey. Wardrobe: Andre-ani. Cast: Conrad Nagel, Renee Adoree, Paulette Duval, Frank Currier, George K. Arthur, Matthew Betz, Helen D'Algy, Claire Dubrey, and Myrna Loy.

Female (1933, First National-Vitaphone/Warners). Executive producer: Darryl F. Zanuck. Produced by Robert Presnell and Henry Blanke. Directed by Michael Curtiz. Screenplay: Gene Markey and Kathryn Scola. Photography: Ernest Haller, George Barnes, John Mescall. Editor: Jack Killifer. Art direction: Jack Okey. Cast: Ruth Chatterton, George Brent, Lois Wilson, Johnny Mack Brown, and Ruth Donnelly.

Viva Villa (1934, MGM). Produced by David O. Selznick. Directed by Jack Conway and Howard Hawks. Authors: Edgcumb Pinchon and O. B. Stade. Screenplay: Ben Hecht and Charles MacArthur. Photography: James Wong Howe, Charles G. Clarke. Cast: Wallace Beery, Fay Wray, Leo Carrillo, Stuart Erwin, Henry B. Walthall, and Donald Cook.

China Seas (1935, MGM). Directed by Tay Garnett. Screenplay: Jules Furthman, James Kevin McGuinness. Cast: Clark Gable, Jean Harlow, Wallace Beery, Lewis Stone, Robert Benchley, and Rosalind Russell.

Tarzan Escapes (1936, MGM). Produced by Bernie Hyman. Associate producer: Sam Zimbalist. Directed by Richard Thorpe. Screenplay: Cyril Hume, Louis Mosher, John Farrow, Wyndham Gittens, Otis Garrett, Edwin H. Knopf. Based on characters created by Edgar Rice Burroughs. Photography: Leonard Smith. Editors: W. Donn Hayes and Basil Wrangell. Art directors: Cedric Gibbons and Elmer Sheeley. Set decorations: Edwin B. Willis. Special effects photography: Max Fabian and Thomas Tutwiler. Special effects: A. Arnold Gillespie, Thomas Tutwiler, James Basevi, Warren Newcombe. Cast: Johnny Weissmuller, Maureen O'Sullivan, John Buckler, Benita Hume, William Henry, Herbert Mundin, and Cheetah the Chimp.

The Garden of Allah (1936, United Artists). Produced by David O. Selznick. Directed by Richard Boleslawski. Screenplay: W. P. Lipscomb and Lynn Riggs. Novel by Robert Hichens. Photography: W. Howard Greene and Harold G. Rosson. Cast: Marlene Dietrich, Charles Boyer, Basil Rathbone, C. Aubrey Smith, Tilly Losch, Joseph Schildkraut, and John Carradine.

The Adventures of Tom Sawyer (1938, United Artists). Produced by David O. Selznick. Directed by Norman Taurog. From the Mark Twain classic novel. Screenplay: John V. A. Weaver. Photography: James Wong Howe. Cast: Tommy Kelly, Jackie Moran, Ann Gillis, May Rosson, Walter Brennan, Victor Jory, David Holt, Victor Kilian, Nana Bryant, Olin Howland, Donald Meek, Charles Richman, Margaret Hamilton, Marcia Mae Jones, Mickey Rentschler, Cora Sue Collins, and Spring Byington.

Gone with the Wind (1939, MGM). Produced by David O. Selznick. Directed by Victor

Fleming. Author: Margaret Mitchell. Screenplay: Sidney Howard. Photography: Ernest Haller. Cast: Clark Gable, Vivien Leigh, Leslie Howard, Olivia de Havilland, George Reeves, Fred Crane, Hattie McDaniel, Everett Brown, Zack Williams, Thomas Mitchell, Oscar Polk, Barbara O'Neil, Victor Jory, Evelyn Keyes, Ann Rutherford, Butterfly McQueen, Howard Hickman, Alicia Rhett, and Rand Brooks.

Duel in the Sun (1946, Selznick Releasing Organization). Produced by David O. Selznick. Directed by King Vidor. Author: Niven Busch. Screenplay: David O. Selznick. Adaptation: Oliver H. P. Garrett. Photography: Lee Garmes, Hal Rosson, Ray Rannahan. Cast: Jennifer Jones, Joseph Cotton, Gregory Peck, Lionel Barrymore, Herbert Marshall, Lillian Gish, Walter Huston, Charles Bickford, Harry Carey, Butterfly McQueen, Otto Kruger, Charles Dingle, Tilly Losch, and Scott McKay.

Ring of Fear (1954, Warner Brothers). Produced by Robert Fellows and John Wayne. Directed by James Edward Grant. Story and screenplay: Paul Fix, Philip MacDonald, and James Edward Grant. Photography: Edwin B. DuPar. Editor: Fred MacDowell. Art direction: Alfred Ybarra. Set decoration: Ralph Hurst. Musical score: Emil Newman and Arthur Lange. Cast: Clyde Beatty, Pat O'Brien, Mickey Spillane, Sean McClory, Marian Carr, John Bromfield, and Twelve Performing Acts of the Clyde Beatty Circus.

Wellman's work on these twelve films ranges from a few days to several weeks in length. Not knowing the exact scenes that he directed and which ones ended up in the final edition, it is nearly impossible to access the impact of his work.

However, there were three exceptions. We have already discussed how his work on Bernard Durning's *The Eleventh Hour* (1923) vaulted him into the ranks of director. *Ring of Fear* (1954) was probably the longest stint of any of these uncredited projects.

In the 1950s, Wellman and John Wayne made six pictures together, three starring the Duke himself: *Island in the Sky* (1953), *The High and the Mighty* (1954), and *Blood Alley* (1955). In 1954, Wayne's production company was making a low-budget, circus murder-mystery on location in Arizona. The film was in big trouble and needed help. Wayne asked his pal Wellman for a favor—to go to Arizona and fix it. Wellman did just that: rewriting, recasting, and shooting for several weeks.

The end result was excellent, as *Ring of Fear* became a complete success. Wellman had accepted no salary, but the Duke, being the generous person that he was, gave his director-pal a piece of the profits.

The third exception was *Gone with the Wind* (1939). No records of Wellman's participation have been uncovered. However, I support my father's contention. I was present at a party at David Selznick's Beverly Hills home in 1956. I was sitting with my father, Selznick, and several guests. Selznick was telling his friends about all the work he and Wellman had done together. When he completed the laundry list, my father interjected with, "Don't forget, I burned down Culver City for your *Gone with the Wind*." Selznick quickly replied, "And that, too!" They, of course, were referring to the burning of Atlanta in the legendary Oscar winner.

ACADEMY AWARD RECOGNITION

Wellman's films earned a total of thirty-two nominations, including seven Oscars.

Wings (1927). Academy Award for Best Picture and Best Engineering Effects (Roy Pomeroy).

The Public Enemy (1931). Nominated for Best Writing—Original Motion Picture Story (Kubec Glasmon and John Bright).

The Star Witness (1931). Nominated for Best Writing—Original Motion Picture Story (Lucien Hubbard).

A Star Is Born (1937). Academy Awards for Best Writing—Original Story (William A. Wellman and Robert Carson) and a Special Award for Color Photography (W. Howard Greene). Nominated for Best Picture, Best Actor (Fredric March), Best Actress (Janet Gaynor), Best Direction (William A. Wellman), Best Screenplay (Dorothy Parker, Alan Campbell, and Robert Carson), and Best Assistant Director (Eric Stacey).

Beau Geste (1939). Nominated for Best Supporting Actor (Brian Donlevy) and Best Interior Decoration (Hans Dreier and Robert Odell).

The Ox-Bow Incident (1943). Nominated for Best Picture.

Lady of Burlesque (1943). Nominated for Best Music—Scoring of a Dramatic or Comedy Picture (Arthur Lange).

The Story of G. I. Joe (1945). Nominated for Best Supporting Actor (Robert Mitchum); Best Screenplay (Leopold Atlas, Guy Endore, and Philip Stevenson); Best Music—Scoring of a Dramatic or Comedy Picture (Louis Applebaum and Ann Ronell); Best Song ("Linda," music and lyrics by Ann Ronell).

Battleground (1949). Academy Awards for Best Writing (Robert Pirosh) and Best Black and White Cinematography (Paul Vogel). Nominated for Best Picture, Best Direction (William A. Wellman), Best Supporting Actor (James Whitmore), and Best Editing (John Dunning).

The High and the Mighty (1954). Academy Award for Best Music—Scoring of a Dramatic or Comedy Picture (Dimitri Tiomkin). Nominated for Best Direction (William A. Wellman), Best Supporting Actress (Claire Trevor and Jan Sterling), Best Editing (Ralph Dawson), and Best Song ("The High and the Mighty," by Dimitri Tiomkin and Ned Washington).

Index

Note: Page numbers for photos are in *italic* type.

Academy Awards (1929), 151–154
acrobatics, 58
Adoree, Renee, 96
Air Circus, 156
aircraft, World War I, 20
Air Eagles, 156
Air Mail Pilot, 156
Air Patrol, 156
Air Police, 156
American Ambulance Corps, 6, 53
An American Citizen, 100
Andrews, Major F. M. *119*
Arlen, Richard (Cornelius Mattimore),
    109–*110*, 115, 119–*122*, 124,
    126–*127*, 138, 145, *146–147*, 156
armistice, 60
Arthur, George K., 96
Arthur, Jean, 146
Art of Cross-Examination, The, 2
Arzner, Dorothy, 92
Aunt Sarah (Wellman's aunt), 39
Aviator, 156
Azire, Captain, 28–30, 36, 38, 42

Badger, Clarence, 68, 104
Balsley, H. Clyde, 53–56
Banky, Vilma, 112
Barker, Reginald, 68

Barrymore, John, 100
Barthelmess, Richard, 156
Barton, Charles, 109, 122–*123*, 135,
    154–155
Baylies, Frank "Jules," 47
Beau Geste, 102, 108
Beaumont, Harry, 68
Beery, Wallace, 145–*147*
Beggars of Life, 145–146, *147*
Belasco, David, 100
Bellamy, Ralph, 156
Bennett, Constance, 95
Beresford, Bruce, 154
Bernhardt, Sarah, 99
Beyond the Rainbow, 107
Big Dan, 86, 90, 96
Big Parade, The, 103, 114
Black Cat Squadron (escadrille N. 87),
    25, *26*, 29–30, 35, 38, 44
Bleriots, 10–12
Bleriot, Louis, 10
Bleriot Method, 52
Blood and Sand, 102
Boardman, Eleanor, 96
Boob, The, 96, 106
Borzage, Frank, *92*, 152
Bow, Clara, 96–97, 103, 107, 109, *110*,
    115, 117, 138–139, 145, 156

Boyd, William "Hopalong Cassidy," 156
Brandt, Joe, 91
Brent, Evelyn, 146
Brian, Mary, 146
Bronson, Betty, 97–98, 143
Brooks, Alden, 96
Brooks, Louise, 145, *146*
Brown, Staff, 47
Bull Moose Party, 52
Busby Berkeley dancer.
    See Coonan, Dorothy "Dottie"

Cagney, James, 153, 157
California, 100
Campbell, Alan, 158
Campbell, Captain S. C., *136*
Capra, Frank, 91–*92*
Caprice, 100
Carroll, Nancy, 146
Carson, Robert, *157–158*
Cat's Pajamas, The, 97–98, 106
Celia I–V (Wellman's planes), *34*–35,
    38–39, 41, 43, 46
Chadwick, Helene, 56–61, 64–65, 67–69,
    78; mother of, 57–61, 63–65, 69
Chang, 152
Chapin, Jacques "Jack," 94
Chapin, Margery, 94–*95*, 98, 106, 113,
    126, 136–137
Chaplin, Charlie, 61
Chauve-Souris, 98
Cheney, Major J. E., *119*
Chinatown Nights, 146, 148
Chow (Wellman's Hollywood dog),
    89–91, 92, 93, 94
Circus Cowboy, The, 86
Clifton, Elmer, 107
Clothier, Bill, 121
Coffin and Gilmore, 15, 17–18, 28
Cohn, Harry, 91–93, 96, 97
Cohn, Jack, 91
Colman, Ronald, 112
Columbia Pictures, 91–94
Coonan, Dorothy "Dottie," *140, 142,*
    158–160
Cooper, Frank James (Gary Cooper or
    "Coop"), 110–112, *111*, 115,
    123–126, 141, 143–146, 156
Cooper, Miriam, 67

Cortez, Ricardo, 97
Count of Monte Cristo, The, 100
Covered Wagon, The, 102
Crawford, Joan, 95–96
Criterion Theatre, 143
Croix de Guerre, 38, 41, 47, 49, 52, *55*
Crowd, The, 152
Cruise, Tom, 156
Crystal Hall, 99
Cukor, George, 144
Cupid's Fireman, 88
Cupid the Cowpuncher, 70

Dangerous Paradise, 146, 154
Dawn Patrol, The, 156
Day in Court, 2
de Curnier, Adjutant, *11*
del Riccio, Lorenzo, 140
DeMille, Beatrice, 100
DeMille, Cecil B., 74–75, 100–101,
    104–*105*, 140
DeMille, Constance, 100
DeMille, William, 100
De Runye, 12
Devine, Mr. and Mrs. Andy, *158*
Douglas, Dave, 8
Dowling, Edward, 95
Down to the Sea in Ships, 107
Driving Miss Daisy, 154
Durant, John and Alice, 51
Durning, Bernard "Bernie" J., 74–75,
    77–79, 82–86, 88, 147
Duval, Paulette, 96
Dvorak, Ann, 156
Dwan, Allan, 104

Eagle and the Hawk, The, 156
Earhart, Amelia, 103
Eleventh Hour, The, 79, 82, 84
Elite Glove Co., 100
Escape, 96
Espagne, 47
Essex Roadster, 148–151, 156
Evangeline, 67
Exquisite Sinner, The, 96

Fairbanks, Douglas, Jr., 156
Fairbanks, Douglas, Sr., 3, *4*, 22, 49,
    61–65, *62*, 67, 68, 71, 152

Fame and Fortune, 107
Farnum, Dustin "Dusty," 74, *76–78*, 84–86, 100
Farrar, Geraldine, 69
Farrell, Charles, 108
Fascinating Youth, 109
Fast Mail, The, 78
Fellows, Rockcliffe, 69
Fields, W. C., 101, 109
Film Reports, 96
Fleming, Victor, 104, 114–115
Folies Bergere, 100
Folies Bergere (nightclub set), 138
Forbes, Ralph, 108–109
Ford, John, 156
Fox, William, 89–90, 152
Frederick, Pauline, 69
French Air Service (also French Aviation, French Flying Corps, Lafayette Flying Corps), 6, 8, 10, 38, 47, 53, 71, 79
French Foreign Legion (Legionnaire), 6, 10, 53–54, 117

Gallagher, John Andrew, 155
Gasnier, Louis, 56
Gaynor, Janet, *149*, 152, 158
Gentlemen of the Jury, 2
Gibbons, Cedric, 152
Gilbert, Jack, 69
Glazer, Benjamin, 152
Gold Diggers of 1933, *142*
Goldwyn, Samuel (Samuel Goldfish), 72, 74, 100–101
Gone With the Wind, 148
Good Little Devil, A, 100
Goulding, Edmund, 95, 154
Grace, Dick, 127, *136*
Grand Hotel, 154
Grant, Cary, 156
Grauman's Chinese Theatre, 79
Greene, W. Howard, 158
Griffith, D. W., 61, 108
Guile of Women, 70
Guinness, Cecilia Lee (Cecilia Guinness McCarthy), 1

Hackett, James K., 100
Hall, James, 156

Hamilton, Neil, 108–109, 156
"Hark the Bells," 145
Harlow, Jean, 156
Hart, William S., 61, 87, *105*
Hattons, Frederick and Fanny, 90
Hawks, Howard, 156
Hearts Adrift, 100
Hell's Angels, 156
Henley, Hobart, 68
His Neighbor's Wife, 100
Hitchcock, Thomas "Tom" or "Tommy," Jr., *37–47*, 52–53, 60, 79–*82*, 117
Hobart, Doty, 90
Honest Hutch, The, 70
Hopper, E. Mason, 68
Hubbard, Lucien K., 104, 108, 112, 116–*119*, 122, *128*, 130–131, 133
Hughes, Howard, 152, 156
Hunter, T. Hayes, 68

I Blow My Own Horn, 109
"I Left My Love in Avalon" (actual title: "I Found My Love in Avalon"), 69
In the Bishop's Carriage, 100
Iron to Gold, 74–77
It, 103, 108
Iveagh, Lord and Lady, 1

Jackson, Andrew, 51
Jannings, Emil, 152
Jazz Singer, The, 144, 153
Jes' Call Me Jim, 70
Joffre, Marshall, 9
Johnson, Julian, 103
Jolson, Al, 144, 153
Jones, Charles "Buck" (Charles Gebhardt), 78–79, *87–88*, 90
Jubilo, 70
Judd, Davy "Juddy," 13, 18, 47

Kahn, Otto, 129–135
Kaufmann, Lottie, 99
Keaton, Buster, 61
King, Henry, 112
Kirkwood, James, 69
Knickerbocker Buckaroo, The, *62*, 63, 67

LaCava, Gregory, 104, 109
Ladies Must Lie, 109

Ladies of the Mob, 144–145
Laemmle, Carl, 137
Lafayette Escadrille (also Escadrille
    Americaine, Franco-American
    Flying Corps), 6–7, 10, 28, 47
Lafayette Flying Corps, The, 44, 58
Lahm, Brigadier General Frank P., *119*
Landis, Cullen, 69
Langtry, Lily, 100
Lasky, Blanche, 100–101
Lasky, Jesse L., 96–106, 108–109,
    118, 122, 141–144, 148, 150–151,
    155–156
Last Command, The, 152
Last Straw, The, 87
Laugh and Live, 22
Law of Contracts, The, 2
Law of Sale, The, 2
Legion of the Condemned, 141,
    143–*144*, 146–147, 150, 156
Legion of the Lafayette, 39, 44
Lighton, Louis D. "Buddy," 103
Lilac Time, 156
Lindbergh, Charles, 143
Lloyd, Frank, 68
Lloyd, Harold, 61
Loew, Marcus, 99
Loew's Consolidated Enterprises
    (Loew's Inc.), 99
Lombard, Carole, *148*, 156
Loring, Hope, 103
Lucas, George, 155
Luck and Opportunity, 2
Lyon, Ben, 156

Mack, Charles, 115
Magnascope, 140
Man I Love, The, 146, 148
Man Who Won, The, 76, 84, 86
March, Fredric, *148*, *149*, 156–158
Marie (French laundress), 30–32
Marsh, Mae, 69
Mason, Shirley, 79
Mayer, Louis B. ("L. B."), 137, 151–153
McCarthy, Celia (mother of William A.
    Wellman), 1–23, 25, 27, 28, 34–35,
    39, 42, 49, 61, 78, 95, *158*
McCarthy, Reverend Charles P., 1
McLeod, Norman, *136*

Meeker, William "Billie," 14, 47
Méliès, Gaston, 113
Men of the Sky, 156
Metro-Goldwyn-Mayer (MGM):
    formation of, 99–101
Miot (French flying ace in Wellman's
    escadrille), 30, 35–36, 41
Miss Wolf (American nurse), 54
Miss Wood (Wellman's nurse in WWI),
    39, 54
Mix, Tom, 87–88
Moore, Colleen, 156
Moore, Tom, 69
Moreno, Tony, 56
Morris, Chester, 146
Mrs. Fiske, 100
My First Hundred Years in Hollywood, 98

Nagel, Conrad, 96
Name Above the Title, The, 91
New York Mail, 96
nickelodeons, 99
Nieuport, 17–18, *22*, 29–30, 38, 44, 53
Normand, Mabel, 69
Norton-Harjes Ambulance Corps
    (also Harjis-Norton), 6–7
Not A Drum Was Heard, 86, 90
Nothing Sacred, 148
Novak, Jane, 69
Novelty Fur Company, 99

O'Brien, Pat, 156
Ogden, Matilda Gouverneur, 1
Old Ironsides, 108, 143
Olmstead, Gertrude, 96
O'Neill, Eugene, 100
O'Neill, James, 100
Orphans Bureau, 99
Oscar (Academy Award statuette), 152

Paramount Pictures: formation of,
    99–103
Parke, William, 68
Parker, Albert, 63
Parker, Dorothy, 158
Parsons, Ted, *136*
Perry, Harry, 113, 119–*121*
Pershing, General John J. "Black Jack,"
    8–9, 72–*73*, 74, 117

Pickford, Jack, 69
Pickford, Mary, 61, 63, 100, *105*
Poilus (Poilu), 20, 43–44
Pomeroy, Roy T., 140
Prisoner of Zenda, The, 100
Public Enemy, The (original title:
    Beer and Blood), 157
Putnam, David, 47
Putnam, George Palmer, 103

Queen Elizabeth, 96, 99

Racket, The, 152
Rainbow Division, 72, 106
Rebecca, 148
Red Cross, 8
Renee (Wellman's first wife), 32–34, 36,
    41–44
Republican party, 52
Revier, Dorothy, 94
Rex Pictures Corporation, 96
Rialto Theatre, 143
Ricketts, Tom, 94
Roberts, Theodore "Daddy," 97
Rochambeau, 4, 5
Rogers, Charles "Buddy", 108–*110*,
    115, 119, 120–121, 124, 126–*127*,
    138–139, 146, 156
Rogers, Will, 61, 69, *70*
Roosevelt, Quentin, 52
Roosevelt, Ted, 52
Roosevelt, Theodore "Teddy," 49,
    51–53, 117
Rough Riders, The, 114–115, 135
Royles, Edwin Milton, 100
Ruptured Penguins, 60

Sally, Irene and Mary, 95
San Jose Juvenile Band, 100
Saunders, John Monk, 103–104, 113,
    115–117, *119*, *136*, 146
Schertzinger, Victor, 68
Schulberg, Benjamin Percival ("B. P."),
    92, 96–98, 104–106, 108, 112,
    118, 122, 143–144, 146–148, 150,
    155
Scorsese, Martin, 156
Scott, Tony, 156
Second Hand Love, 86

Selznick, David O., 137–138, 148, *150*
Selznick, Lewis J., 137
Selznick, Myron, 137–*138*, 140, 143,
    148, 150–151, 154
Sennett, Mack, 61
Seventh Heaven, 152
Sgt. Jeannot, 35–36
Sheehan, Winnie, 84
Sheik, The, 102
Sheldon, E. Lloyd, 104
Shosberg, Max, 99
Since You Went Away, 148
Sinclaire, Reginald "Reggie" Duke,
    19–20, 47
Skelly, Hal, 146
Sketton, Francis, 8
Sky Devils, 156
Sky Hawk, 156
Sky Raiders, 156
So's Your Old Man, 109
Spad, 21–23, *27*, 58, 61–62
Spellbound, 148
Squaw Man, 75, 100
Squaw Man, The, 74–75
Stanley, Forrest, 94
Star Film Company (Star Film Ranch),
    113
Star Is Born, A, 148, *149*, 157–158
Star Wars, 1, 155
St. Clair, Malcolm, 104
Steene, E. Burton, 119, 139
Stralem, William, 129–135
Street Angel, 152
Stuart, Gloria, 156
Sunrise, 152
Sutherland, Eddie, 104
Swanson, Gloria, 101

Taffy (Wellman's childhood dog), *4*, 13,
    49
Talmadge, Norma, 61
Ten Commandments, The, 102
Tess of the D'urbervilles, 100
Texas Hollywood, 131
Thaw, William, 28
Thompson, Frank, 131
Tommick, Captain Frank, *136*
Top Gun, 156
Tracy, Spencer, 156

United Artists Corp., 61
U.S. Air Service (U.S. Aviation), 6, 39, 52–57, 158

Vagabond Trail, The, 86
Valentino, Rudolph, 61, 101
Variety, 96, 98
Vengeance of the Deep, 109
Vickers machine gun, 16–17, 56
Vidor, Florence, 98, 146
Vidor, King, 114, 152
Vignola, Robert, 96
Virden, Doris, 111–112
Volcano, 109
Von Sternberg, Josef, 96, 149

Wales, Ethel, 94
Wallis, Hal, 156
Walsh, Raoul, 67
War Department, 104, 114, 116–117, 122
Warner, Jack, 98, 153, 156
Warner Brothers, 153–154, 156–157
Way of a Girl, The, 96
Way of All Flesh, 152
Wellman, Arthur Gouverneur, 1–23, 28, 40–41, 49–51, 61, 78, 158
Wellman, Arthur "Arch" Ogden, 3–23, 25, 28, 39, 49, 78, 158, 159
Wellman, Celia. *See* McCarthy, Celia
Wellman children, *160*
Wellman, Francis L., 2
Wellman, Gloria, 106, 113, 126
Wellman, Joseph, 2
Wellman, Mary Fairlie, 2

Wellman, William Augustus, 1–3
What Price Glory, 103
When Husbands Flirt, 92, 94–96, 106
White Rose, 108
Whitney, Flora Payne, 52
Wild Bill Hollywood Maverick, 156
Wild Boys of the Road, 159
Williams, Ben Ames, 90
Williston, Samuel, 2
Wilson, President Woodrow, 42, 45, 52–53
Wings, 1, 6, 103–107, *108*, 109–147, 152–156, 161
Winning of Barbara Worth, The, 112
Wiseley, Cadet Charles M., 131
Wiseman, Sir William, 129–135
Woman Trap, 146
Wood, Cyrus, 95
Worsley, Wallace, 68
Wray, Fay, 112, 144–*145*
Wurtzel, Sol, 84, 88

Y.M.C.A., 13
Yosemite Trail, 78–79
You Never Know Women (original title: *Love – The Magician*), 98, 106, 143
Young Eagles, 146, 154, 156

Zanuck, Darryl F., *153*, 154, 156–157
Ziegfeld Follies, 94, 100
Zukor, Adolph, 96, 98–104, 122, 137, 143–144, 152
Zukor, Hannah, 99
Zukor, Jacob, 99

About the Author

WILLIAM WELLMAN JR. has written articles for *Film Comment*, *Films in Review*, *Action Magazine*, *Memories Magazine*, and *DGA News*. An actor with more than 180 screen and television credits, he has also worked as a screenwriter and producer of independent features. He created and executive produced *Wild Bill Hollywood Maverick*, an award-winning documentary about his father. *C'est la Guerre*, a biographical film of his father's life, is currently in development.